P9-AQC-314

Equal Opportunity In A Free Society:

The "Libegalitarian" System

By
Kaj Areskoug

Dorrance Publishing Co., Inc.
Pittsburgh, Pennsylvania 15222

Copyright (c) 1991 by Kaj Areskoug
All Rights Reserved
ISBN # 08059-3184-8
Printed in the United States of America
First Printing

The world is governed too much.
Unknown; motto of the *Boston Globe.*

A wise and frugal government, which shall restrain men from injuring one another . . . leave them otherwise free to regulate their own pursuits . . . and not take from the mouth of labor the bread it has earned—this is the sum of good government.
Thomas Jefferson

We ought not to be quite so ready with our taxes, until we can secure the desired destination.
Edmund Burke

To the extent that the rules allow everyone to play on equal terms, the pattern of outcomes, including the distribution . . . of goods and services, cannot be adjudged to be 'unfair.'
James M. Buchanan

CONTENTS

INTRODUCTION

The main rationale for reading is that it can inform and educate, or amuse and entertain. If a book informs or educates, it is a tool for investment in what we can call informational human capital. The investment can create more direct, consumable benefits later on—perhaps through a better-paying job or smarter management of personal affairs. If a book entertains, it is, by contrast, an immediate consumption item.

At least this is how a modern economist would explain why people find reading a useful activity, worth its costs in money and time. This is also how every author should try to justify why he has devoted some of his personal resources to producing a book, and why he expects other people to apply some of theirs to buying and reading it.

This book aims primarily to inform and educate. It wants to become a tool for investment in a certain type of knowledge capital. The knowledge, and the intended "education," belongs in the department of political economy or comparative ideological systems. Under the right circumstances, such knowledge can pay off by helping us make better political decisions, as voters or as public officials—with the ultimate hope of A Better-Run, More Productive America.

More bluntly, this book will try to change your political views. It will try to convince you that we could devise a much more attractive political system than the one we have today in the United States, one that better reflects the social values that most of us hold. You might call this book a blueprint for economic-political reform. Or you might call it a "how-to" book, if you let "how" refer to a prescription for broad national constitutional reforms.

The book argues that we could simultaneously realize the two most basic ideological requirements of all Western democratic nations: individual freedom and equality of opportunity. We could do this by adopting an ideology that will here be called **libegalitarianism**—essentially a hybrid between libertarianism and egalitarianism. Like other fully developed ideological schemes, it tries to define the rights of the individual in all social conflict situations. It defines the proper roles of government, and it outlines how society ought to redraw the boundaries between public-sector and private action.

The central creed of the **libegalitarian** ideology is that every citizen should be entitled to a "maximum equal lifetime opportunity." That is, society should grant every person the largest possible opportunity for lifetime personal well-being, provided that such opportunities are also given to everybody else. Far-reaching reforms will be necessary if we decide to adopt this as our guiding constitutional principle.

The resulting new society would look very different from the United States of today or of the past. By contemporary definitions, it would be neither right- or left-wing. It would, in effect, combine elements of free-enterprise conservatism, civil libertarianism and social democracy. These features would, it will be argued, combine to create a true "opportunity society."

One way of characterizing an ideology is by describing how it defines and distributes the citizens' rights and obligations. The **libegalitarian** society would offer all individuals two basic rights, or "entitlements": One is the right to an equal start in society (an egalitarian aspect of this society); the other, the right to participate freely in the private economy, supported by certain crucial government-provided services (an essentially libertarian aspect). Sustaining these rights would require a set of matching obligations— basically, to honor the like freedoms of others and to foot the bill for government services received. Together, these rights and obligations define a unique system of "distributive justice."

The **libegalitarian** society will have a government that is:

■ neutral in its treatment of different citizens and different activities—it will be nondiscriminatory in all matters; and

■ cost-effective in that it will undertake only those programs that are worth their costs to the taxpaying public.

But meanwhile, individuals will be accountable for:

■ all failures to respect the property rights of others, by having to make full restitutions for such rights infringements; and

■ the prorated costs of the government programs they benefit from.

This kind of society would have consistent, equitable resolutions for just about any type of socioeconomic conflict situation. Its ideological foundations would be strong and broad enough to provide answers for a nearly unlimited range of socioeconomic questions, such as:

Should the government provide a basic education to everybody? Do the elderly deserve publicly financed health care? Do pollution controls fairly balance the interests of industry and the public at large? Should government agencies take steps to eliminate shoddy or dangerous consumer products from the marketplace? What should the authorities do to lessen the amplitude of the business cycle and the extent of national unemployment?

The fact that this book is devoted to a single theme and a single cause will, of course, influence its tone and attitude. You may find the book insistent and doctrinaire. You may also find it provocative and radical, in that some of its policy implications are sharply at odds with conventional thinking. Or you may find its policy prescriptions utopian, in that the recommended reforms stand little chance of being undertaken in the near future. Indeed, the time perspective is long-term, and you will find little or no discussion of gradual implementation strategy or transitional adjustment problems. These are some of the trade-offs that the author has made in favor of singularity and consistency in the basic ideological message. The reader should be so forewarned.

Chapter I
TOWARD AN IDEOLOGICAL ALTERNATIVE

THE PURPOSE OF IDEOLOGY

Ideologies are schemes for social organization, based on particular, deeply held values or top-priority interests. Explicitly or implicitly, they lay down ground rules for how rights and obligations are to be assigned among different socioeconomic groups. They typically outline how the boundaries are to be drawn between government and private activity. Ideologies guide the resolution of conflicting private and public claims on society's resources.

Each actual, well-functioning social system can be described by its underlying social values. These can usually be summarized by some ideological label. And the national constitution will normally embody these values.

Ideologically, the United States is in a mess. So are most other non-socialist countries. To be sure, the United States is by and large a capitalist democracy, in which a popularly elected government coexists with a large decentralized private sector and where many individual rights are acknowledged in the law. And there has been too little public displeasure with this system to produce any lasting tendencies toward revolution and reformation.

But the public-private boundary in America is thin and unstable, and rights are often redefined or redistributed. Moreover, the actions and

1

policies of the government obey no clear, permanent set of principles. Quite possibly, if the American people were offered a clearer delineation of ideological alternatives and socioeconomic possibilities, they would no longer tolerate the current state of affairs.

Most of our elected Presidents and legislators are also guilty of a great deal of ideological ambiguity, misunderstanding and obfuscation. They may in the past have publicly subscribed to one of the two traditional centrist American ideologies, liberalism or conservatism. But today most of them are afraid of any ideological labeling at all, or they assert that they are both liberal and conservative, in some unspecified and noncommittal blend. Recall all the silly, disingenuous references to the feared "L-word" during the 1988 Presidential campaign.

American election campaigns are dominated not by competitive comparisons of ideological values and their policy applications, but by questions of personality, style and imagery. When they do address some substantive issues, they often concentrate on exploiting special-interest concerns that are fashionable enough to get the mass media's attention; but they do not place these concerns in the broader context of conflicting socioeconomic rights and relative public priorities. Admittedly, small-party candidates often present clearer, ideologically based messages; this is true both of avowed socialists or communists and of libertarians or right-wing radicals. But these candidates command much less public attention, and their views rarely get a fair hearing.

Meanwhile the media, especially television, do little to clarify or analyze the broader ideological implications of the candidates' or parties' policy proposals. Have the major networks ever presented a balanced analysis of the loss of individual freedoms because of the federal budget deficit, the highway speed limit or the professional licensing of physicians? Have they ever sorted out how big-city rent controls tend to redistribute individual opportunities among current and future renters, landlords and other members of the community?

Yes, there is a strong and unfortunate anti-ideological streak in the United States today. It is fashionable to denigrate ideological concerns. This is exactly what Governor Dukakis did when he announced that his Presidential campaign would be about "competence, not ideology" (a statement that, however, in the end did not seem to benefit him). "Ideologue" has become a pejorative term.

It is often thought that ideologies are too rigid and mechanistic to allow for individual circumstances, or too abstract and unrealistic to serve as guides for actual policy making. Why not look for pragmatic commonsense solutions to our social problems and escape the straitjacket of unbending, preconceived rules? Don't the examples of such doctrinaire regimes as Hitler's Germany, Stalin's Russia or Castro's Cuba tell us something about the dangers inherent in ideological zealotry?

No, that is not really what those examples tell us. They illustrate the implications of particular ideologies, not of ideological theorizing, analysis or argumentation per se. In fact, if we have some faith in the long-run power of good ideas over bad ones (and we agree that "ideas have consequences"), historical experience should lead us to favor more, and not less, ideology: A fuller, clearer popular debate over the merits of those intolerable regimes might arguably have caused them to be rejected in advance, for the benefit of untold millions.

All political actions require a common set of guiding purposes, or they will have no ethical justification. If an ideological foundation is lacking altogether, the effects of political actions can be judged neither good nor bad; government becomes an exercise in arbitrariness. Without ideology, we will have no general yardstick for evaluating political programs.

We all know that we can be strongly affected by government policies, and most of us have some private notions about what is right and fair in this respect. We are untrue to ourselves if we do not try to translate these personal values into a broader political ideology and judge political action accordingly. An outright rejection of all ideological concerns and ideas would thus be intellectually untenable and morally apathetic.

Much of the public skepticism toward ideology seems based on an overstated, badly drawn contrast against pragmatism. While the ideologue seeks to fulfill some general, abstract ideal, the pragmatist supposedly is content with doing simply what "works." But almost every government program or policy produces some trade-offs, with some bad consequences for some social groups along with benefits for others. Nearly all policies thus turn out to be distributive or redistributive; the socioeconomic pie is not very elastic, and its reslicing will leave some parties with smaller pieces than before. Policies therefore cannot be said to "work" unless we presuppose a value system that permits us to weigh their benefits and costs for different socioeconomic groups and to evaluate their overall net effects. Defining and articulating that value system is of course the task of ideological analysis.

Some of our leading political figures (e.g., Ronald Reagan) have repeatedly been criticized for being much too ideological—too dogmatic to be sensible or too rigid in their pursuit of a few basic values, at the expense of other interests.[1] Those who make these complaints would be more credible if they really dissected the ideological values—or exposed the ideological contradictions and ambiguities—that permeate the views or actions they are criticizing. They would be even more credible if they managed to contrast the implications of alternative ideologies, including, possibly, their own. For instance, they might then be able to explain to us how seeming contradictions in a political candidate's views can be reconciled in terms of a hidden, deeper principle, or how an apparent consistency actually represents an untenable straddling of disparate political goals.

The American electorate seems to be dominated by two nonideological attitudes toward the political process. One is the political personality cult, which substitutes devotion to an admired leader for substantive political choice. Recent history is replete with examples of such cults. At best the trusted leader may be an approximate symbolic representation of the values of his followers; but ascertaining this requires some measure of ideological sophistication. At worst the public's trust in him may be based solely on his personal charisma, and his followers will be at the mercy of his unpredictable, unprincipled programs.

Another attitude is that of eschewing the broad ideological questions by selective position taking, issue by issue. Each position will then tend to reflect highly personal values, based on a limited perspective, whether "selfish" or partially altruistic; and many issues will remain outside the individual's own frame of reference or concern. This exclusionary, personalized attitude may certainly be expedient and self-gratifying, even as it might accommodate some favorite charity causes. And one might think of it as a micro ideology of personal-interest maximization. But it is analytically uninteresting and, to most of us, ethically inadequate. Furthermore, it surely could not serve as a banner for a broad reform movement, based on shared values, worthy of enshrining in a national constitution.

In short, we need more ideological debate, not less, or we won't be able to sort out, articulate and achieve our goals for the nation. This is where political science, and particularly the science of political economy, should step in and lead the way. The analytical tools—concepts, theoretical structures, illustrative economic data—certainly exist. But they need to be better applied, and the results need to be better demonstrated and communicated to the general public. There is big educational and promotional job waiting to get done, primarily by political scientists, economists, journalists and political office seekers. Without such efforts, the American political marketplace will remain ideologically disorganized, deceptive and, communicatively, inefficient.

FREEDOM AND EQUALITY

The dominant ideological principle in American political history, and in the American consciousness, is that of individual freedom. We hardly need not remind ourselves how this principle is invoked in the Declaration

4

of Independence or, to a more limited extent, in our Constitution. For further evidence, we might peruse some recent Presidential speeches or partisan political platforms. Or we could draw attention to some contemporary liberation movements.

Unfortunately the popularity and overuse of the term "freedom" has expanded and trivialized its meaning, so that it now can sound trite and corny. But we have nothing better to replace it with. "Liberty" would also do, although it suffers from quaint, history-book connotations. Whichever term we pick, we must clarify its contemporary meaning, or we cannot use it as a practical policy norm.

Freedom and Opportunity. Sometimes freedom means to suggest an absence of factors that constrain our socioeconomic behavior. These factors may involve coercive behavior by other individuals, operating on ourselves or our belongings: robbery, rape, embezzlement or arm twisting. Or they may involve actions by private or governmental organizations or groups: gangs of thugs, government agencies or invading foreign armies. This is a "negative" definition of freedom.

Yet sometimes freedom is loosely equated with personal possibility or ability. This suggests something more—not just an absence of specific obstructions but a presence of positive, enabling circumstances as well. This is, logically, a "positive" definition.

We will find that the former, "negative" interpretation of the word is preferable and better suited to the semantic requirements of our ideological analysis. It permits us to draw a critical distinction—that between the absence of external obstacles to human action and the personal capabilities to carry out such action.

These capabilities can be summarily characterized as "resources," which are the personal prerequisites for all useful human action. Resources, in turn, are the productive faculties embodied in our persons or in our physical and financial belongings—or assets, in the accounting jargon. They can, by definition, potentially generate income, satisfaction and pleasure for us—as long as we have the necessary freedoms to accomplish this; if they could not, we would not count them as assets or resources.

Let us illustrate: Each of us may be "free" to travel to Mars, yet we lack the financial and legal means to acquire a suitable transportation vehicle. Conversely, we may have the monetary means to buy half a pound of marijuana from a local drug dealer, but the risk of apprehension by the police puts a big dent in our freedom to do so. The former is a case of freedom (in the "negative" sense) without matching resources; the latter, one of adequate resources but incomplete freedom to use them.

When a person has both the requisite freedom and adequate resources to exploit that freedom, he has, in our terminology, a true "opportunity." Opportunity is the key social ingredient in personal satisfaction and well-being. It is the totality of what society has to offer us—an invitation, so to speak, that society extends to us and which is waiting to be accepted and exploited. And in our view, this is all that anyone should expect from society, at least if we believe in individual responsibility and respect the needs of others. In such a society, it should be up to each one of us to make the most of the opportunities given to us.

Our ideological scheme will thus be designed to create an "opportunity society." In itself, this concept might seem like little more than an empty, populist-romantic cliché. But we will, in due course, spell out what, specifically, we want this concept—and the notion of "equal opportunity"—to mean.

The Distributional Aspect. But let us admit right away that one person's opportunity gain is usually another person's loss. Society's total resources are severely limited, especially in the short run. And even if we can enlarge them in the future, their maximum potential size will still, at any one moment, be sharply limited. So it makes some sense to characterize society's total resources as an economic pie of a fixed short-run size, to be sliced up by our chosen ideological formula. This is, admittedly, a tricky balancing act.

Similarly there are upper limits to the freedoms that can be created by eliminating or preventing obstacles to human action. Most such obstacles have some positive benefits for some members of society—i.e., for those who seek support or protection through barriers on other people's freedom; and "absolute" freedom for some could easily entail a loss of freedom for others. So if we wish to respect the interests of all members of society, and ideologically favor no particular group, we will have to explain how competing freedoms are to coexist, justly and equitably.

It should be apparent that the ideological prescriptions we are aiming for involve both distribution and maximization. How to divide existing resources among the citizens is, of course, a distributional matter. How to expand their freedoms to exploit those resources is a matter that involves both distribution and maximization: Instituting hitherto suppressed freedoms can add, even on a net basis, to our overall opportunities (maximization); yet we will seek not to unduly disadvantage anybody in the process (a distributive matter). The distribution-maximization distinction closely parallels the conventional differentiation between "equity" and "efficiency": We want to be fair in dividing things up, but at the same time, we want to have as much as possible to divide.

How, then, should we, the citizens of America, enlarge our socio-economic opportunities while at the same time making their distribution more equitable? How should we let the nation's resources be distributed, and how far should we go in freeing their use (and thereby enhance their productivity and their potential future growth)?

Our basic egalitarian instincts predispose us to favor a system that gives everybody an equal amount of opportunity, or an amount as equal as possible. The goal of equal opportunity, of course, happens to be widely shared in all democratic societies; and in the United States, it probably is nearly coequal with that of individual freedom.[2]

At the same time, we know that individual actions can change any initial opportunity distribution. Some people will squander their opportunities. Others will cultivate and enlarge theirs, through work and saving, or through the operation of chance, luck or the whims of the gods. Thus a person's opportunities over time are to a large extent subject to his personal control, through his handling of his resources. Therefore, if we were to constantly equalize opportunities, we would have to redistribute the resources of different individuals again and again—taking away from those who have husbanded their resources and giving to those who have forfeited most of theirs. Would this be fair?

This writer says no; it would be grossly unfair, as well as administratively messy and complicated. Instead we should figure out how to give everybody an equal amount of resources for use throughout his lifetime, and leave it at that. But we should also allow him the fullest possible freedom to use those resources. These conditions could be achieved through what we will call a **libegalitarian** system. Such a system will distribute an equal amount of resources to everybody on a lifetime basis and, thereafter, give everybody the freedom to exploit those resources as completely as he or she can.

Efficiency versus Equity. It is helpful to recall the traditional distinction between "equity" and "efficiency"—two goals that social scientists have found difficult or impossible to simultaneously attain within any given political system. Will not we, too, be caught in this dilemma?

Equity traditionally suggests equality, either of outcome or of opportunity. But even those who are more concerned about opportunities usually end up comparing income levels or other "outcome" variables. The latter are much more easily measured. And it often seems that outcomes must directly reflect opportunities that existed in the past, while, at the same time, helping define opportunities in the near future. We have often heard that "nobody chooses to be poor," so almost all poverty would have to reflect a lack of opportunity.[3]

Yet we can influence our circumstances—not just our own socio-economic conditions but perhaps also the way we will be treated by government and society. Depending on our own actions, government might give us a more, or less, favorable treatment, and government will then enlarge, or reduce, our future opportunities. So our choice of outcome will affect opportunity, in a reversal of the generally assumed relationship.

Consequently, if government stands ready to correct future outcome disparities, it will almost inevitably reduce the individual's incentives to maintain and build up the resources he already has. In a sense, the individual will then "invest" some of his resources in future claims on the taxpaying public—claims that offer new opportunities at the expense of others. Such "investment" tends to be socially unproductive. It pushes resources away from their most efficient uses and reduces the overall productivity of the national economy. It also seems unfair.

It is obvious, then, that enforcing even a partial equality of outcomes will damage society's macroeconomic incentive mechanism, while also violating basic notions of mutuality and equity. Equality of outcomes should therefore not be a primary ideological goal. Put differently: Outcomes are to a large extent expressions of personal choice and should hence not be societally regulated. In particular, transitory outcomes are ethically inconsequential in the long-term context.

That is why, instead, we prefer to define social equity as equality of opportunity. This definition can make equity compatible with the overall economic efficiency that can be obtained in an environment of extensive individual freedom. And that is why we want to extend the time dimension of "opportunity" so that it refers to the full lifetime experience. Only through this interpretation can we avoid all the efficiency and ethics problems concerned with shorter-term opportunity concepts, or with a social program for repeatedly adjusting the individual's opportunity position.

Consequently the **libegalitarian** scheme proposed in this book provides that equality of opportunity should be an initial individual condition, not subject to repeated renewals by society. Yet the individual should be allowed to create additional opportunities for him or herself—in effect, by reinvesting some of the "dividends" he receives from his initial opportunities—through his own, subsequent actions, without any societal penalties. And in choosing his preferred strategy, he ought to enjoy as much freedom as is compatible with the like freedom of others, or some opportunities will unnecessarily, and unfairly, be forgone.

The scheme gives priority to equity over efficiency in that the former principle is the ethical starting point. In particular, no efficiency argument is allowed to disturb the basic provision of lifetime equality of opportunity. But within that constraint, our scheme gives full weight to the efficiency goal: Each individual economic agent is permitted to seek maximum satisfaction of his private goals, in the market or elsewhere (and we believe him to be capable of doing a generally good job in this respect).

Our ideological scheme will repair a major macroeconomic efficiency flaw in contemporary democratic systems. It will remove the moral hazard exposure that results from their standing offers to correct unequal outcomes through repeated redistribution measures.

By singling out equality of opportunity and freedom as our two basic equity norms, we have automatically pushed aside other potential values, and this ought to be acknowledged. Some societies have put high priorities on national cultural traditions, external conquests, religious and transcendental concepts, or law and order. Up to a point, such values might be accommodated also within a **libegalitarian** framework. But such values will rank no higher than private preferences and will have no rightful claim for government support. Collective projects based on such values would have to be privately financed, and they must not be allowed to violate the freedoms and opportunities of those who do not subscribe to those values.

HOW THE ARGUMENT IS PRESENTED

This book attempts to describe a comprehensive alternative social system based on one premise: the ethical superiority of the norm of maximum equal opportunity. All judgments made in this book are intended to illustrate the merits and consequences of that system, nothing more nor less.

That norm is treated as an axiom that should not, and cannot, be proved; it is in the nature of an assumption, even though it happens to reflect rather commonly held values (and could therefore be viewed as having some empirical validity). Some political scientists try to go one step further, searching for a more fundamental, unchallengeable basis for their ideological preferences. They often claim that their socioeconomic schemes are based on "natural rights." Yet these claims are, in essence, metaphysical.

The values underlying any ideology have no greater logical validity than personal preferences, however noble or permanent they may sound to many of us. In comparing the merits of different political systems, we cannot, really, do any better than examine our innermost ethical values and appeal to others to adopt them and to live by them. This is a subjectivist approach, with no pretensions of universal, objective validity. But it seems to be the only honest approach possible.

Apart from postulating our basic value premises, we will make a number of relatively uncontroversial assumptions about human behavior: Individuals have distinct personal needs and preferences, which they try to satisfy through purposeful individual or group actions. They are not aimless zombies or irrational morons, but generally know what they want and how to try to get it. This requires material and mental resources that are, for the most part, in scarce supply. Individuals compete for these resources and try to develop new or better resources.

The implications drawn from these various premises are in the nature of logical deductions. They are not free-floating opinions or reflections of other, unspecified values; nor are they in any sense empirical observations. The "proof" of those implications lies in their logical connections with the initial premises and not in the world of facts.

Let's illustrate. When, later on, we find that certain government programs—say, pollution controls or tax rules—are unfair or inefficient, we are demonstrating particular applications of our basic equity norm. We are showing that this norm could be more fully adhered to if these controls, or tax rules, were modified or abolished.

Those who disagree with these conclusions will have to do one of two things: show a technical conceptual or logical error in the way we have derived these conclusions, or admit to not sharing the underlying equity norm. Simply disagreeing on the specifics will not constitute a convincing counterargument. And the possibility that the government program under scrutiny might perfectly satisfy an alternative ideological scheme is beside the point; that scheme is irrelevant to us.

In illustrating our conclusions, we will refer to social conflicts that have recently generated public interest and debate. We can then draw distinctions between our conflict resolutions and those proposed by other ideological camps. At times we will pick relatively minor, obscure or even ridiculous examples. These may have some expository shock value. But more important, they will help us show how far, at the extreme, our ideological norm will take us; it is, after all, meant to be exceedingly general.

Also, by addressing obscure or hypothetical conflicts, we can define the perimeters of the affected socioethical territory. If we determine that people should be allowed to undertake actions as controversial and offensive as A and B, certainly they will be permitted to do a number of more innocuous things. The way we deal with A and B will then help define the boundaries of the individual rights embodied in our ideological scheme.

One last methodological note. To convey our ideological message, we need a terminology that communicates effectively. The most suitable technical language is that of economics, supplemented by some political science terms. Economic concepts will be useful to us because we are essentially concerned with the employment and distribution of scarce resources —the central question in economics. Those concepts will prove especially convenient because of the breadth and generality of the social and political questions that nowadays are addressed by the economics profession, from family matters to crime to the pleasure of leisure.[4]

As we look at the world through the lens of economics, we will interpret individual human action as an ongoing effort to maximize personal welfare, satisfaction or happiness—three terms of equivalent meaning in this context. Thus the "economic man" strives to better his life by constantly reassessing his socioeconomic opportunities and trading off less-valuable resources for more-valuable ones. Economically speaking, his end goal is to maximize his benefits from consumption, optimally distributed over his lifetime. However, he may be only partially successful, as his information about existing opportunities will be incomplete, and information—in itself, a valuable resources—is costly to come by. And he will make mistakes, or reap unexpected windfall gains, depending on chance and luck. Even so, most of his economic optimization efforts will usually pay off, and he will learn from his mistakes.

Our focus on consumption as the individual's innermost concern within society may seem peculiar. Surely we all have higher aspirations, and consumption seems merely one ingredient in human welfare. Yes and no. Note that we will use the term consumption very broadly. We will, in fact, let it represent any welfare-generating human act that requires the use and partial depletion of some valuable resource.

If a human endeavor is both directly beneficial and costly, it is, by definition, in the nature of consumption, never mind how it is conventionally labeled. We consume when we use our homes to entertain guests; this consumption includes a small amount of housing (which could, instead, have been rented out to somebody else), as well as, typically, some food and beverage supplies. If we join a health club, we are probably making a conscious decision to invest in a healthier future with extended and more satisfying consumption prospects; we are trading off valuable cash and leisure time today in exchange for more productive bodies and higher, more satisfying consumption levels tomorrow.

National defense programs consume, directly, a great deal of materiel, fuels and maintenance services. Alternatively, they can be said to indirectly consume all the private goods that could have been produced if the required resources had been allowed to enter the private sector instead. All of these situations revolve around the key socioeconomic issue—that of some type of consumption, now or later. This explains why we need a consumption perspective, and an economic perspective, on our entire ideological discussion.

Economics is not "everything." But it provides us with a helpful analytical and verbal framework. It permits us a consistent view of all facets of social interaction, whether in the traditional marketplace, in informal person-to-person settings or in the political arena. If we communicate accurately and easily by using economic terms and ideas, we are, in fact, practicing good communications economics; and this is something every author ought to do.

Chapter II
LEGITIMATE FREEDOMS

FREE OR UNFREE

If freedom, along with opportunity, is to be the cornerstone of our ideological system, we will have to define, characterize and identify it. If we find that freedoms carry costs as well as benefits, we ought to be able to show that the costs are outweighed by the benefits. If we are going to criticize other social systems on this score, we will need to show that they, in effect, are guilty of suppressing certain freedoms that we could restore.

In the political and ideological context, freedom is almost always a matter of interpersonal or intergroup relations, and ultimately of the societal rules that govern those relations. Ideologies regulate socioeconomic behavior and establish methods for conflict resolutions, and in so doing, they protect, modify or rearrange the freedoms of the affected parties. Freedoms tend to clash, and society often steps in to redraw the battle lines. (Generally ideologies do not touch on relations between humans and other living organisms; however, some political scientists have raised their voices on behalf of the freedom of animals, even at the expense of humans, and the animal-rights movement has been gaining ground lately.[5])

Whether we are dealing with "negative" or "positive" provisions for freedoms, a central ideological question is: Should society allow individuals in situation X to perform acts of type A, even though this may lessen the possibilities for individuals in situation Y to perform similar, or functionally related, acts (of type A or B)?

Assume our answer is affirmative. We will then be sanctioning the former individuals' freedom to perform those acts (type A). And we can consider this freedom, by our ethical standards, a "right"—i.e., a socially sanctioned freedom. At the same time, we will implicitly be restricting the freedom of individuals with conflicting aspirations (in situation Y), thus denying them potential rights of their own. (For instance, X and Y might represent competing efforts, by a man and a woman, to fill a particular job vacancy; or while the person in situation X wants to manufacture handguns, Y represents a police force wishing to preserve gun ownership for itself.)

In short, ideologies are, to a large extent, conceptual frameworks for a definition, distribution, protection or denial of rights. These rights include, in particular, the rights not to be prevented from exercising a variety of wanted, beneficial freedoms ("negative" freedom provisions). They can also include guaranteed access to some of the resources that make freedoms exploitable and economically useful (sometimes classified as "positive" provisions).

Production and Exchange. Freedoms, and the associated rights, can be classified in many different ways. One way is to apply the standard distinction between the two basic socioeconomic functions, production and exchange, and hence between production freedoms and exchange freedoms. This two-way classification of socioeconomic functions can provide us with a useful analytical starting point. It will allow us to differentiate between different freedom-threatening situations or policies, and between different policy approaches through which freedoms might be preserved.

A few definitional relationships might need to be clarified. Production transforms inputs—of labor, raw material, energy or machine use—into outputs of other goods (or services). Producers (firms, individuals or public agencies) undertake such transformations when they believe that the outputs are more valuable—or command higher prices—than the needed input combinations. Exchanges allow us to alter the composition of goods at our disposal, as producers or consumers, so that they will, jointly considered, be more valuable to us. They might be able to produce more output for us, because of their complementarity in a production process (e.g., between a PC and a skilled PC operator). Or they might "produce" greater consumer satisfaction when enjoyed together (e.g., a meal complemented by a suitable wine).

All useful human activities can be placed in either of these two categories, whether they involve single individuals or formal, or informal, groups. Automobile assembly, space exploration and warfare are productive activities or at least intended as such. So are TV watching, house cleaning and ball games, even though they may not appear in the national product statistics. Exchanges (or trades) include not only purchases and sales in the ordinary marketplace, typified by shopping malls or electronic trading networks. They also include many unstructured, informal transactions in other settings, in which individuals or groups "barter" goods, services or simple favors. In all of these, some freedoms are at stake; and political theoreticians or practitioners might see reasons to restrict these freedoms.

Freedom to Produce. Should society generally allow us the freedom to produce? Should this freedom be unlimited? One is almost tempted to answer with an unequivocal yes. If humans act with clear, well-conceived purposes, any production they undertake will, it seems, have a beneficial purpose. Even if some activities—from the manufacture of Edsels to the baking of a collapsing soufflé—should prove misguided and ultimately unproductive, this ought to be the producers' own responsibility; at least this will be our preliminary analysis.

Generally, disallowing production would violate our ideological desire to maximize worthwhile opportunities. So we will tentatively conclude that everyone should be allowed to decide for himself what to produce, and how and when.

Furthermore, production seems, in itself, to create no direct interpersonal or social conflict. It is mostly a technical, engineering-type process, without those interpersonal implications that can prompt immediate ideological scrutiny. However, production feeds exchange, through formal and informal distribution channels, as products are sold to consumers and users on the final-goods markets. Moreover, production usually presupposes exchanges in the input markets (especially of labor for wages and of raw materials for cash or credit). Therefore the freedoms granted to producers will have complex spillover effects on other, related parties, and these effects can enhance, or restrict, the rights and opportunities of these parties.

However, some productive activities generate social counterpressures, based on moral, humanitarian or pecuniary concerns. Some activities are perceived to produce negative side effects on third parties—effects broadly categorized as negative "externalities." For instance, some people strongly object to the publishing of pornographic magazines. Production through the use of child labor, or under unsanitary conditions, is widely disapproved of and has been declared illegal. In addition, there are, today in the United States, bans on certain quasi-industrial activities in the home that compete with unionized factory work (including, until recently, the knitting of ski caps). So production is, in the predominant con-

15

temporary view, not a purely private matter but an interpersonal, social phenomenon of potential ideological relevance.

Should we accept this view? Or should we stick to our essential belief in the usefulness of production and in the strong case for producer freedom?

In developing a complete answer, we must, to start, preserve the producer's need for immunity from interferences that seem purely gratuitous—interferences that clearly violate individual freedoms or their mutual coexistence. No one should be entitled to restrict the productive activities of others on purely private-esthetic or private-moral grounds in the absence of contractual obligations with such implications. Moral or esthetic concerns not founded in our basic ideological value scheme are irrelevant; acknowledging such concerns would introduce perfectly arbitrary restrictions and create an unstable rights structure; and so, they deserve no official, constitutional sanction.

But shouldn't we regard the personal offense we might take, say, from barbaric factory conditions or the ugliness of many consumer goods as negative "externalities" that ought to be curbed? No, these consequences must be tolerated in an individualistic society—or we would not respect the freedoms and rights that inhere in our goal of individual opportunity maximization. These rights require a clear delineation of property ownership, and no personal moral or esthetic claims on other persons' property can then be officially honored.

A purely psychological offense is not comparable to an invasion of property or the destruction of another person's assets. We should have no "psychological property rights" in each other's property, for all property could then become ambiguously co-owned, and property management would then be hopelessly inefficient. In other words, moral-esthetic standards should not be accorded property-like protection; production freedom ought to take precedence.

Moreover, as we analyze various types of activities that are by many regarded as offensive, we will find that legitimate ideological concerns might be raised on another plane—about the associated exchange transactions. It is possible that offensive job conditions, shady production methods or harmful exploitations of natural resources reflect violations of labor contracts or commercial rental agreements, or an unwarranted expropriation of public property. These are matters of exchange, or should be so regarded, rather than production questions per se. They might indeed be illegitimate by our ideological standards, once we have assumed the right perspective on these questions. So while production processes in themselves tend to be ethically innocuous, there might be critical questions of how the associated resources were acquired, or how the final products were disposed of.

Freedom to Exchange. The exchanges we are concerned with include sales, rentals, lending and many other types of bilateral give-and-takes of goods or services. They can occur either through traditional commercial transactions in recognized markets or through noncommercial *quid pro quos* in other contexts. But they all involve at least two interacting parties who are presumed to seek and attain some benefits from their transactions. Thus we find exchanges, not just in shops, offices and auction halls, but also in homes and recreation facilities.

One example is baby-sitting for free room and board. Another is a mutual sharing of information about grocery prices or job market conditions. Also consider social dancing, sex or card games: These activities all contain elements of exchange, as well as production. So does marriage—a long-term contract for the exchange and production of a broad range of mutually beneficial services. And if we are lucky, we will also have a bilateral exchange relationship with every level of government: Under the best of circumstances, the government provides us with useful services in exchange for the taxes we pay. In performing any one of these exchanges, we, of course, need the requisite freedoms; yet society has raised a variety of objections.

Purposeful exchanges normally make both parties better off, unless one party turns out to have made a serious miscalculation. We are therefore strongly inclined to declare exchanges ethically permissible and not to be restricted. The burden of proof is on the side of those who wish to interfere or restrict.

Exchanges permit a useful redistribution of goods, from those with lesser needs (for the goods they give up) to those with greater needs (for the goods they acquire). Ideally both parties to a particular exchange find themselves in that desirable situation. Furthermore, exchanges help make production worthwhile: If I cannot sell my output, I could as well give up most of my organized productive activities (unless I am one of those rare self-sufficient providers, like Robinson Crusoe without Friday).

Disallowing the freedom of exchange would normally mean that both of the trading parties would suffer a loss of opportunity to enhance their welfare. If we reject that approach, we will have to permit prostitution, gun sales and heroin traffic—unless we find other, ideologically convincing grounds for not permitting such transactions.

Implicit in the right to exchange is that the exchange is freely and voluntarily entered into. Forced recruitment of labor does not constitute a voluntary exchange. Nor does a business deal arranged under the threat of physical abuse or through deception. There will certainly be some ethi-cally gray areas in this regard, particularly with respect to acceptable ad-vertising and bargaining tactics. But the principle is clear enough: The freedom to engage in voluntary exchanges should be a very basic social right, while forced, coercive exchanges should not.

Voluntary exchange perfectly satisfies the old—and much more gen-eral—maxim (attributed to Herbert Spencer) that each person be granted all freedoms compatible with like freedoms for all other individuals.[6] It is the central element of any ideology based on mutually compatible indi-vidual freedoms; and it is also the best avenue available for enhancing individual opportunities. The "free trade" principle applies not just among nations but even more strongly among individuals and private firms. This has long been recognized by all the leading political scientists in the capitalist, free-enterprise tradition, from Adam Smith to Milton Friedman.[7]

OBSTACLES TO FREEDOM

Alternatively we can analyze freedom more indirectly—by examining the forces that can restrict or destroy it. We can then decide which of these forces, if any, ought to be considered illegitimate. When they are not, we will give the threatened freedom the status of a social right, de-serving of official protection.

Let's start with those obvious cases in which individuals apply outright coercion over others to achieve their ends. Murder and bodily assault re-strict the victims' freedoms to use their bodies, and possibly their minds as well, both while the attack is taking place and often even longer. Economically these are incomplete exchanges, with a taking of personal physical assets (human assets) in return for nothing. Similarly, incarcera-tion, deportation and military conscription constitute lopsided exchanges, with expropriations of physical human assets, or their use, on highly un-favorable, unilateral terms.

Such violations of a person's freedom obviously imply an immediate loss of opportunity for him—the opportunity that coercion forces him to forgo. This opportunity might be related to his immediate consumption: He simply cannot enjoy himself to the extent he had anticipated. Or the lost opportunity might involve the production and buildup of assets that he had hoped to draw on in the future; in this case, there is an infringe-ment on his freedom to earn, invest and potentially consume later on. The former situation could occur, for instance, if we are forbidden to eat our preferred meal or undertake our preferred vacation travel. The latter situa-tion might occur if we are prevented from taking our preferred, best-paying job, and thereby are prevented from saving some of the hypothetical earnings from that job.

In either case, a loss of freedom will mean a loss of opportunity, a loss of actual or potential consumption possibilities and a loss of human satisfaction. Certainly we will have to declare such violations of freedom illegitimate—or we will not be able to meet our goal of opportunity maximization.

Freedom is similarly restricted if somebody is deprived of some of his already accumulated assets—a possibility that especially involves such tangible assets that can be disposed of in the marketplace. Theft, robbery, embezzlement and confiscation obviously entail involuntary sacrifices of physical or financial assets in the victim's ownership. As such, they lessen the victim's ability to enjoy the freedoms normally associated with such assets—most fundamentally, his freedom to preserve or accumulate wealth, with subsequent opportunities for future consumption.

It may seem obvious that these freedom-destroying acts should be considered illegitimate; most ideologies have prescribed that, in principle, they should. However, each society tends to set up its own rules about what is legitimate in this regard, with varying effects on the structure of freedoms and rights.

Even basically freedom-oriented societies are up against one common ideological problem—that of reconciling freedoms with their half-hearted, often ineffectual, efforts to equalize opportunities. Many freedom infringements are justified by a perceived need to offset weaknesses in the distribution of resources and the associated opportunities. In lieu of policies that would directly correct the resource distribution, policymakers will be tempted to recommend second-best solutions that interfere with the market mechanism. This is true of rent controls and some aspects of "affirmative action" programs. Yet these market interferences will undermine some of the freedoms that government otherwise claims to honor.

Many societal obstacles to freedom thus consist of government regulations that interfere directly with the freedom of exchange. Yet others stem from governmental programs that aim for a redistribution of resources, primarily through taxation. These latter programs tend to encroach on the individual's freedom to dispose of his income and to allocate it to his preferred uses—at least this is a strong possibility that we must explore.

In any case, it is natural to hold up government for special scrutiny. Government is easily the biggest potential destroyer of our freedoms, as well as their best potential guarantor. Naturally, almost all social systems have given the national government exceptionally large prerogatives in the definition and granting of freedoms. Actually we might try to construe our relations with government as a set of benign "exchanges," not entirely unlike those we undertake in the market; government activity may then, at first blush, seem to enhance, rather than restrict, our freedoms. But this would be a very special kind of government, one that we may never see the likes of (except in our own **libegalitarian** vision).

To sort out the positive and negative aspects of government is undoubtedly the toughest job for an ideological critic. So let us not yet try to draw the line between its freedom-creating and freedom-destroying aspects or to generalize about its net effects on individual opportunities. Let's be content, for the moment, to assume that such distinctions can be satisfactorily drawn and that we may be able to design a better alternative.

Effects of Government. Any institution is potentially open to charges of either omission or commission. So is, of course, government. It is either doing the wrong thing or not doing the right thing; or it is doing too much or too little of what is essentially the right thing.

Government can destroy freedoms by taking away some of the resources that individuals have built up through their own work and saving; it then destroys some of the freedoms related to the transformation of individual skills or muscle power into future consumption opportunities. The effects can be similar when government leaves resources in individual hands but circumscribes their use. If government supplies no fully compensatory freedoms or resources, the affected individuals will suffer net opportunity losses, and we are inclined to regard this as illegitimate. So government is then excessive, at least by our **libegalitarian** standards.

But we will find that government can, in other situations, create freedoms (even though the anarcholibertarians hold the opposite view). These freedoms have to do with our ability to access the very services that government, and government alone, can provide. Briefly, the chance to draw on government can be regarded as a composite, multifaceted freedom all in itself. Conversely, a prohibition against all government, or against government activities that are truly warranted, restricts the freedom to participate in the organization and operation of government. Similarly, an insufficient amount of government can destroy freedom for those who thereby fail to get adequate access to its potential freedom-supporting services.

Only the most extreme ideologies postulate that government is never excessive—as do some versions of full-fledged socialism. And only the most extreme ideologies claim that government is never insufficient—as does the school of anarchist laissez-faire. We will not fully agree with either position—not because we fear being "extreme," but because we think we have a more discriminating understanding of the possibilities and limitations of government.

Government activities, like private activities, can be separated into the two broad classes of production and exchange. Government is a multiline producer and, as such, competes with the private sector for the nation's available resources. Its productive activities tend to preempt and replace potential private activity, for better or for worse.

The goods or services output of government, as we have experienced it so far, may be relatively similar to that which could have been produced privately with the same resources; consider the U.S. national park service or a state police force, each of which seems to fill some private or quasipublic needs. Or the government's output may be very different from what private parties technically could have produced or would have wanted to produce; consider some of the U.S. government's major recent foreign policy adventures or the moon landing in the early 1970s.

Government involvement in exchange transactions may seem much more innocuous by comparison. If the government enters into voluntary, businesslike exchange deals with private parties, there is no direct, obvious violation of anybody's freedom. Both the public and the private transactors may seem to gain, at least if the exchanges are linked to useful public activities.

But our conclusion will be different if the government sets its selling price too high (e.g., by charging too much for postal services or imposing excessive professional or business license fees), or if it coerces unwilling persons into unattractive exchanges (e.g., through a military draft). The reluctant, overpaying private buyers will then lose some of their freedoms and opportunities. Government is then overstepping the boundaries of its mission. It is, in fact, destructive.

Taxation is a major aspect of the citizen's "exchange" relationship with his national government. Of course it destroys the taxpayer's freedom to directly control the use of his entire income and to acquire the individual goods and services he wants. To judge whether this is legitimate, we have to ascertain whether the taxpayer, indirectly, gets his money's worth anyhow—by receiving government services that he actually desires but could not have bought in the private market.

Needless to say, taxation can be excessive in our kind (and almost any kind) of society; and this is a major aspect of potential governmental destruction of freedom. But let us not be blind to the converse possibility: Taxation of some or all taxpayers could be too low to permit government activities that might be sufficiently beneficial to them. The fundamental political questions are, thus, both how to decide what services the government ought to offer and how it ought to charge the benefiting public. From our ideological perspective, the answers will depend on the government's effects on freedom and opportunities.

All governments, in addition, rely on regulations and controls to achieve its production- and exchange-related ends. Almost by definition, controls are freedom restrictive; the only meaningful exceptions involve controls that are entirely ineffective or which impinge on freedoms that nobody, ever, would care to exercise. Controls on offshore drilling, medical practice and deer hunting unquestionably restrict some people's freedom of production. And import quotas, rent controls and food quality inspections limit the abilities of some people to buy and sell, sometimes to the advantage and sometimes to the disadvantage of the other party to the exchange.

Such government policy measures indeed violate the ideal of free voluntary exchange. Like excessive taxes, they seem to make some people unnecessarily unfree. One is thus tempted to flatly declare them ideologically illegitimate.

Yet we should keep an open mind to the theoretical possibility that there are compensating benefits to the public in one form or another. The two big problems are: Will the benefits accrue to those individuals whose freedoms are restricted? And, could these benefits not be produced at lower costs in the private sector and, therefore, with less severe losses of freedom and opportunity? To get a better handle on these questions, we must first reach an understanding of the general nature of all "collective action"—the key concept in the analysis of government.

GROUPS AND COLLECTIVE ACTION

Freedom is an individual condition or an individual experience. It might therefore seem to follow that freedom can be enjoyed only by individuals, acting on their own behalf. In the extreme, freedom could then never be enjoyed through any sort of cooperative activity; instead every joint pursuit would seem to hinder freedom's maximization.

A society conforming to such an atomistic model would, economically, have to be based on individual entrepreneur-workers like the old-style farmer, the solo artist or the individual consultant. These one-person firms would interact, at arm's length, solely through exchange transactions, without any organizational commitments to other workers or resource owners.

But we know that the modern reality is very different, and we cannot attribute that reality wholly to the unfortunate presence of excessive, repressive government. Modern societies are dominated by large or small private and public group organizations that attract and pool resources originally belonging to their individual members. We must suspect that some of these organizations are useful and productive, perhaps by offering their members freedoms that otherwise would be unavailable to them. We could hardly picture a modern society without them. And a free society could hardly, without special justifications, be allowed to restrict the freedom of individuals to form such organizations or to join them.

What, then, should group organizations be permitted to do in a free society? How should organizations operate if they are to avoid engaging in freedom-destructive activities? Can we, accordingly, separate legitimate from illegitimate organizations or legitimate from illegitimate group actions? Is the nation a legitimate group and the national government a legitimate spokesman for it?

Modern political economists have developed a sophisticated theory of groups and collective action.[8] This theory helps us answer the preceding questions. Since it will be one of the cornerstones of our **libegalitarian** ideology, it deserves to be summarized and restated here.

Collective Goods. The rationale for all organized groups is that they produce collective goods for their members. A collective good is a good that cannot be produced and made available to selected individuals only; it is, by its nature, shared among the group members. This is mostly a technological matter in that the technique does not exist for producing and distributing the good in individual units; and so the individuals who would want to purchase it could never find it in the private market. Collective goods come only in multiuser varieties and not in individually negotiated bundles.

Collective goods exist on many geographic planes, from the neighborhood to the city, the state, the country and the whole world. Sometimes collective goods have little or nothing to do with geography, but instead are based on shared values among the group members.

People who live in the same urban neighborhood may have a shared interest in the physical characteristics of the area, and they therefore constitute a natural locational group. They may or may not be organized; in either case, improved neighborhood conditions would represent a collective good to them. When conditions change for the better, everybody, in varying degrees, will share in the benefit of the change. There would be no way of channeling this benefit only to certain members of the neighborhood, since everybody will enjoy it automatically.

Stockholders in the same corporation share in the benefit of increased profits. To them the corporation's profits represent a collective good, until the profits have been distributed or until they choose to sell their stock. Or consider a nonpecuniary good: To those who would like to see reduced poverty in Alabama, a reduction in that state's poverty will be a shared, collective good of yet another kind.

In many cases, the group members can leave the groups they belong to. This clearly applies to the person who moves out of a neighborhood or sells his corporate stock. In other cases, the members cannot, psychologically or physically, leave their group. This applies to people with strongly held permanent values (such as family loyalty or religious beliefs) that predestine them to particular group affiliations. Their need to organize themselves will then usually be so much greater, for the chances that they could satisfy those values in other, substitute circumstances will be so much smaller.

A free society must clearly tolerate, or even encourage, group organizations as long as they have clear, useful missions and confine themselves to those missions. Yet groups, like individuals, should have to respect the freedom of others to pursue their interests, individually or collectively. And a free society might perhaps also encourage group organizations to treat their own members in a similarly respectful manner—at least, by its own, governmental example. Ideally, there ought not to be any systematic violations of freedoms either among the group members or between them and outsiders; yet society's obligation to prevent such violations will, of course, be much greater, and much firmer, when they involve the government itself.

As members of the nation-group, we should insist that the government, in its own activities, respect the freedom of all of us. We might also prefer that similar constraints be imposed on trade associations, bridge clubs, boy scout organizations and the Ku Klux Klan. But publicly forcing these latter organizations to do so would be coercive. After all, disgruntled members could work to effect changes within their own organizations. Or, as a last resort, they could cancel their memberships and establish new, better-run organizations.

It thus seems that government does not have an intrinsic right to control these matters, except by maintaining the freedom of voluntary exchange at all private—individual or organizational—levels. However, this rule does not, in itself, define the complete boundaries of government. If the government is to protect essentially all citizen rights, how, precisely, do we define these rights? So we still need a definition of the government's own mission, apart from that of passively protecting the private sector.

It is commonly believed, almost as an axiom, that governments should look after the common interests of the general public, not those of "special interests" or individuals; that this belief is so readily compromised in practice is another matter. National governments should take care of national needs, state governments of state needs, and so on. This is also a simple, short-hand description of collective-good theory, as applied to the public sector.

Translated into the language of collective-good theory, this will mean

24

that governments derive their justification from two coexisting conditions. One, some collective goods are geographically or territorially based. Two, governments can be regarded as legitimate organs of our major territorial groups—the nation, states and localities—and possibly also of other geographic entities with broadly shared interests. Governments are therefore well positioned to produce some of those goods. They are usually better positioned for this job than private organizations, which normally lack a definite, permanent territorial base.

This view of government seems relatively well accepted, even though group theory and collective-good language has not penetrated the public consciousness or the media vocabulary; and, unfortunately, contemporary economists and political scientists rarely approach governmental problems from this basic theoretical angle. But if we go ahead and apply these theoretical norms, we will automatically have a way of identifying what is wrong with our current political system. And we can proceed to sketch a better, drastically reformed society.

The National Government. The nation is a territorial club. Its boundaries may not be just right, but let's not consider how they might be perfected right now. States, counties and cities are, by extension, examples of smaller territorial clubs; and we sense immediately that there are tricky problems of potentially overlapping functions among them. But the nation obviously commands most of our ideological interest—partly because it is much more ambitious and powerful and partly because, in the United States and elsewhere, it establishes many of the legal boundaries for state (provincial) and local government action as well.

What, according to the theory of groups and collective goods, should national governments be doing? They should produce the collective goods desired by their member-citizens—whom we presume to be cost-conscious maximizers of their personal welfare. By contrast, governments should refrain from producing purely individual goods, i.e., goods that can be produced and distributed in a normal, individualized fashion in the marketplace or via private group arrangements. So what collective goods should they, then, produce? Especially those that are national in nature, i.e., those that ultimately accrue to, or benefit, essentially all the citizens. This is a tough requirement.

But we first need to establish that by producing according to this rule, the government can enhance the citizens' freedoms and opportunities. We have already suggested that there is an element of freedom in the right to receive the services of a supportive, productive government (a freedom of exchange, of sorts). Or we could think of this right as a potential indirect method for creating new resources, obtainable from the government—which also presupposes a kind of freedom (a freedom to produce). Moreover, the collective goods obtained in this way can potentially reinforce valuable freedoms in the private sphere—freedoms to accomplish things that might not otherwise be possible. For example, a government-operated police force may expand, first, the freedom of property owners to prosecute burglars and collect damages, and, second, the broader freedoms of safe private commerce or peaceful urban living.

Cost Aspects. Yet government is costly, both in terms of money and in terms of resource use or forgone activity in the private sector. So we need to weigh the costs of government action against its benefits. Only in this way can we determine how much production is really worthwhile or whether any production at all is called for. The territorial club members will of course have to pay these costs, and they would feel cheated if they didn't get their money's—their cost contributions'—worth.

There will, in theory, always be a break-even-point at which production, via government, is just barely justified and beyond which further production will be too costly or inadequately beneficial. Economists (foremost among them, Paul Samuelson) have shown mathematically where this point lies, based on the marginal (last-unit) costs and benefits of each line of government production.[9] Essentially it is analogous to the point of production for the well-run firm that tries to maximize its profits via individual-good production in the free, competitive market.

In short, the government ought to be run in a cost-effective, business-less manner. The government should simulate the business firm's behavior in the market, for only then can it efficiently cater to our collective needs.

And how should the citizens share the costs of government activity? In accordance with the extent to which they benefit from government-made services, just as the buyer of individual goods pays the cost of his own purchases—this is a corollary of the neoclassical collective-goods theory. If the citizens don't benefit, they shouldn't pay either.

With this cost rule, however, we realize that governments might not need to confine themselves to producing goods that are enjoyed by everybody within their respective territories. If nonbeneficiaries do not have to pay, they will hardly have any reason to object to government programs they do not benefit from. Even in a free society, governments might hence be allowed to produce more limited, selective collective goods as well—as long as they do a better job than the private sector, and as long as they properly charge the beneficiaries and only them.

There would surely be great implementation difficulties with this kind of rule. But if techniques can be developed for identifying the true beneficiaries, perhaps these parties could be made to bear the entire costs—for instance, through service or user fees collected in exchange for those benefits. The **libegalitarian** system launched here is amenable to such possible arrangements. (The anarcholibertarian model, definitely, is not. Liberals, by contrast, seem to have very few qualms about such "microcollective" goods programs; their notion of what government may do is fluid enough to accommodate a variety of narrow, nonterritorial collective-goods demands.)

The best traditional example of government activity with legitimate collective-good justification is defense. By defending the nation, the government can produce security that benefits just about everybody within the country. Freedom from attack or external threats increases our freedoms and opportunities in many respects. Adequate defense could not possibly be provided by the private sector in sufficient amounts, and the resulting freedoms and opportunities would be too limited. This is a generally accepted view, except within anarchist circles.

One serious objection against this reasoning is worth considering. It is sometimes claimed that the analogy between nations and private clubs, or other private organizations, is false. Governments are coercive in that they have taxation powers, and membership in the national territorial club is not really voluntary. By contrast, we can quit a private club that we are unhappy with. At least so say the diehard libertarians.

But surely this distinction is grossly overdrawn. All club memberships carry certain obligations, as well as rights. Once we have joined, we have committed ourselves to fulfill those obligations. The nation is similar—in kind, if not in degree: Once we decide to live in a certain country, we assume certain obligations. We could, after all, vote with our feet and emigrate, even though this would be a rather drastic step.

All club management has the potential for being coercive and tyrannical, whether private or public, and we may have to fight against such tendencies by exercising our club rights to protest and seek reform from within. By the same reasoning, we will be better off if we concentrate on redefining and improving what government, as well as our favorite private organizations, are doing, rather than rejecting these institutions altogether.

Government, at its best, is a cost-effective producer-seller of worthwhile services to the public at large. Taxpayers are buyers of government protection and many other services whose values ideally outstrip their tax costs—even though, in practice, many of the person-to-government exchanges have seemed grossly wasteful or unbalanced. In turn, government employees and its product suppliers are of course sellers to the government, and these transactions also need to meet businesslike cost-effectiveness criteria.

If government carried out these production and exchange functions efficiently, with proper attention to individual benefits and costs, it would indeed perform an entirely constructive role. It would conform to the opportunity-maximization and equality requirements of our **libegalitarian** constitution.

THE SATISFIED CONSUMER

The individual performs a number of economic functions, and his abilities to perform these functions are interdependent. The freedom he enjoys in one function will tend to be more valuable if, at the appropriate time, he is equally free to perform other, complementary functions. These interdependencies must be kept in mind when we try to design a superior, opportunity-maximizing social system.

Each individual, with no exceptions, is a consumer. He uses up some of his resources in the direct, immediate satisfaction of his current needs, wants and desires; this is what the term consumption means. As we have already noted, consumption is a key tool for personal well-being, satisfaction and even happiness. It is the managerial instrument through which we can directly satisfy our personal needs and desires. Consumption is the final economic step in the disposition of our individual and national resources.

The consumer function is therefore, ideologically, the central one. Assigning a key role to consumption is not philistine or crass. Rather it is a way of celebrating the individual. It reflects a recognition of his varying personal needs and promotes the best possible societal accommodation of these needs.

Consumption freedom is a primary requirement of a free society. Without it, other freedoms will become meaningless. Freedom to work and to seek the highest-paying job available would lose its value if the fruits of the labor could not be used for the acquisition of consumer goods. Similarly the freedom to engage in profitable investment would not translate into any personal benefits unless the investment returns could someday be consumed—by the investor, of course.

If consumption freedom were permanently absent—luckily, an absurd situation—rational humans would stop working and investing, in preparation for death. To be sure, no known ideology or regime has dared to go nearly this far. But on the other hand, there is distressingly little recognition of consumption in either the theoretical or the everyday political debate, at least outside narrow libertarian circles. This is something we specifically want to rectify and account for in our proposed **libegalitarian** system. We want to identify some of the major encroachments on consumption freedoms that occur today or are proposed by other political systems, but which we would wish to escape. We want to ascertain how these freedoms can be restored and safeguarded.

Two key aspects of consumer freedom can be distinguished. One has to do with access to different types of consumer goods, the other with the timing of their acquisition or enjoyment. In either regard, freedom is legitimate only if it satisfies the general mutuality requirement and thus leaves the interests of others unimpaired; recall Spencer's rule.

That is—to pick a couple of crude examples—we cannot endorse the unauthorized eating of other persons' food or the uninvited occupancy of their homes. But we can fully endorse the individual's right to consume goods that are already in his possession, whether he himself produced them (e.g., homemade cakes) or acquired them through bona-fide non-coercive purchases (take-out dinners). And we can as readily sanction the right to consume on credit (consumption not yet paid for) as long as others voluntarily provide that credit—in effect, by deferring their own consumption.

Such consumer freedoms should therefore be construed as social rights. These rights might, at first blush, seem wholly uncontroversial; yet, in actuality, they are not, as we shall see.

Choice of Goods. The freedom to consume should imply a full, unrestricted choice among available consumer goods, as long as these are legitimately acquired. There must be no coercive governmental or private restrictions on the right to satisfy one's personal consumption preferences—at least not in a society that claims to respect individual freedom. All such preferences and choices ought to be equally legitimate, without discrimination. Society must be neutral in this regard—or individual opportunities cannot be systematically maximized.

This freedom must emcompass the eating of bad food as well as good, the wearing of ugly, as well as beautiful, clothes and the watching of stupid, as well as intelligent, movies. It must include consumption acts that some people may regard as immoral or otherwise offensive, whether undertaken in the dining room or in the bedroom. This includes cigar smoking, reckless drinking and the taking of dangerous drugs. And we might add suicide: the consumption of a nonreproducible body and mind.

But shouldn't harmful and immoral consumption acts be considered illegitimate? Shouldn't we protect people against their self-destructive urges? No, not if we respect the sanctity of individual freedom and the opportunities created by freedom. There is no foreordained notion of what consumption acts are individually destructive or harmful, and societal authorities should have no right to impose the particular consumption standards that are favored by the current officeholders or their constituents. The national constitution of a free society cannot permit discriminatory restrictions against certain consumption preferences and consumption acts, regardless of how few people share these preferences or how repulsive or dangerous the vast majority may find these acts.

Unfortunately the U.S. government does not operate in accordance with these proconsumer principles: Instead it imposes a large number of restrictions on consumers who, it is claimed, threaten to damage their own health (through allegedly malnutritious food or insufficiently safe medication), foul the environment (through smoking) or waste natural resources (through off-season hunting)—or who break other anticonsumer rules.

Timing. In regard to timing, consumption freedom must imply the right to consume more now and less later, or vice versa, in any quantitative combination that can be sustained through voluntary exchange.

Each of us should be allowed to pick his preferred consumption time path, or he will be unnecessarily unfree. Some of us are impatient, early consumers who wish to spend most of our incomes or use up most of our resources as soon as possible. Others prefer to postpone their consumption gratification, relishing the anticipation of a good future life. Neither group of consumers should be favored by the government. It is true that the conventional Judeo-Christian work-and-save ethic tries to tell us that the latter, postponement-prone type of behavior is ethically superior. However, an individualistic, freedom-loving society cannot let such an attitude hold sway at the constitutional level.

Intertemporal preferences—i.e., sooner-versus-later tastes—are as legitimate as intercommodity preferences, say, in the choice among wines, clothes or taped concert pieces. They are an important manifestation of individual choice.

If the government restricted the freedom of such choice—say, by putting a ceiling on permissible annual consumption levels for particular age groups—the impact on the individual members of these groups would vary, and there would occur discriminatory losses of well-being among them. True, those who would voluntarily have stayed within the prescribed limits, even in the absence of such restrictions, would not sense any losses. But those who, as a result, had to rearrange their consumption paths would, indeed, suffer losses. Similar inequitable results occur if the government imposes tax penalties on those who exhibit particular intertemporal consumption tendencies—as if these individuals were out of step with a societal timing norm.

But are these examples realistic? Does the government in reality ever pursue such peculiar policies? You bet. Intentionally or unintentionally, it is extensively engaged in influencing and complicating our intertemporal consumption choices. In many complex ways, the authorities penalize us for trying to spend and consume at the time we want to. They set up inducements for us to spend and consume at times when we might otherwise not have wanted to. The resulting intertemporal spending shifts tend to make many of us worse off—not just during particular phases of our lives, but in the total summation of our lifetime consumption experience.

Almost every aspect of the U.S. government's spending, tax or regulatory policies has some intertemporal consequences for some income or citizen groups—some minor, some significant. The government is pervasive enough to change the availability over time of almost all types of private-market goods, as well as public-sector goods, and public policies therefore have distinct intertemporal implications for different socioeconomic groups. For instance, tax-financed federal health care programs obviously favor the unhealthy, who are numerically overrepresented among older citizen groups. And in this sense, they force a delay in the average citizen's consumption, from the time of tax payment to the time when those health care benefits can be enjoyed (if ever).

Tax policies and income support programs also contain many provisions that result in similar distortions in the timing of consumption. One clear example is high marginal income tax rates—they penalize savings and delayed consumption. Low-interest government loan programs are another instance: By making cheap funds immediately available, they subsidize an acceleration of consumption.

Many of these examples may in themselves seem trivial. But they add up to a pervasive pattern of government control over consumption timing. And since a less desired timing makes the real value of consumption smaller, those controls similarly reduce the overall value of our lifetime consumption opportunities.

Personal Consumption Management. Barring governmental obstacles, a grown-up person can manage his lifetime consumption path in several ways. First, he can delay his entry into the labor force after he has completed his basic schooling, e.g., by continuing his education. Such a decision usually produces low income (which, officially but unrealistically, might be recorded as zero) for a prolonged period; and he may temporarily be dependent on others for support. In compensation, he usually earns relatively large incomes later on as the added education produces positive income returns. Typically, this results in considerable consumption sacrifices during his school years and extra consumption later in life.

Secondly, a person can decide to work more (or fewer) hours, especially if he has opportunities to take paid overtime work (or to take leave without pay). Or he can moonlight. His decisions in these regards will help govern his choice of consumption levels over time—perhaps expanding his consumption during his remaining nonwork hours or during vacations, or perhaps after retirement, or a bit of both.

In other words, a person who carefully plans his work and life will consider the questions of how much to work and when to spend the added income at the same time. He will view his prospective life as a whole, and he will appreciate the many potential trade-offs between work and leisure and between consumption now and later.

Thirdly, our prototypical "economic man" can temporarily, perhaps for several years, expand his consumption by borrowing from banks, friends or relatives. Of course, repayments of these borrowings will curtail his net spendable income and his potential consumption levels later on. Conversely, if he refrains from consuming his entire income, he will be a saver now. The savings, including the cumulative returns that they generate over time, will, in all normal circumstances, augment his consumption opportunities in the future.

To enjoy the full benefits of these opportunities, the individual must have unrestricted freedom, both as a consumer and as a saver, investor and borrower. In particular, he or she must have full consumer-market and financial-market freedom. He must be allowed to live in the residence of his choice, eat his preferred food, dress as he sees fit, use the transportation facility most convenient for him and take the medications that the available expertise indicates he needs—provided, of course, that he pays the costs of producing and delivering these items.

The government must not forbid or restrict such individual consumption choices, or freedom will be incomplete and unevenly available. This is one of the main messages of the libertarian tradition, one that we can wholeheartedly subscribe to and incorporate into our **libegalitarian** system.

But we should not forget that the enjoyment of all these consumption benefits also depends on each person's initial resources (acquired through birth or upbringing), which lay the groundwork for his income and consumption opportunities later in life. Today those who were born poor have much less scope for personal consumption management than the rest of us. By and large, they cannot reach the same consumption levels as those who start out better off. And they do not have the same flexibility in choosing their preferred time paths of spending. Consequently our goal of maximum equal opportunities requires both that we all have free spending choice and that all of us, initially, get access to the same amount of spendable resources.

In short, as consumers in a free equal-opportunity society, we should expect

- to receive an adequate amount of initial human-capital resources, on which we can base our efforts to generate income and consumption later on;
- to be able to acquire any consumer goods the full costs of which we are willing to pay, and to be allowed to consume these goods;
- to be allowed to freely decide when to make such acquisitions, or to engage in such consumption; and
- to grant other individuals the same consumption rights.

THE WELL-EMPLOYED WORKER

We are all workers, in one capacity or other, regardless of our nominal employment status or job description. All of us, therefore, have an interest in worker rights, broadly defined. Without such rights, we might not be able to fully exploit our opportunities as workers. This assertion should not seem particularly surprising or controversial. But in truth, those rights are often violated in the United States today, sometimes in the very name of worker rights.

History has sensitized Americans to the horrors of slavery, and freedom of choice in job matters seems like a well-established democratic right. Our society, indeed, has a deep-seated respect for our freedom to decide our own whereabouts and our own career paths, contrary to conditions in some communist systems. We take it for granted that we can freely choose our own careers, even though we may be subject to parental or social pressure in this regard. And we are usually free to apply for jobs that become available, even though we might have doubts about how objectively and thoroughly each application will be considered. But matters are, of course, a bit more complicated.

Basic Job Rights. Those who seek employment with others are potential sellers of labor services, looking for potential buyer-employers. It would seem natural that job seekers should have the same fundamental rights as other market participants to freely conclude exchange agreements with their chosen contract parties. They should hence be permitted, singly or jointly, to negotiate whatever employment terms they wish, without interference from any governmental body. Or, at least, we need special justification for such interferences.

Yes, exceptions may be needed for child labor, as children cannot be given full membership in a free society for grown-ups; but this exception is not unique to the labor market, as it will have parallels in other transactional situations that are also reserved for adults. Morever, the employment rights of aliens may deserve separate analysis, connected with their rights to enter the country in the first place.

33

Otherwise workers and firms should be able to develop their own mutually preferred packages of job requirements and job compensation. This may seem self-evident, especially on this abstract ideological level. However, there are many current American examples of government restrictions on worker freedom and other types of labor market freedom. Until not long ago, we could have referred to military conscription. Should the draft, as seems likely, be reinstated in a future armed global confrontation, this would definitely be a severe restriction on our labor market freedom.

Today actual government interferences with labor market freedom are not quite so drastic or so conspicuous. They are, however, numerous. And, in some instances, they are serious enough to push individuals out of the jobs that the market otherwise would have provided them. More typically, the government imposes rules that effectively alter the conditions of employment at the expense of either or both of the parties to the hiring agreement.

For example, federal or state laws prohibit many types of work considered unsanitary or immoral. They prohibit certain activities involving both employee and employer rights from being performed outside the favored, union-approved factory setting (e.g., small-scale textile production). Furthermore, various labor-related laws alter the relative bargaining positions of labor and management or otherwise skew the contents of permissible labor contracts (e.g., by protecting the interests of striking workers); compulsory medical insurance may soon be another, major retrogressive step of this kind.

But one might suspect that these laws, in many cases, capture the interests of the affected workers quite well—and may, in fact, accommodate employer interests too. They often seem to reflect nearly universal worker demands for "better" job conditions, and such conditions might make workers both happier and more productive. Therefore, in the absence of such labor protection laws, many similar provisions might, instead, have been embodied in private contracts.

Perhaps so. But we can't really tell, since the law destroys the preference-revealing power embodied in free-market bargaining over job conditions. At least some workers would prefer to do without some of the protective legislation (e.g., in matters of relative safety), if they knew its indirect costs—especially if they were aware of the laws' negative effects on the employers' ability to offer cash wages. One extreme example of such an outcome—in which regulatory "improvement" turns into exactly the opposite—is the loss of entire jobs because of the minimum wage.

Worker preferences are too varied to be accommodated through nationally standardized restrictions on employers. Furthermore, these preferences change in response to changing worker incomes, habits and family obligations. We need to let these shifting preferences find market outlets so that workers can maximize their employment opportunities accordingly. This is a matter of both efficiency and equity.

But some willing workers are handicapped in their job searches because of unfortunate family backgrounds or poor early schooling. There is then a built-in equity problem that needs to be dealt with; "affirmative action" is intended to do that in a broad-scale, roundabout way. Yet this equity problem ought to be addressed directly and separately—say, through remedial training or other compensation to workers with such long-standing handicaps and through fundamental reforms of child care and public schooling for the benefit of the next generation.

The medicine should fit the illness and should not be applied, unnecessarily or harmfully, to some of the presumed secondary consequences of that illness. Misguided labor laws that interfere with labor market freedom tend to compromise both the efficiency and the ethical neutrality of the labor market. Ultimately the overall economy will suffer, and so will long-run job opportunities.

Aspects of Worker Freedom. In a free society, the worker's freedoms ought to extend to all aspects of his labor market involvement: type of activity, hours of work, form of compensation, work place conditions and so on—subject, of course, to his ability to successfully bargain for those terms. Rarely, if ever, will there be any demonstrable national or communitywide collective-good complications that could overrule that principle. His freedoms should be limited only by the need of others for like freedoms. This Spencerian restriction will be satisfied only through an unobstructed right to free contract making in all labor markets (and in markets that are linked to these markets, e.g., those for the services of employment agencies, for legal advice in labor matters or for job-related insurance).

If a person is working for himself, he is both a worker and a producer. The principle of free voluntary exchange requires that his combined worker-producer freedoms allow him to produce whatever he wants as long as he does not infringe on the like rights of others. A few examples: He should be allowed to produce gold, hunt deer or sell pornography as long as he does not trespass on anybody else's domain, violate any contractual agreements or interfere with anybody else's work efforts.

Some national or international resources may be judged especially scarce and precious, and we might wish to somehow discourage work that absorbs a great deal of them; endangered species come to mind here. But no restrictive government intervention is really needed, once property ownership has been fully established. The free market can then account for this scarcity through appropriate resource pricing. He who pays the price should then be able to use that resource to the extent he wishes, in his work or otherwise. The scarcity of whales would certainly be no reason for putting whaling company employees in jail. But if scarcity-based pricing of whales reduces both whale product demand and whaling job opportunities, so be it.

Proper Government Role. The appropriate involvement of government in labor matters in a **libegalitarian** society can easily be summarized. By equalizing the educational investment in all children and adolescents, the government will fulfill its essential obligation in the matter of employment opportunities. Each person, when reaching maturity, will then be as prepared for work as his natural personal characteristics permit. After that the government should keep its hands off and let private parties undertake their own training, job planning and labor negotiations. These rules reflect the realization that labor market freedom creates both the most efficient job markets possible and the most ethical system of balancing the interests of different market participants.

The social goal ought to be well-employed workers, where "well" refers both to qualitative job conditions and the workers' quantitative productivity. This goal requires adequate basic schooling coupled with free markets in labor and all labor-supportive activities. It does not, however, require government programs that try to match available labor supplies with the evolving labor demands of private American business.

There will, even in this ideal society, be a variety of public-sector jobs. These ought to be filled in a manner that will minimize the costs of producing the needed public goods. Thus the government should definitely not restrict access to public-sector jobs for particular citizen groups, whether racial, sexual or age-based; even foreign-born people ought to qualify for the Presidency. Yet if particular categories of job seekers are unqualified, they should of course not be hired, never mind their relative statistical representation in government jobs.

Nor should the government force the private sector to obey racial or sexual quotas, or to undertake "affirmative action" that gives preferential treatment to specific applicant types. Rules such as these impose unfair disadvantages on other job applicants, as the notion of "reverse discrimination" has finally made clear to the general public. Such rules are also not cost-effective and thus not consistent with the maximation of opportunities. And once society has attained equality in the provision of basic schooling, there will be no ethical reason for disturbing the competitive positions of different worker categories.

What, then, becomes of "workers' rights?" This concept should definitely not imply that the government somehow has to guarantee every citizen a particular type of job or some job with a minimum salary. If it tried to do so, it would have to create jobs that, by the market's standards, were not sufficiently productive and hence not economically justified. This would distort the overall utilization of the national labor force, with reduced overall productivity (and a diminished pie). As a consequence, many jobs would offer unnecessarily low pay and would be poorly tailored to individual ambitions and interests. And in practice, a federal job-and-pay guarantee would be a huge burden on the taxpayers, who would have to finance the extra wages that exceeded the monetary equivalents of the workers' productivities.

Rather, the worker in the **libegalitarian** society should expect

- to be able to enter the adult labor force having received the same basic schooling as the labor force at large;
- the right to seek and negotiate whatever job he wants, without government interference;
- not to be deprived of any part of his wages through taxes that exceed the value of government services received; and
- to have to grant other workers these same rights.

THE WELL-REWARDED INVESTOR

Investment, in the broad sense of the term, is a central aspect of our lifetime socioeconomic behavior. To invest is to acquire assets, of whatever kind, that promise to produce income or other future benefits in return; and this is a goal we all share, in varying degrees. We are all investors, at least during part of our lives. As such we want to be well rewarded through extra income or other benefits—sufficiently well to be compensated for the sacrifices that our investments require.

The Choice to Invest. Like all beneficial economic acts, investments are costly. The investor must obtain sufficient funds (cash, credit or, generally, purchasing power) for their financing, and he or she can do this by borrowing, by saving part of his current income or by selling other assets.

The rational person or firm invests only if and to the extent that the prospective returns seem at least adequate relative to the costs—provided, of course, that he is allowed to do so. He will invest if and when he expects to be sufficiently well rewarded for the costs and risks of so doing. His expectations might not always be borne out, but he will learn from experience and adjust his investment behavior accordingly. So over time, his behavior will approach the model of the smart, well-informed "economic man."

Investment creates a deliberate link between the present and the future, economically speaking. It reflects an appreciation of the continuous, time-interdependent quality of all human life: We need to look ahead, even though the precise future will never come under our full personal control; but we occasionally have to tap into the reserves we have built up through past investments to meet urgent needs today.

For individuals or families, it is often hard to draw a sharp line between consumption and investment. Sometimes the delay between an asset purchase and the accrual of benefits from it is too short to warrant any special attention. If I purchase a can of sardines today and eat them the next month, I have technically undertaken an investment with a one-month maturity. Or if I put money in the bank, use part of it now and then, and occasionally replenish the account, I will be engaged in a continuous process of short-term financial investment and divestment. It is hardly worthwhile to distinguish the investment aspects of such food purchases or cash management steps.

The benefit delay, and thus the investment element, is much more pronounced in regard to purchases of homes or acquisitions of pension plans. The same holds for education—which is usually an investment in income-, consumption- and pleasure-producing capital; it represents a buildup of human capital.

The opportunity to invest is essential to just about every person and every firm; and it can also enhance the benefits of government activities, through public-collective provisions for delayed public-collective benefits. Investment can enrich us or enable us to restructure our spending in better accord with our private and public time preferences. It is a crucial tool for intertemporal personal or organizational economic management. In the private sphere, it presupposes adequate investor freedom, so that we can choose the best available investment opportunities. In the public sphere, it presupposes a competent evaluation of public investment needs and costs and of the possibility of equitably financing such investment.

On the individual level, investor freedom can fruitfully complement worker freedom and consumer freedom. A person's freedom to invest in his skills can improve his marketability as a worker and add to his earnings. It can make it easier for him to acquire human capital, real estate or financial assets—all means for expanding and improving his consumption time profile. One can hardly see any reason for denying him these rights.

On the corporate level, the right to invest is tantamount to a right to build new and better factories, machines and tools; to set aside liquid-asset reserves for future expenses, and to train employees needed to produce goods—and thereby to generate profits for investors and entrepreneurs. The general merits of such rights are hardly in doubt. And those who advocate specific limitations on some of these rights should be called upon to justify the associated damage to the investment process.

On the governmental level, investment should be undertaken whenever future public goods needs are strong enough to warrant the associated taxpayer expense today. This evaluation requires that proper consideration be given to potential alternative resource uses in the private sector, something that involves a comparison of the expected public-project returns (adjusted for risks) with the market-determined interest rate. This is a shorthand description of public-investment planning that tries to emulate the behavior of rational private investors in the competitive marketplace.

Current Restrictions. Nobody really questions the general merits of investment that produces adequate future returns. But our liberal-conservative society has so many other demands on available national resources, and tries to satisfy so many other criteria in resource-use decisions, that the merits of investment freedoms are easily overlooked.

Investor freedom seems incompatible with many of the tax and regulatory provisions in current American law. It is not that the U.S. government is philosophically or consistently anti-investment. Nor is it generally proinvestment for that matter. Rather, existing tax and regulatory restrictions have other purposes, which collide with general investment interests. Typically these indirect investment impediments are the result of pressures from worker, consumer or taxpayer groups with little stake in the affected investor freedoms or with little understanding of the social merits of the affected investments.

Strict zoning restrictions obviously destroy the possibilities for investments in property beyond the prescribed limits. Those who had discovered advantageous opportunities for property investment will thereby be deprived of some potential wealth. At the same time, other investors may gain. Thus already established commercial property owners may benefit from not having a new competitor setting up shop. And some residential property owners may, by virtue of zoning regulations, be able to continue enjoying unobstructed views. As a consequence, both these categories of property owners may see an appreciation of their property values; and the improved view will constitute an immediate consumer benefit to the favored house owner.

These results are, however, of very dubious merit. It is unlikely that the restrictions will be economically efficient in the sense of balancing the interests of different property owners and the public. Zoning is much too crude a tool for that; since it is based on legislative or administrative edicts, it is incapable of negotiated accommodation and graduated cost-and-benefit-conscious trade-offs. Also, zoning regulations are almost bound to produce inequities: They tend to favor particular investors over others, through discrimination based on such a secondary factor as the geographic location of their property.

Similar losses of investor freedom occur when the government regulates particular activities in factories, on farms or in homes, or in the markets that cater to them. Production and exchange transactions then become *de facto* investor restrictions.

If I am, from now on, not allowed to make widgets of a certain popular size, my widget manufacturing investment will be correspondingly impaired. If I have to start paying an import tariff on the best available widget-making tools, my production costs will go up and my profits will go down; I may then have to scale back my investments in this enterprise. Of course I will usually be able to channel my efforts and my investible funds elsewhere. But this will be an inferior, second-best solution, with reduced prospects for income and wealth generation.

The government has in cases such as these stepped in to tilt the balance of rights and opportunities among different categories of investors (and, ultimately, among all those whose fortunes are linked to these investments). This is contrary to the free-market method of conflict resolution and will normally be illegitimate in a free society.

The only qualification needed here is that all property rights must be fairly assigned at the outset so that there are no built-in biases in the investible resources that different parties have at their command. That is, nobody ought to have a preferential investment status from birth or upbringing, with access to vastly more, or vastly superior, assets invested in him or her or on his behalf. Thus nobody should have extra investment opportunities just because he was born into the ownership of a farm or a factory or had better access to a business education.

Taxes and Subsidies. Income and property taxes are, of course, burdens on investors in the taxed activities. To judge if such taxes are illegitimate encroachments on freedom, we must first examine the whole question of what role taxes are to play in a free society. For now let's be content to agree that at least some tax levels will be overly high and hence illegitimately destructive of investor freedom.

Taxes can, for instance, be a powerful tool for preventing firms from financing their planned investments in plant and machinery in the market's preferred way—through what would have been mutually beneficial financing deals with savers and lenders (e.g., through stock or bond issues or bank loans). The government then drives a wedge between the investor-borrower and the saver-financier, and both sides will be worse off as a result.

Let us, however, also admit that government undertakes some useful investments of its own and that it might create private investment opportunities that could not otherwise have existed. These public or publicly-in-

40

duced investments ought to be scrutinized on grounds of both efficiency and equity.

If these public investments do not produce overall national returns commensurate with their tax costs, they must be judged inefficient. This criterion ought to be applied both to defensive missiles and to waste-disposal facilities. A wasteful use of taxpayer money is, in this situation, a sign of excessive, counterefficient public investment.

The equity test should be directed toward the relative distributions of investment benefits and investment costs. In accordance with public-good principles, beneficiaries should pay, and nobody else. Conversely, government involvement in investment should be regarded as inequitable whenever it creates net benefits for selected socioeconomic groups at the expense of other groups. This can occur when an investment is targeted to produce just such selected benefits at general taxpayer expense, or when the tax structure is such as to undercharge some members of the public for benefits in which they fully share. The beneficiaries then, in effect, receive subsidies, disguised under other policy labels.

The subsidy element is especially easy to detect in regard to human-capital investment, as through health care or education. Public health facilities, for example, help some people maintain or expand their physical investments in their own bodies or minds, thereby permitting them to lead more remunerative, more enjoyable lives. Those facilities thus provide bodily or mental subsidies from the taxpaying public.

What is wrong with that? Two things. One, healthy taxpayers will have to pay most of the costs, and their investments in their own educational or professional human capital will thereby bring lower after-tax returns. This seems *prima facie* unfair. Two, the patients using those facilities will be encouraged to lessen their own efforts to manage their minds and bodies, perhaps taking fewer medical or nutritional precautions, or otherwise adjusting their life styles. This is one of the serious moral hazards inherent in a social system that fails to maintain personal accountability and encourages dependency on the public purse.

Compared with a free-market situation, the national investment pattern will then be distorted, and some less-valuable investment will take the place of more-valuable investment. Granted, public health facilities may sometimes compensate for some of the unfair disadvantages connected with a poor upbringing. But this would be an inefficient, roundabout way of dealing with a problem that requires its own, separate solution.

In principle, the freedom to invest should be a fundamental constitutional right in a free society—and with it comes the obligation to foot the bill. Without such freedom (and such obligations), some investors will unduly cut back or reorient their investments, the productive capacity of the national economy will be reduced, and our long-term national consumption opportunities will be reduced.

Potential investors in a free, equal-opportunity society should thus expect

- to have entered adult life with a standard foundation of human-capital investment;
- to be allowed to undertake the amounts and types of investments (or disinvestments) they wish, on freely negotiated terms and without government restrictions or punitive taxes;
- to have to contribute their fair shares of the taxes needed over time to finance productive public-goods investments; and
- to grant other potential investors the same rights.

Chapter III
EQUAL OPPORTUNITIES FOR UNEQUALS

THE BENEFITS OF FREEDOM

Freedom often seems to be in conflict with equality. If we want freedom, perhaps we can't have equality, for freedom breeds change, difference and unpredictability. And if we want equality, we can't have as much freedom as otherwise possible, for equality requires control. We therefore cannot adopt both of these two political principles as basic ideological norms; we will have to choose one or the other—or so it appears, judging from the political debate.[10]

The Alleged Conflict. The perception that the principles of freedom and equality are incompatible with each other probably stems from their distinctive associations with capitalism and socialism or with governments of different size and influence. Freedom is the cornerstone of capitalism, and it suggests little or no government. Equality, on the other hand, is popularly thought to be a basic aspiration of socialism, and it usually connotes a strong and active government with a mandate to redistribute and equalize.

One might, in addition, see a formal, logical contradiction between the two principles. They both embody constitutional goals, and each goal seems to require its own set of policies. Yet different sets of policies cannot coexist and be effective in the same society since they will operate at cross-purposes. So one of them has to be discarded or compromised. Or, in other words: Society cannot serve two ideological master principles at the same time.

Moreover, it must be taken for granted that freedom will be utilized differently by different individuals, with unequal results for them. The strong, smart or lucky will usually be able to carve out bigger slices of the socioeconomic pie for themselves, while the weak, dumb or unlucky are deprived of their "fair," equal shares.

Look at the early stages of the industrial revolution, the pre-New Deal United States, or most of contemporary Latin America. Free enterprise, without the leveling effect of vast public poverty-relief and redistribution programs, appears to have produced large inequalities in income and wealth. Similarly the Reagan administration's promarket, tax-reduction and deregulatory reforms, modest as they were, are now claimed by their liberal, Democratic critics to have caused a serious widening of those income gaps. Contrariwise the egalitarian redistribution programs undertaken in Western Europe and the United States in earlier decades have led to extensive restrictions, especially in the form of income taxes, on the freedoms of those with superior skills and earnings capacity. These negative correlations between freedom and equality would not seem to be entirely accidental.

Nevertheless one should not uncritically accept the idea that freedom and equality are truly incompatible—logically, ideologically or pragmatically. Rather, we will show that the two principles can, indeed, be constructively reconciled as long as we interpret them correctly, i.e., in accordance with our own basic ideological values. We will then be able to fuse these two principles within our own **libegalitarian** structure. But before we do that, we need to consider how freedom serves the broader purpose of opportunity—which is the variable we really would like to equalize.

Purposes of Freedom. If, like the die-hard libertarians, we were just concerned about the condition of freedom per se, we would not need to worry about how this condition is exploited by different individuals or what results it will have on individual circumstances. Equal freedom in the marketplace would then represent sufficient equality, never mind what this freedom can be used for or what relative individual handicaps exist in exploiting it. Observable inequalities of results would be analytically uninteresting and ideologically irrelevant.

However, most of us want freedom not for its own sake but because of what it can do for us. We want the freedom necessary for the maximum satisfaction of our wants and desires (even though most of us will accept the constraints resulting from the similar aspirations of others). Freedom is not in itself a primary, consumable good that automatically produces personal well-being. It is, rather, an environmental situation that allows us to interact beneficially with other individuals and organizations. The ability to benefit from that situation depends on what resources we have at our disposal and can employ. Without appropriate resources, freedom will go to waste.

Freedom plus Requisite Resources. The main type of freedom that can be mutually shared with others is the permission to engage in unrestricted voluntary exchange. Exercising freedom in this way requires that we have something to offer the other party, or no exchange can occur. This requires personal resources.

To conclude such exchanges, we have to be able to deliver the assets (often consisting of cash) or services desired by our counterparts in the market. The more assets we have, the more acceptable they are to others, and the more easily they can be liquidated (for cash), the bigger and more valuable will be the purchases we can make; also, the greater will usually be the benefits that we can derive from such exchanges. This is perhaps self-evident; yet it needs to be said so that we can untangle the merits, and limitations, of the freedom of exchange.

For all decision makers (individual, private-organizational and governmental), freedom thus needs to be coupled with adequate resources in the decision maker's hands. Our ideological scheme must allow for this linkage: Only through access to adequate resources will freedom translate into valuable opportunities—and our ideological goal of maximum equal opportunity will therefore have normative implications for the distribution of resources. Logically, freedom and resources are two necessary, and jointly sufficient, conditions for opportunity; individually, they are insufficient.

A few simple examples: The freedom to acquire a luxurious home is naturally of value only to those who can afford to do so. Without adequate financial means, this freedom will be worthless. Conversely, if government regulators or coercive neighbors effectively destroy my freedom to acquire a particular house, no amount of resources will suffice for me to get it (short of a special resource in the form of political influence or a private police force). Even free speech, to be usefully exercised, requires some resources—a soapbox, funds for purchasing pencil and paper or for renting a printing press or, at a minimum, a set of vocal cords.

However, the two interacting factors, freedom and resources, are rather different in nature, and their differences could affect the way we would like society to parcel them out.

Freedom is both activity-specific and person-specific: Freedom is meaningful only in reference to specifically identified activities of potential human benefit, and its value (to a person with sufficient resources) is a matter of personal preference, circumstance and need. Preferences, circumstances and needs vary, of course, among individuals, and they can change over time for any particular individual (and our ideology wants to be especially sensitive to these variations and changes). Freedom is not fungible, interpersonally or intertemporally. To attain maximum opportunities, we thus need the specific freedoms required to engage in the particular transactions that would make the largest contributions to our opportunities.[11]

This quality of freedom makes it unsuited for rationing or selective distributions; its varying individual values would make any conceivable distribution scheme inherently unfair, in innumerable, incalculable ways. Equity—as well as efficiency—therefore requires that freedom be as widely and fully available as possible. If, however, freedom is unevenly offered across different activity types or socioeconomic groups, some groups are bound to be discriminated against, and equal opportunity will be impossible. This is one reason we take such pains to criticize limitations on particular, often trivial-seeming freedoms of special concern only to small subsegments of the population. And this is why the **libegalitarian** constitution stresses the provision of all types of freedoms for the benefit of everybody.

By contrast, most resources are highly fungible, especially in an economy based on free, voluntary exchange: One type of resource can generally be sold for another, so that particular, individual resource needs can be met. (Exceptions mostly involve the more personal aspects of human capital, such as those that do not easily translate into favorable exchange opportunities. Instead, their value stems primarily from their use in the individual's own consumption activities—this can be true of many intellectual or artistic qualities, including a subtle appreciation for good food, wines or music.)

Therefore, if society is to allot particular amounts of resources to particular individuals (under our scheme, to ensure equal opportunity), it can do so in lump form. And the most easily transferable good is of course money, which has perfect fungibility in all mature economies. So money (e.g., the U.S. dollar) is clearly the preferred means of government-to-person resource transfer—which should not be a surprising conclusion. (Incidentally, money is also the most efficient and equitable means of citizen payment to the government, in the form of taxes or fees; having to pay by giving up nonmonetary resources—or, worse, freedoms—would often be discriminatory and wasteful.)

Resources, in contrast to freedom, have another, very relevant characteristic: They are personally renewable. The resources we acquire through birth, childhood and early schooling can be augmented through our own efforts, in different ways and degrees—through personal savings, appropriately invested. At any moment in a person's life, it should, in theory, be possible to differentiate a person's "initial" resources—what is left of the resources given to him at birth or during his youth—from his self-acquired re-sources. Similarly an individual's opportunities are of two fundamentally different kinds: those given to him by society and those he has built up himself, for himself.

The two components of resources and opportunities do not, by our standards, carry the same socioethical weight, and they need to be ideologically differentiated. Our preference is for equalizing the initial, society-provided component, while letting each individual take responsibility for the other, self-acquired component himself.

By taking this view, we are setting ourselves apart from almost all other contemporary political thinkers and practitioners, except those in the libertarian camp. It has, unfortunately, not been fashionable, even theoretically, to differentiate the resources—or the incomes and wealth—provided by government from those generated by the individual himself.

The essential contemporary mistake, especially on the part of the modern liberals and socialists, lies in a tendency to look at equality from a "time slice" perspective. While today's liberals might proclaim a goal of equal opportunity, they usually ignore the fact that each life is an interdependent, continuous whole, with controllable interlinkages between resources and opportunities then, now and in the future. They suffer from a kind of temporal myopia, devoting most of their attention to temporary conditions in particular calendar, or budget, years. Admittedly they have made some efforts to equalize basic, initial opportunities as well, especially through family assistance and educational facilities; but these modest, quasiegalitarian programs have not been accompanied by follow-up efforts to adjust the beneficiaries' rights to entitlements later in life.

Furthermore the social-liberal failure to find a way to equalize the long-term distribution of resources has led them to repress freedom in unnecessary and discriminatory ways—and they have often done this in the false or superficial name of equality. Among the most conspicuous measures of these kinds are punitive income taxes, which, in effect, repress the right to manage and augment legitimately acquired resources. They also include certain regulatory programs with special redistributive purposes (e.g., rent controls). The inadequacies or perversities of these measures confirm that the freedom-equality conflict needs a more realistic, equitable and macroeconomically efficient solution.

THE LIFETIME PERSPECTIVE

If we agree that society ought to treat all persons "equally," how should we apply this norm to individuals at different stages of their lives? Should we have equality, however otherwise defined, for the newly born? For

47

those who are just reaching maturity? Or for everybody, regardless of his age? Should equality be a renewable right, not just a "start-up" right?

And if we want to provide equality of opportunity across all age groups, how do we compare twenty-year-olds with sixty-year-olds? Should they enjoy "equal" opportunities, even though the sixty-year-old has had forty more years to build up, or squander, the opportunities he enjoyed earlier in his life?

Continuous Equality? If we were traditional, simple-minded egalitarians, we might opt for a system of continuous equality, as measured by the actual living conditions of each person or socioeconomic group. We might then eschew the usual distinction between equality of outcome and of opportunity. After all, "opportunity" is awfully elusive, and individually generated opportunities usually presuppose an accumulation of positive outcomes in the past (e.g., in the form of invested earnings or self-financed professional training).

Fully implemented, this system would imply a kind of socioeconomic standardization throughout the population at each moment in the nation's history. All Americans would have to be allotted, each year, the same bundle of goods. Or, more practically, they would have to receive monetary incomes that enabled them to acquire identical bundles of goods; and the amounts of these incomes would have to be assessed through reference either to actual market prices in each location—however distorted by government interventions in the market—or to a set of hypothetical "shadow prices" estimated by the government for this purpose.

Such an arrangement would imply a standardized real consumption or income level, provided or guaranteed by the government; yet statistically differentiating consumption from savings would be difficult, so the focus might have to be on income. If income equality, consequently, were to be perfectly enforced, nobody could be allowed to supplement that income through personal efforts, either through extra work or through personal saving. Either the government would have to force everybody to save the same amount of his income and pay everybody an identical return on these savings thereafter—a tough policy assignment. Or it would have to tax away (at a 100 percent rate) all returns on personal savings (while perhaps allowing people to delay the spending of the principal of those savings).

Of course, if the national economy grew faster than the population (as it typically does in most years), an increase in real personal incomes would become possible over time. This would tend to make later generations successively better off. Some intergenerational inequality would thus result, even if efforts to equalize income or consumption contemporaneously were fully successful. This, in itself, suggests something about the absurdity of the absolute equal-income message.

That system would be fundamentally socialistic: It would make income levels a matter of rigid social planning while effectively prohibiting private accumulation of income-producing resources. Even if factories, farms and manpower were nominally in private hands, the fruits of their employment would not accrue to the nominal owners, but to the nation as a collective whole. So the nation's resources would in reality be national collective property. And the income derived from it would be distributed as social entitlements, not as rewards to those who built up these resources and figured out how to gainfully employ them. This seems intuitively very wrong.

On efficiency grounds, such an ultraegalitarian system would have some highly negative features. It would have very little in the way of incentives for work effort, savings accumulation or a search for productive investment opportunities. This would lessen chances that each worker would find the type of job in which his talents and skills could be best applied. It would persuade many not to train for better-paying jobs. And it might keep them from trying to provide for their own economic futures.

Nationally many opportunities for improving the allocation of human and physical resources would thereby be neglected. If the government were to try to remedy these problems through its own centralized labor-market and investment planning, it would have an impossibly difficult task. And it would have to interfere even more aggressively and coercively in what ought to be private endeavors.

On equity grounds, this system would also, despite its ostensible equality features, seem unappealing to most of us. It would suggest limitations on both worker freedoms and saving-and-investment freedoms. Particularly objectionable is the implied prohibition against the postponement of consumption spending and the accumulation of income-generating wealth, through investment in tangible assets (including, possibly, homes) or in one's own human capital (through professional development). In short, it would deny us the freedom to determine our own preferred consumption paths over time.

Consequently, a guaranteed government income (whether equalized across the population or not) would, by necessity, violate very basic human freedoms. It would force us to slice the total economic pie in a particular fashion, while stopping or discouraging people from enlarging their own slices and, indirectly, the total national pie. Naturally, partial measures in this direction will have similar, though more limited, consequences. One must suspect that many socialist-egalitarian sympathizers would have strong second thoughts if they realized that these are the implications of their distributive prescriptions.

There must be a more reasonable way of construing the equality requirement. Especially, there should be some way of comparing the total lifetime economic prospects of different individuals or social groups. This comparison ought to be made at the outset ("ex ante"), before individual actions have altered these prospects, and it should not be confused with the varying "outcomes" produced by such actions over time. Put differently, we need a technique for summing up different time paths of income or consumption (or other indexes of our evolving socioeconomic conditions), before we can tackle the question of how these paths ought to be equalized.

The Capital Concept. The best available concept is that of capital, as understood in modern financial and economic theory. If we stretch it to its fullest, we will be able to encompass nearly everything we regard as "opportunity." And we will be able to conceptualize the notion of lifetime opportunity so that it can become our basic ideological building block.

"Capital" generally refers to accumulated wealth, set aside for future use, by its owner—a person, a firm or a nation. It looks backward in that it reflects investments undertaken in the past, through acquisitions of factories, homes, skills, technologies or indirect claims on such assets (through holdings of stocks, bonds, bank deposits, etc.). It looks forward in that it denotes future income or benefits (or at least a reasonable prospect thereof), derived either directly through the use of real assets or through monetary returns on financial assets.

But those benefits must be discounted at a rate reflecting the going interest rate, or the "time value of money," so that we get a measure of their present value. As a result, benefits expected to arrive soon will count for more than those arriving later; and if their arrival is uncertain, their present value will be adjusted further downward.

This dual perspective can be applied to a retail store, or to an M.B.A. degree. Both required capital expenditure when they were "installed." Both typically hold prospects of generating earnings for their owners, as long as they are intelligently used and the overall economy continues to function.

But conceivably they might have been badly planned to begin with. The store might have been located in the wrong, nonprospering neighborhood, or the business degree might have been conferred on a student who ultimately decides to become a poet. In both cases, prospective incomes from the invested capital will be much reduced; and when we put a value on it, we will have to depreciate it well below its acquisition costs.

Even if the investments turned out to be well planned, they will usually wear out or become obsolescent over time—a different reason for a gradual write-down of the capital.

Analogously, a person's capital can be viewed as the summation of his prospective future income or consumption levels, properly discounted— i.e., discounted by the interest rate prevailing in the financial market for similarly long-term loan transactions. The discounting process reflects the fact that near-term consumption, or spending generally, tends to be worth more to us than spending in a more distant future; most of us tend to be a bit impatient, and we really cannot know for sure that we will be around when that future arrives. It also reflects the fact that postponed consumption makes room for investment (by ourselves or by those we lend our excess funds to) that can generate positive income returns. And it is precisely the pressure of saving and investment opportunities that tends to curtail current consumption and give it an extra "scarcity" value relative to future consumption.

Individual capital is individual opportunity today, tomorrow and later on without any specific limit in time. My future lifetime opportunities are my current capital, at least as long as I plan to stick around long enough to enjoy them. If I don't, my remaining capital will go into other hands. And if I allow this to occur, I will be exploiting another worthwhile opportunity— that of enriching my heirs. So the life of my capital might exceed my own; but this possibility creates no analytical problems as long as we value capital on a long-run, transgenerational basis.

Capital embodies resources, or assets, and presupposes their relative freedom of use. Those resources must be not only usable but also preservable and not subject to immediate self-destruction. The more resources one has, or the greater freedom one has to use them, the larger his associated opportunities over time and the larger his associated stock of capital. Recall that this is also how we previously defined "opportunity"—the product of resources and their freedom of use. The concepts of capital and opportunity are thus, from our perspective, synonymous.

Let us illustrate further, so that we may begin to appreciate the value of the many freedoms on which capital and opportunity depends. In a non-socialistic society, each person normally owns a wide variety of assets, each representing one aspect of his total capital; and most of them have been accumulated through his or her own efforts in the marketplace (the obvious exceptions being the assets of children, young adults and some handicapped persons).

An individual's physical assets may consist of a house, furniture, appliances and other objects with significant life spans, and they have

51

typically been purchased, indirectly, through his or her prior sale of labor services. His financial assets may include stocks, bonds, future pension rights and cash, and he may also have various outstanding financial liabilities, typically in the form of loans (which are, of course, negative items in this tally). His human assets will consist of his innate intelligence, plus his accumulated muscle power, useful skills and work experience.[12]

Each of these assets is potentially income-, consumption- and benefit-producing; this is why they were installed in the first place. Altogether, the individual's total capital, if properly calculated, should sum up the time-discounted future benefits that he or she, or an impartial observer, expects him to derive from these assets, net of liabilities. The larger the benefits, the sooner they arrive and the more certain their magnitude, the larger will be his capital.

The capital in different persons' possession varies for many personal and social reasons. The young, healthy and recently educated are *de facto* richer; the old, sick and senile, poorer—unless these discrepancies in human capital are offset by the latter's larger holdings of nonhuman capital. Some people want to use up most of their nonhuman capital early in their lives, while others like to pass on much of it to their heirs. If there is freedom to exercise these intertemporal or intergenerational preferences, individual capital positions will differ even more sharply and unpredictably.

Furthermore, government, in effect, reduces or increases the capital positions of particular socioeconomic groups. It does so either by redistributing resources or by changing the extent of the freedoms provided for their exploitation. Almost everything the government does today has some of these distributional consequences, intentionally or not. This is true of the federal income tax system, consumer regulations, import quotas and the "war on drugs," to mention a few major examples.

What provisions, then, should society make for the distribution of resources and capital among different groups and individuals? Should it, via government, directly distribute such resources, as in the form of grants or subsidies, or in kind (to be financed by the general taxpayers)? Or should it be more modest and confine itself to laying down ground rules for how private parties can redistribute resources among each other? Or should it leave this matter entirely in the hands of private entrepreneurs, savers, donors and testators, without any government involvement?

This is the essence of the ideological equity problem. And it can be more easily solved if we analyze our total lifetime opportunities from the standpoint of the inherent capital and the prospective returns thereon—this is the **libegalitarian** approach.[13]

SOURCES OF SOCIAL INEQUALITY

If we are to equalize individual resources in some way, we will have to make sure what they consist of and how they originate. Take a grown-up American, male or female, preferably still at a young age, and let's ask ourselves the following questions: What socioeconomic factors determine his or her prospective lifetime levels of income, consumption and personal well-being? Can they be neatly fit inside the broad concept of resources? Can the origins of those resources be identified? Are they subject to sufficient governmental or societal control so that they could potentially be equally distributed across the population?

We will find that, yes, there are definable resource categories to which we can attribute much or most of our personal prosperity and well-being. Yes, at least some of those broad resource classes are subject to public distributional control. So, yes, the equal-resource and equal-opportunity goal might be meaningful and realistic enough to form one of the pillars of a new, **libegalitarian** ideology.

A person's resources can best be classified in accordance with their origins, which can be put in four distinct categories: nature, family, government and personal effort. Each of these four elemental forces can, in its special ways, generate investment. That investment can add to a person's capital and his opportunities for future income, consumption and well-being. The various resources embodied in this capital tend to be unequally available to different individuals.

Part of this inequality is due to the way we have organized society, while part of it is not. Government and family are, of course, matters of societal organization and, as such, amenable to political control or influence. But society has essentially no control over nature. And personal effort is, by definition, an individual matter; and, at least from our ideological perspective, society should not be held responsible for it.

Nature and Family. Some capital is innate. Nature bestows on each of us a genetic endowment of innate qualities that influence our potential future physical and mental capabilities. To be sure, nature does not dictate our future health; but it certainly affects our individual probabilities of avoiding disease and enjoying physical and mental strength at almost any stage of our lives.

Nature helps some people, through their genetic heritage, look more attractive than others, think better than others and live longer, or more happily, than others. It probably also endows us with different amounts of innate potential intelligence, even though this matter is still subject to a great deal of scientific controversy. These potentialities represent some of nature's initial investments in us, undertaken before our birth.

Whatever the exact biological linkages may be, nature seems, at least indirectly, to make us socioeconomically different. It contributes to making some of us richer than others by making us healthier, smarter and thus more employable. It helps make some people more popular and more marriageable, and hence more productive in some of the noncommercial arenas. Innate qualitative differences can consequently put us on different life paths in regard to income, consumption and personal well-being. This reality will strike many as inherently inegalitarian and offensively undemocratic, yet it cannot honestly be denied.

After a person's birth, society starts to interact with nature, reinforcing or whittling away what was there at the beginning. For the small preschool child, society is nearly synonymous with the family, although family is gradually complemented or supplemented by playmates and school. Of course, the family usually invests extensively in the child's physical, psychological and intellectual development. It thereby adds, in varying degrees, to the child's innate capital, except in the rare cases in which parents or guardians are nonexistent or utterly negligent. Part of that investment is required for the child's physical survival; it is in the nature of pure maintenance or a kind of gross investment that just replaces the ongoing "depreciation" of the original capital. When the family does not provide even this level of investment in its child, there will thus, by definition, result a net "depreciation" of child capital.

In more normal cases, this human capital continues to grow as the child benefits from parental care, a supportive, family-dominated environment and, later, school. Thus, as all of us have observed, the child's prospects for a productive, enjoyable life improves. By how much, we need not to worry about just yet; and we could never come up with a very exact measurement anyhow.

Yet new inequalities may emerge, because of the varying efforts and abilities of parents and teachers. Some inborn inequalities might actually be mitigated through private or public "remedial education," as it is called in other contexts. But otherwise the distribution of capital endowments across the young population can often become less uniform over time, through the gradual influence of conditions within the family. Some young people seem doubly blessed by nature and society, while others seem doubly cursed.

Personal Effort. As a child matures, its own attitudes, decisions and actions will of course carry greater weight in its development. The typical teenager is, with his parents and teachers, a cooperative investor in himself, and he gradually expands his relative participation in this joint capital accumulation venture. For instance, graduate school can be a major long-term investment project with substantial commitments by the student, his family and society at large. If the education is successfully planned and carried out, the student's intellectual and skill capital will be vastly augmented. This will push him further toward the richer end of the individual capital endowment spectrum.

In our mature years, we might still be accumulating skills on the job while reaping continuing rewards from our past physical and intellectual investments. We may also struggle to reduce the rate of physical depreciation that tends to occur through impaired health and a loss of sexual and social appeal. We usually become financial accumulators, through pension plans and growing personal stock or bond portfolios, at least until late middle age or early retirement; and for may of us, our residential real-estate equity grows too. But intellectually, we slowly turn into "de-cumulators," through the creeping obsolescence of our basic mental skills, a reduced IQ and ultimate senility.

Some previous capital inequalities will disappear as people mature and age. This is especially the case when some high-living people with large initial capital endowments gradually dissipate their assets while some of the frugal poor slowly enlarge theirs. Other inequalities may be sustained or accentuated—this occurs when the initially wealthy go on saving while the poor go into debt and squander what meager resources they initially had.

A relatively free society will have to tolerate these seemingly inegalitarian conditions. More to the point, ideologically speaking: Many of these disparities might actually not represent inequalities in the broader lifetime context. Rather, they might merely indicate different individual ways of using the resources that society originally allotted to us.

Government. The fourth major source of personal resources, government, operates both through the investment-producing services provided directly by the public sector and through its indirect effects on privately undertaken investment. The latter effects might be positive or negative. This, naturally, depends both on the overall directions of government policies and on their impacts on particular socioeconomic groups.

Whether our particular government is a net contributor to a particular person's capital, or a net drain on it, is nearly impossible to tell. Technically, to find the answer, we would need to compare the current situation with a hypothetical "control" society—except we don't really have one at our fingertips. Yet it is reasonable to believe that, across the overall population, these net contributions tend to be negative. This must be a manifestation of the wealth-destroying tendencies of our existing political system, as compared with a freer, more individualistic one.

The broad facts in today's United States are, however, not in serious question. At present, some types of government contributions to our individual resources are offered to almost everybody, including free public schooling and heavily subsidized public college education. Other types are made available only on a selective basis, typically to those who are sufficiently poor, sick or old to qualify; they are "means-" or "needs-tested." These programs of resource transfer come under labels such as income support, family assistance, Medicaid or, simply, "entitlements."

Most of these programs tend to benefit those who fall substantially below certain income and wealth standards—and who thus seem to lack personal resources. The benefits are in this simple statistical sense regressive.[14] But what these programs equalize are conditions at particular moments, i.e., approximately when the welfare checks or food stamps are distributed, or when the hospital doctor sees his Medicaid patient. They focus on current income conditions rather than on wealth; and they are based on data pertaining to very limited, partial aspects of income. These "entitlements" are thus distributed with little attention to the recipients' past or future socioeconomic situations. They may hence do little to equalize true capital ownership.

Similarly the costs of these entitlement programs are recouped without much attention to the taxpayers' longer-term income and wealth situations. Most of these programs are paid for through personal (and, to a less extent, corporate) income taxes—and the income tax base is only a very partial indicator of different persons' true relative wealth, or their lifetime capital endowments. Ostensibly the personal tax income structure is meant to be progressive, thereby complementing the regressivity of the benefit program for maximum redistributive effect. Whether those taxes truly are progressive, once we measure lifetime income positions more accurately and completely, is on open question.

Contemporary U.S. egalitarianism can therefore be said to be "present-oriented." The government's program of transfers and income taxes is based on a "time slice" principle, as if the government was just taking a snapshot of the conditions defining our rights and obligations. It fails to view each person's life as a whole or as an extended continuum (which would seem to require a motion picture, not just a snapshot).

Perhaps this would be too much to ask of our legislators or public administrators. But our egalitarian government policies, as currently designed, produce some very anomalous results for that very reason. Some of their results may actually be quite antiegalitarian in a more meaningful sense of the term. In particular, they often redistribute in favor of those with superior or adequate initial capital endowments, yet with little inclination to preserve, enhance and utilize these endowments.

Sources of Moral Hazard. Unfortunately there is, in all the major industrial nations, a well-established tradition of such artificially and narrowly egalitarian policies. The overall direction of these redistributional programs is there for everybody to see; and even though the expansion of some of these programs was halted in the 1980s (most clearly in the United States and the United Kingdom), the long-term trend still seems more upward than downward.

People naturally feel they can count on these programs and policies to continue to exist. Every rational person will take them into account in his personal economic planning. He knows that if he begins a steep economic slide, the social safety net will catch him. He knows that he is automatically insured, thanks to the taxpayers. If he denied these approximate realities, he would be foolish; and acting as if he was unaware of them, or too self-sufficient to care, would not bring him much public admiration or gratitude anyway.

This means that the public and private aspects of personal capital accumulation have become negatively interdependent, i.e., competitive instead of cooperative. The prospect of receiving capital transfers from the government reduces the individual's incentive for private capital accumulation. Instead it encourages him to squander some of his own capital, in particular, the kind of capital that would reduce his ability to qualify for government benefits (most conspicuously, capital that brings him monetary income in the form of higher wages, dividends or interest). The strong possibility of such consequences constitutes a huge macroeconomic moral hazard that is built into the incentive mechanism of the present social-policy structure. (It is not unlike the traditional moral hazard faced by an insurance company, whose promised compensation lessens the insured's incentive to avoid risky, loss-creating behavior.)

Of course, sometimes the disincentive for a person to employ his own capital productively may be too weak to affect his behavior. The talented and devoted do not easily alter their careers even if they face severe income taxation; they will continue to receive a lot of psychic income that escapes the Internal Revenue Service. But for others, the cost-benefit balance among available career options will tilt in the other direction if one option entails much larger future tax liabilities, or if it holds much less promise of financial public support.

Some individuals will thus choose, knowingly and deliberately, or in a socially conditioned reflex, not to work, not to educate themselves or not to save as much as they otherwise would. Consider a worker who engineers his own layoff so that he can collect unemployment benefits—a pleasant vacation subsidy, as it were. Or one who abandons his wife and children, and skips town, so that they can collect family assistance.

At worst these individuals might become professional welfare chiselers, habitual loafers and public freeloaders—or true social parasites.[15] Others will be content to moderate their work and saving behavior: They may just scale back their professional ambitions and capital accumulation efforts, while being prepared to cash in their public-assistance chips if and when they cross the border of eligibility.

Meanwhile others, with innate advantages, a strong work ethic or a habit of thrift, will have to foot the extra tax bill. They are consequently being penalized for their talents, their productive work or their atypically large savings.

Note again the parallel with insurance and the social costs of these moral hazards: Those who are careful and prudent will have to pay higher premiums to help defray the additional costs of compensation payments that result from the irresponsibility or outright fraud of others. But also note that in a free private insurance market, insurance companies can adjust their premiums for those who—like accident-prone automobile drivers—take extra advantage of their policies. Our government has not shown any similar differentiated cost-responsiveness.

These potential public responses to existing transfer and transfer-financing programs can thus negate much of the programs' intended egalitarian consequences, especially in the longer haul of a full adult lifetime. Those responses permit individuals to obscure their true lifetime resource or capital positions, thereby breaking any negative link between initial opportunity and "net entitlement" (entitlement receipts minus tax liabilities connected with the financing of entitlement programs).

Just as, today, some transfer benefits might truly turn out to be progressive (relative to basic, initial resource endowments), so many tax liabilities will turn out to be regressive. This occurs, for example, when somebody manages to overcome the handicap of childhood poverty and poor basic schooling and gradually becomes a high-salaried, highly taxed worker—and does not live long enough to collect much Social Security. He, too, becomes a net loser in the game of exploiting government. His true lifetime opportunity would most likely have been closer to the national average—the theoretical egalitarian norm—in an America without these redistributive programs.

Even if we ignore occasional policy aberrations and mistakes, we can hardly characterize contemporary American redistribution policies as egalitarian. Do we "equalize" when we give to those who waste or misapply their resources while taking from those who are frugal, ambitious or creative? Hardly—especially not if we take a lifetime perspective on our socioeconomic circumstances, and not if we think every functioning adult has a responsibility to manage his own, private economic affairs.

THE ROAD TO SOCIAL EQUALITY

How, then, could the **libegalitarian** society see to it that its resources will be equally distributed, on a lifetime basis, among its individual members? How should we define the resources to be distributed, and how large should each person's resource "entitlement" be?

These are profoundly difficult questions, for several reasons. One, they require a precise notion of what kind of resources we are talking about. Two, they will require that we outline a plausible method for measuring current resource inequalities, so that we can judge the need for corrective, equalizing measures. Three, we have to suggest a program for eliminating these inequalities that does not, in the process, violate individual freedoms. For if freedoms had to be sacrificed, opportunities to exploit those resources would be reduced, and other inequalities or inefficiencies would unnecessarily be introduced.

Equality of What? The equality we seek is definitely not one of individual "outcomes," as this term is usually construed.[16] It is not equality in terms of personal income, consumption or any other index of actual living standards at particular moments. None of these concepts fit any reasonable definition of resources, the variable we wish to equalize across the national population.

As we have demonstrated, equality of income, consumption or other socioeconomic outcomes will, by necessity, imply that individuals are not allowed to keep the full rewards for their own efforts to achieve particular outcomes. Equality of any of those kinds erodes the benefits we otherwise will reap from our personal exertions. Contrariwise, the **libegalitarian** position is that inequalities attributable to our own legitimate behavior ought not to be governmentally removed. The freedom to expand one's resources and improve one's opportunities should be an inalienable right. Call it the freedom of capital accumulation, or, more broadly, the freedom of intertemporal consumption choice.

However, society ought to remove and prohibit those inequalities that it currently imposes upon us without our personal cooperation. This requires that society do two things: one, equalize the conditions under which all individuals begin their responsible, adult existence; and two, stop interfering with this basic equality later in their lives.

To meet the first requirement, society should attempt to equalize all young persons' "start-up" capital, i.e., their initial endowments of capital before it has been used up, recomposed or augmented through individual actions. This is the only way we could even begin to equalize the lifetime opportunities that society provides us, for any subsequent equalization efforts are bound to be ineffectual or inequitable.

So we need to sketch a basic constitutional program for equalizing the resources, or capital, that society initially allots to each person. We will then have to differentiate the three sources from which our initial personal resources originate: nature, family and government; resources that stem from personal effort are, of course, neither "initial" nor ethically relevant. And we will have to try to disentangle the interconnections among those three resource categories, so that we can discuss how they should be mobilized, singly or jointly.

Equalizing Nature? Ethically and constitutionally, nature—the basic physical properties of man and his surrounding physical environment—deserves to be treated very differently from man-made institutions. Historically, nature has run its course largely undisturbed by political and socioeconomic arrangements. It is too big and strong a force to be controlled by man. It demands special respect and should not lightly be tampered with. Of course it can be temporarily exploited; but the costs of exploitation can be large, unpredictable and difficult to repair, and policymakers are rapidly learning to suppress their urges to take that route.

To be sure, the appearance, character or productivity of some of our basic natural resources has occasionally been altered by human action—by infantry wars, oil spills, acid rain, waste disposal, weather modification programs, nuclear explosions and other localized man-made events. Such events may have caused some shifts in nature's long-term contribution to the flow of income and in the supply of a healthy, attractive environment, and the productivity of particular communities or regions might thereby have changed. Yes, it sometimes seems as if nature retaliates against those who invade or attack it. But the geographic mobility of people has mitigated the effects on individual economic circumstances. In all, man's clashes with nature have rarely left any deep marks on the relative distribution of personal resources and capital.

Instinctively, one thus has to respect the nature-society dichotomy, as a physical reality and as an ideological premise. Consequently, one will hesitate to recommend any government schemes that would attempt to correct innate, nature-based inequalities. Ideology hardly appears to be a way to change the laws of nature or man's natural characteristics. The idea of official bioengineering on humans, or a governmental genetics program, is especially unappealing to most of us. Apart from science-fiction fantasies, we don't look with favor on any societal plans to alter the human brain or body—especially not if those plans smack of racism or genetic selectivity.

Perhaps technological advances in bioengineering will give man the power to control nature much better in the distant future than today. Our political attitude toward nature might then also need to be revised. For now, though, it seems more sensible to treat nature as a worldwide resource that ought to be used for the benefit of all people of all generations, but not to be tampered with for distributive purposes. We do not, today, have the capability for even remotely equalizing nature's influence on the characteristics of different individuals or groups. We do not even know very precisely how to distinguish the effects of natural forces from those of social forces, since they blend and interact.

This implies that, however reluctantly, we will have to leave natural interpersonal inequalities out of ideological consideration. There should, accordingly, be no public-policy compensations for substandard intellectual, mental or physical capabilities—i.e., for inborn shortages of these important human-capital ingredients. Nor should those with above-average capabilities of such kinds be subject to any corrective taxes or regulations. Instead we should tolerate the inevitable favors and disfavors that nature bestows upon us in varying degrees.

The alternative would be to require government to grant compensations for incorrectable natural handicaps. It would have to give those with substandard innate human-capital endowments compensatory allotments of nonhuman capital. Presumably these would have to be distributed in the form of cash, discount vouchers for remedial training, free insurance policies, plastic surgery in publicly financed clinics, subsidized access to medical facilities or other assets or services.

But this approach would raise some very awkward questions: How should we erase, if not the direct distinctions of race, gender or looks, at least the personal well-being differentials attributable to these factors? Are we ready to push equality so far as to tax the good-looking and subsidize the ugly? Should we really try to ascertain the average community esthetic standards in these respects and classify our citizens accordingly? Should circus freaks, by the same token, be deprived of their freakishness-related incomes? This writer tends to answer in the negative.

Inequalities that are attributable exclusively to gaps in innate human-capital endowments or to subsequent uncontrollable natural events will therefore have to be accepted. In particular, we should not expend large public resources trying, sometimes successfully but often in vain, to bring every child with a birth defect up to the nondefective par. Nor should we try to educate the retarded so extensively that they can successfully hold middle-income-producing jobs. Doing so would not be cost-effective, given the alternative uses of those resources in private or public hands. It also would force us to impose governmental standards in highly subjective matters. Before somebody received a remedial payment, he would of course have to be declared naturally deficient—and this would, in itself, be a humiliating experience to the affected individuals.

Leaving natural inequalities alone has implications also for adults. Those who can get better-paying jobs because of greater innate intelligence, or a more congenial or attractive appearance, will then be allowed to do so without penalties; they will be able to cash in on the extra personal capital endowments implicit in those characteristics. Those who, for similar reasons, can marry more advantageously will similarly be able to exploit this favor from nature with impunity. So will those whose potential circle of friends and acquaintances will thereby be wider. None of these inequalities will be deemed inequitable from a societal standpoint. They do not, after all, represent societal arrangements.

Natural inequalities among groups and individuals can be a source of creative tension and stimulating variety. Efforts to suppress these inequalities could lead to dangerous experimentation or stifling homogeneity. Compensating for some of them might sometimes seem humanitarian, but doing so systematically on the large political plane would cruelly brand certain groups as inherently substandard.

Roles of Government and Family. There remain two sources of personal capital and opportunity, the effects of which we would prefer to see equalized: government and family (or family surrogates). Our goal should thus be to equalize the aggregate joint contributions by government and family to each person's "start-up" capital—the resource endowment that becomes the basis for his future capacity for earnings, consumption and economic well-being.

As a first approximation, this means that personal capital provided through physical and psychological care, basic schooling and, possibly, the first stages of higher education should be subject to social equalization. And, ideally, so should all other benefits received exclusively because of familial ties, including large-scale intergenerational property transfers and financial inheritances.

Such provisions in the egalitarian direction would go a long way toward achieving greater lifetime equality of opportunity. The equality will be incomplete, since natural inequalities will be left uncorrected; one should therefore describe the equality as "social."

Whereas the natural components of different persons' start-up capital cannot be equalized, most of the other components can. These include, especially, the human capital components provided by government and family.

The timing of the societal capital distributions is important too. It seems obvious that provisions for adjusting these capital items on the personal balance sheet ought to be completed before each person reaches maturity. After that, the individual can and should take charge of his own life; and no fair comparisons could, in any case, be made between the capital positions of individuals who have already reached a more advanced age.

So even though "maturity" is not a sharply fixed point in our life spans, a standardized cutoff age at which societal obligations generally cease will have to be established. Yet we need not, just for the sake of ideological neatness, draw a sharp dividing line at an age of, say, eighteen or twenty-one. Different age limits could be established for different purposes, reflecting the growing decision-making competence of typical adolescents.

Let us, then, nail down the principle that society is responsible for providing each person the upbringing and education that he needs to enter the adult world with a "normal" amount of socioeconomic capital. Let's call it developmental capital, to be endowed in each person by society. This capital should be evidenced by the young person's health—unless he has willfully, during his incipient maturity, let his health degenerate through dangerous habits or a reckless lifestyle. He should have been given a "normal" education, one that provides the typical young person with a standardized amount of education and a "normal" opportunity for future skill development and gainful work.

Needless to say, educational investments should be made when they are likely to be most productive—neither too early in life, nor too late; this is mostly a matter of applying cost-benefit analysis to various educational technologies and strategies. Generally these human-capital investments ought to be completed in time so that each individual will be optimally prepared for the next steps in life, including the possibility of higher education. Conversely, if some distributions of educational (or other personal developmental) capital were delayed until middle or old age, their long-term returns would usually be reduced, given the reduction in the person's expected remaining life. He would then be unable to collect what is due to him; the intended lifetime equality would then not be achieved, after all.

Yet each person could perhaps be allowed, once he reaches a certain age, to request delayed delivery of some of the social capital allowances due to him. For instance, he might be permitted to postpone some publicly provided schooling until later in life (perhaps by delaying the use of governmentally provided school vouchers). Such flexibility in timing, established in accordance with the recipient's needs and wishes, could indeed enhance individual freedom and opportunity.

No Replenishment. Once each person has received his fair share of social capital, he should not be entitled to any new social capital infusions, whether in cash or in governmental services. Such infusions would of course upset our carefully devised equality. In particular, nobody should be permitted to get fresh access to the public purse by squandering his initial resources, as by refusing to work and to cultivate his skills, by mismanaging his health or by impoverishing himself in other ways.

The social investment in each person must be a nonrenewable, once-and-for-all transfer—or government will be subject to extortion of repeated, unearned favors. If an individual wants to replace some capital that he has, somehow, lost, he should have to rely on his own work and saving efforts.

This principle is sharply at odds with the contemporary American approach to poverty relief, public health care and other "needs-tested" social programs. Those programs generally allow people to qualify and requalify for public assistance by demonstrating that they, suddenly, meet current eligibility criteria. Few questions are asked about how they managed to achieve this status, beyond such matters as their most recent job or health history, their current home ownership or the status of their bank accounts. Their own contributions to these conditions are treated as irrelevant or forgivable.

To be sure, some assistance programs encourage schooling and training. Also, recent attempts to introduce "workfare" as a more constructive alternative to traditional "welfare" are a small step in the right direction, with some promise of potential self-help. And many individual social workers might do all they can to wean their clients from the welfare trough. But unfortunately, present American policies in this area are not generally based on a principle of ameliorating lifetime inequalities. They are almost entirely oriented toward momentary relief, and they often have perverse longer-term effects.

In the proposed **libegalitarian** system, self inflicted poverty, diet-related health problems or other preventable misfortunes will be no reason for government favors to the adult population. Mature grown-ups will have full responsibility for their own actions and their socioeconomic situations. They will never qualify for public assistance—provided they have been given equal social lifetime opportunities, embodied in their social capital endowments, to start with. Remaining social inequalities will then be of their own doing, and not a social responsibility.

Altogether, the equality prescribed by the **libegalitarian** ideology
- refers to opportunities, the exploitation of which is an individual responsibility;
- refers to potential conditions throughout each person's lifetime, as they appear before he reaches maturity; and
- translates primarily into standardized child care and adequate basic education for children and teenagers, along with an equally shared right to free voluntary exchange among adults.

Chapter IV
PROPER GOVERNMENT FUNCTIONS

REALIZATION OF FREEDOM AND EQUALITY

Translating ideology into a functioning socioeconomic system normally requires a central political authority. Except when the ideology prescribes anarchy, there has to be an authority that can establish the appropriate institutions, policies, laws and enforcement mechanisms. This is, generally, how a society gives meaning and reality to the various citizen rights and obligations that the prevailing ideology calls for. Government—not church, tribe or family—is nowadays the main authority that enforces these rights and obligations.

The central questions in modern political ideology thus concern what the national government should try to do, and what institutions and policies it needs to get it done. Not all ideological questions are necessarily governmental; some center on purely private behavior and may depend on the power of nonpolitical authorities, divine or secular. However, most of the large, contentious ones today are, indeed, governmental. And, conversely, when governmental questions arise, they must be referred to the ideology department before they can be systematically and intelligently resolved.

Both ideology and government concern resource allocation and income distribution on the broad, societal level. Explicitly or implicitly, ideologies provide overall distributive and allocative norms; and government is in most societies the largest single distributor and allocator, in partial competition with private organizations that may coexist with it.

Our special concern is the role that government, as allocator and distributor, and as an enforcer of rights and obligations, would have in a hypothetical **libegalitarian** society. It should already be obvious that such a government will occupy an intermediate position between that in an ultralibertarian system, where it is nonexistent, and that in a fully centralized socialist system, where it is all-embracing and all-pervasive. But that intermediate position is not just a midpoint along an axis stretching between two extremes. Nor is it just a convenient compromise solution that accommodates pressures from two ideological corners.

Rather, the principles underlying the **libegalitarian** society—freedom and equality, invoked in the name of maximal individual opportunities—have more subtle and complex governmental implications. **Libegalitarianism** is not altogether antigovernment and certainly not especially progovernment. Possibly, one could characterize it as a prescription for a special type of "minigovernment"; but that label would beg a lot of questions.

Promoting Freedom. Consider first the freedom aspect—the requirement that government permit and promote the full, mutual realization of individual freedom. In this respect, the **libegalitarian** government might at first blush seem to play an entirely passive, or nonexistent, role. Most governmental activities seem antifreedom, as they usually require taxes or controls and make preemptive claims on scarce resources; they might seem invariably to deprive some parties of some freedoms.

But group and collective-good theory has confirmed our suspicion that the truth is not so simple. Government can be a producer; and production can be regarded as an expression of freedom, at least if it is efficiently and uncoercively carried out. Government may also, under the right circumstances, be able to support, guarantee or enhance freedoms that otherwise, in the jungle of anarchic laissez-faire, might be at risk; and it might, just possibly, be able to create entirely new freedoms. Besides, the freedom to establish and use a government may in itself be a legitimate part of the total freedom package that we wish to maximize—although this suggestion will surely offend every diehard free-marketeer.

The key concept capturing the potential for freedom-through-government is, again, collective or public goods. Certainly, if freedom is to be universal, it must include the freedom to produce, or support the production of, public goods. This freedom can be indispensable to macroeconomic efficiency, thus adding to our overall socioeconomic opportunities and to the national economic pie.

Promoting Equality. With respect to the goal of equality, the need for government is perhaps easier to appreciate. It is precisely because of some of the striking inequalities inherent in a perfectly, permanently laissez-faire system that government must step in. To be sure, a laissez-faire system may provide a great deal of equality when it comes to market access and the chance to exchange already acquired goods and services. But it does not ensure equal purchasing power at the outset—when we enter the laissez-faire world—and inequalities in this respect may accompany us throughout our lives.

Full socioeconomic equality—whether of outcome or opportunity—could possibly be attained only through a central coordination of the distribution of resources across all population groups. Only a central authority could command enough power to enforce rules about overall resource distribution; and only such an authority could ensure that resource distribution would be equal. This big coordination job thus, unavoidably, becomes a function of government.

Yes, government is needed as the common provider or guarantor of initial equality, for no other institution is potentially available. No other existing or conceivable institution can speak so consistently for society as a whole. And if we embrace the principle of equality, we are creating a task facing the whole of society.

While other social forces may produce some egalitarian pressures and some egalitarian results, these results will be inadequate. Individual or private group efforts to redistribute resources will almost inevitably be insufficiently large and insufficiently reliable, since they would have to be matters of private choice, and choice is inherently variable and capricious. Our individual egalitarian motivations are not strong enough and are not shared broadly enough to ensure anything like privately engineered equality. And even if they were, no private organization could conceivably handle the job of redistributing enough resources on a permanent basis to meet long-run constitutional requirements. These simple points would not have had to be made had many libertarians not insisted that private charity could adequately perform all essential distributional functions.

In particular, there is no way of inducing and enabling parents to give their offspring identical care and attention, at least not without extensive government involvement or pressure; ideas about parental rights and prerogatives are painfully ingrained in almost all societies, including ours. And the capital invested in the young through education outside the home could also not be equalized without government control.

So government, in a **libegalitarian** society, will have to be given the assignment of equalizing individual opportunities, or at least their social components; and it should be done for life. The professional tools for achieving this will be found in education, psychology, sociology and medicine. But the techniques must be consistent with the individual freedoms that government simultaneously is to protect and enhance—in particular, the rights to engage in voluntary exchange and not to be subject to excessive taxes.

The way to achieve this is through policies and programs that try to equalize our initial lifetime socioeconomic opportunities while permitting us subsequently to freely use, alter or augment these opportunities through voluntary exchanges. Equality first, freedom thereafter—this two-step ideological program is a logical implication of our goal of maximum equal lifetime opportunity. This program also seems eminently appealing from an ethical standpoint. It should, furthermore, be practically feasible, through a package of gradual, long-term reforms.

CHILD DEVELOPMENT

The government must involve itself in child development. The intuitive rationale behind this proposition is that not all parents or guardians can do a uniformly adequate job in this respect. The existing community of grown-ups must therefore act as a collective guardian for the new generation.

Children obviously cannot take care of themselves, and their parents may be unwilling or unable to play the guardian role required to ensure equal treatment. Many parents do not have sufficient material or psychological resources for that role; and even when they do, they do not generally have the incentive to bestow equal amounts of developmental capital upon their respective offspring. Therefore the whole parent institution might need to be fundamentally reformed, if not abolished. At a minimum, parents need to be made subject to extensive oversight or performance pressure—much more oversight and pressure than applied today in the United States.

A Market Solution? But perhaps one could devise a market solution? Couldn't the competitive market select the best, most cost-effective guardians for each child, regardless of natural parenthood? Half-seriously, we could let children and potential guardians compete with each other for familial affiliation, pretty much the way men and women now compete for one another in the marriage market. That competition might create the best parent-child matchups. Meanwhile, truly unqualified persons would, as they should, be left without any children in their actual custody.

If we take this idea to its full extreme, we would presumably allow each child to run away from his home and look for better, adoptive parents in a

68

free child-placement market. We would, in effect, advocate a children's right to parent substitution, or to guardian exchanges—an extensive form of "kid lib." But this right would not quite meet our general mutuality requirement, because of the obvious imbalance between the negotiation powers of the two parties. The child would, needless to say, be comparatively unprepared for the job of parent search and parent selection; this function, too, presupposes adequate prior knowledge and experience, which of course the child does not have. And when children are old enough to run away, they will already be unequally cared for and unequally positioned in bargaining with potential new guardians.

Consequently such laissez-faire child care would only provide a wickedly charming caricature of freedom in the extreme, without the nearly universal benefits we otherwise attribute to the free market. This kind of system would be inimical to equal opportunity, since it would leave some children in underprivileged homes. Our conclusion stands: The ultimate responsibility for guardianship and child development must fall on the community, i.e., on some branch of the government.

Control of Parents. That obligatory community involvement in child care will encroach on parental prerogatives and restrict some parental freedoms is obvious. But why should they not? Why should children be at their parents' mercy—as they substantially are today (despite some legal protections against outright abuse and severe neglect)? Why should parents be allowed to deprive their children of some of the potential lifetime opportunities available to other children? Why should some children have to suffer developmental impoverishment because of their parents' incompetence, poverty or lack of concern?

In a **libegalitarian** society, such parental privileges would have to be abolished—an idea that may seem very drastic or irresponsible. For most Americans (and people of other Western nationalities), traditional family arrangements represent greater values than equal opportunity for the next generation. And the suggestion that a loving father or mother could possibly be incompetent in the child-rearing function will seem absurd and offensive to millions of self-satisfied parents.

To be blunt—and economic-analytic—about it, the family is an institution of grossly uneven quality and sharply varying social productivity. At its best, it can be an extremely useful, low-cost resource, whose productive services cannot be fully, and as economically, duplicated by any other institution. Long-term parental affection can make those services even more abundant, while allowing the responsive child to offer its gratitude and affection in return. Therefore it would be counterproductive not to mobilize that parental psychological resource, for the benefit of both parties. The ideal family will exhibit that neat coincidence of care demand (by the child) and care supply (by his parents), and it will constitute an efficient arrangement for mutual, intergenerational service exchange.

The matter of supply quality actually arises before the birth of the child. It concerns prenatal care as well, and the health and habits of the expecting mother; her actions will help determine the developmental prospects of her baby. But societal oversight will, again, be necessary to lessen the risks of innate, but preventable, child inequalities.

One urgent problem is drug use by pregnant women, and how to deal with it. A balance must be struck between the colliding interest of individual women and their offspring. But the mother should certainly be held financially responsible for any damage that her chosen behavior inflicts on her child.

How, then, can we satisfy the contradictory requirements—that for equalized child care and that for a productive use of the varying child-care capabilities of natural parents (and other adults)?

Certainly we must not do it by severely compromising on children's rights to care, even on a nondiscriminatory basis, for this could undermine our goal of maximizing their prospective opportunities. Instead, we will have to redefine the relationship between parents and society (represented, in this case, mostly by government). We will have to let society step in and correct the interchild inequities that varying parental circumstances and characteristics unfortunately produce.

If most parents do a good job (by some yet-to-be defined standards), the societal job will be easier and smaller. If they do not, this job will be so much bigger and more complicated. It is also pretty obvious that the job will vastly exceed the boundaries of present American government policies involving child care, education and health. And the task will be much bigger than envisioned even under the expanded U.S. child-care programs proposed in the late 1980s.

Government Involvement. The appropriate child development policies will have to be designed along the following lines. First, we must try to define what the typical child would want if it had the requisite maturity and knowledge to make that decision, including an appreciation of the costs. After all, it is the child's interests we, the community—its temporary spokesman—are trying to identify and meet. This is a matter of defining the right amount and composition of the child's needed human capital investment, considering the investment's anticipated future returns and costs. The investment decision should center on the extent and type of health care, education and psychological support that all children need. From the child's standpoint, these are demand matters.

The second question concerns methods of production and delivery—or the matter of society's supply. That is, how are the needed child-care services to be provided? The question is, to a large extent, technological, and outside the realm of ideology. But the job has to be cost-effectively done, or there will be an unnecessary waste of resources—and either the old or the new generation will have to suffer opportunity losses.

This implies that the job should be delegated to those units of society that are best equipped to perform these functions, considering their skills and interests, and their service prices—including primarily wages. By that criterion, child service operations might be either publicly or privately run, depending on which is more cost-effective. There can thus be no *a priori* rule, divorced from cost and quality considerations, about who should provide the child care. That is, century-old family traditions should count for very little—unless they demonstrably satisfy our standards for care quality, interchild equity and cost containment.

But there must also be a system of public oversight, feedback and control—a reliable correction mechanism that can serve as a surrogate for a nonexistent competitive child-care market. The mechanism might best be centered on a network of neutral, unbiased community representatives, drawn from the entire adult population and perhaps organized like juries. Citizen committees could oversee the production and distribution of all relevant child-care services, ensuring that each child got its full allotment. On their recommendation, the appropriate government agencies could be empowered to demand changes in the way a child is being brought up, for instance, by insisting that it be transferred to a foster home or spend more time in a child-care center.[17]

But—it might be objected—there is really nothing about government that makes it an especially good educator, let alone nurse or playmate. There is also nothing about government that makes it a good doctor or psychiatrist. So how can we entrust government officials with these sensitive and delicate matters?

Herein lies a deep dilemma. Government, as we know it, has no obvious comparative advantage, relative to the private sector, in performing child-care tasks. Yet equality of opportunity requires centralized societal control over the dispensation of care, or gross inequities will result, in childhood and long thereafter.

The optimal solution almost certainly lies in a public-private collaboration, with mutual checks and balances, for the entire underage population. The public sector should then concentrate on ensuring national equality and overall generational cost-effectiveness, i.e., on determining overall child-care principles and societal cost constraints. The private sector, for its part, should be slated to provide most of the actual service, working within the setting of families or community centers.

Actually it ought to be a requirement that all children, however well provided for at home, spend part of their time in day-care facilities, together with children from a broad variety of other parental backgrounds. Otherwise two distinct classes of children will emerge—one "democratic," publicly bred class, and one "elite," family-bred class. The result could hardly be equitable.

However, the private-public dichotomy needs to be bridged through the involvement of local governments and quasipublic agencies that are willing to listen to advice from both sectors. For instance, government agencies could be involved in recruiting and supervising teachers, physicians and psychological counselors and in organizing and administering the needed educational and medical facilities—much more consistently than is the case in America today. One attractive alternative is a national child-care ombudsman, to whom suspicious cases of deficient care could be referred by relatives, neighbors or other observant parties. After all, children are everybody's business—especially when the natural parents are grossly out of step with national norms.

On the one hand, the system we are proposing will require sufficient standardization of services to provide the same overall social investment in every young person. On the other, there is no reason to transfer judgment about the detailed nature of these services to a group of government bureaucrats, subject to no free-market cost or quality pressure and accountable only to other bureaucrats or, remotely, to the electorate. There is something to be said for diversity even in childhood, as long as it accommodates different needs or adds to the overall productivity of public education in a fundamentally nondiscriminatory fashion.

We thus have to grope toward a system that avoids both the unresponsiveness and inefficiencies of state-selected programs or state-administered delivery systems and the arbitrary inequalities of conventional parental guardianship. Certainly, the compromise is likely to include privately run schools, day-care centers and hospitals, all subject to community or government quality control, along with supervisory public agencies whose work is ultimately coordinated in Washington, D.C. Indeed, this would be an enormous mixed public-private venture without parallel in our society.

Current Reform Plans. Child-care questions have recently begun to receive a great deal of attention in the national political debate. The reasons are several. Child-care specialists and sociologists have increasingly been able to demonstrate the long-term consequences of childhood conditions for a person's chances to complete his schooling, find adequate jobs and lead productive, noncriminal lives.

At the same time, existing family assistance programs do not seem to have been effective in reaching the children with the greatest remediable socioeconomic handicaps. It is extremely difficult to monitor the use of government assistance—specifically, a Federal program like Aid to Families with Dependent Children—considering the overwhelming prerogatives given to parents; and this is an important lesson that American society has not yet learned. Moreover the increased number of women who desire to take paid jobs has reduced the effective supply of maternal child care in the home. So it is legitimate to ask whether society ought to discourage women (and a small minority of men, especially single-parent men) from employed work because of their obligations as guardians. But the absence of well-defined ideological positions has made the public debate awfully muddled.

Many of the ideas now bandied about push in different directions: Let's try to equalize care, at least to such an extent that the most disadvantaged children will be less badly off; but let's not move in the direction of stifling homogeneity or bureaucratic, quasisocialistic control in child-care matters. Let's recognize that many poor families, especially one-parent families, cannot do the job; but let's not do anything to further weaken the much-cherished family institution. Let's acknowledge a woman's right to, or need for, gainful employment; but let's not entice her to neglect her children at home.

Several innovative child-care proposals emerged during the 1988 Presidential campaign. The most far-reaching one was the Act for Better Child Care Services (the "ABC" bill), drafted by a coalition of public child-care providers and child-care advocates and supported by liberal Democrats. It would give grants to state governments for new child-care services to lower and middle-class families, supplied through a "child-care infrastructure" centered on licensed child-care centers. Republicans responded by offering cheaper, more family-oriented alternatives, with proposed tax breaks to companies offering child-care services to their employees. The Bush campaign pressed for expanded, refundable tax credits, going to both poor and middle-class families.[18]

Especially the ABC bill showed a welcome concern about the current system's unfairness to many children growing up in poor, broken and irresponsible families. Child-care centers can play a constructive role in correcting these inequities by substituting for what parents fail to provide and complementing what they do provide. But the ABC bill preserved a lot of inequity by not making such institutionalized care mandatory. Rather, it was a plan for two classes of citizenship: those who have been privately versus publicly cared for as children.

The tax-credit approach—supported by the Bush administration in 1989-90—has other pluses and minuses. By offering some tax-financed monetary support to families, it would take a small step toward more equal economic conditions in homes with and without children. And giving cash to "nonworking," as well as working, mothers would also ensure somewhat greater fairness, both among different categories of mothers and among their children. But this approach would preserve even greater family child-rearing prerogatives, as there would be no real pressure on families to offer their children similar services. There would be no way of earmarking the tax credits for child care, and all the inequalities that reflect varying parental competence and motivation would remain.

Overall, none of the new child-care proposals goes far enough—especially not the Bush administration's. They all would retain an excessive amount of parental child-rearing control and thereby perpetuate most of the inequalities existing today. None of them have dared to propose the most effective equalization step—that of compulsory child placement in standardized community-run care centers. Such a scheme might indeed turn Uncle Sam into a national baby-sitter (as the *Wall Street Journal* sarcastically has pointed out); but he can certainly be forced to do a much better job than many of our present, near-autonomous mommies and daddies.

The Financing. One additional aspect of a **libegalitarian** child development program has broad enough ideological implications to deserve attention. That is its financing.

Unquestionably, the total amount of human capital investments required nationwide is large enough to profoundly affect the overall distribution of income and opportunities, both among care-receiving children and among care- and resource-supplying adults. Those who will have to pick up the tab will of course lose a commensurate amount of spending power and spending rights, and the equity of so burdening them will need to be examined. The system of financing these costs must be ideologically acceptable, or the entire system will be internally contradictory.

In the 1990s, the cost of bringing up and schooling a young child amounts to hundreds of thousands of dollars; no precise figures that could be nationally averaged are available. This cost includes expenses typically borne by parents and expenses incurred by various levels of government—costs that, overall, are now shared in very haphazard, inequitable ways. How can we fairly distribute a financial burden on this order, without disturbing the delicate balance of economic rights that we have tried, in so many other ways, to establish? The answer: By charging the costs to the beneficiaries of—i.e., to the children themselves.

The child in whom a social investment is placed should be recognized as having an implicit debt to society, and he should be obligated to repay this debt in due course. If we prefer, we could regard the investment differently: as a societal equity acquisition in the child, on which society deserves to earn dividend. Or we could think of this investment as a loan in kind, with an indefinite maturity approximated by the average child's average remaining life, or about sixty years or so. The formal structure of the underlying "debt" is only a secondary, legalistic question, especially since no equity holder or creditor would gain any personal power over the human capital (or human-capital recipient) that he finances.[19]

The needed funds could be raised in the competitive private capital market through issues of stocks or bonds. The funds could be paid to those parties who actually incurred the expenses, or delivered the services, on the child's behalf, i.e., parents, schools, child-care centers, hospitals or public supervisory agencies. Consequently, parents providing above-average amount of services would receive larger public compensations (as in the form of children's allowances), compared with those families whose children spent more of their time in child-care centers. This means that mothers who decided not to take full-time jobs (other than home care) and instead devoted much of their time to the care of their children would be compensated for this—and much more adequately that they would under the Bush administration's new, refundable tax credits.

Regardless of the financial label attached to these child-development securities, one could structure the interest or dividend payments on these securities so that the average person, with an average life span, would fully return the capital (principal plus interest or dividends) to the securities holders over the course of his life.

But most investors realistically would be unwilling to finance the upbringing of a child not in their own personal care, especially if the child was anonymous; the investment would normally be too risky, and an exceptionally high interest rate would be required to offset this risk. To remove this obstacle, the financing could be collectivized: It could be handled by a national trust acting as an intermediary between all the beneficiaries and the private child-care investors. The latter could receive long-term bonds issued by the trust, and each annual bond issue could be made repayable by persons born that year.

No bondholder would then be subject to the risk that individual beneficiaries would fail to meet their repayment obligations, whether due to incapacity or unwillingness to work, early death or other circumstances. The default risks would be diversified away in the national pool of child-development trust money. No significant risks would remain, except for those connected with extreme national economic calamities that could bankrupt an entire generation: potential wars, revolutions, epidemics or deep, prolonged economic depressions; and these risks will somehow have to be absorbed anyway.

This financing scheme would be eminently consistent with our goal of equal social lifetime opportunities. Equal child-care and education access would be matched by equal lifetime burdens of financing these services. The scheme would avoid the enormous inequities that now exist because the taxes that people pay to finance public education and child support are unrelated to their prior receipt of such services (a feature that the current Congressional child-care proposals would, unfortunately, preserve). The productive hard worker would then no longer, in effect, have to assume some of the debts that society incurred in bringing up his unproductive, leisure-loving former schoolmates, on top of his own societal debts. This would be a giant step toward greater socioeconomic equity.

EXTERNAL AND INTERNAL SECURITY

Government clearly has the potential for doing some useful things that individuals cannot do, or cannot do as well, either directly or through private group activity. Those things involve the production of broadly collective goods—goods that can be adequately provided only through the intermediation of a central public producer-distributor.

If it is the duty of government to equalize our lifetime socioeconomic opportunities at the highest possible level, it must help us acquire the right amounts and qualities of such goods; otherwise some of those opportunities will be out of reach. Of course, the "right" amount will, in some cases, be zero—because the public costs are too high. In other cases, positive amounts of public goods will make net contributions to our individual opportunities.

Unfortunately there exists no definite list of existing or potential collective or public goods, let alone a ranking of their relative value. Our ideological scheme therefore cannot prescribe exactly what productive activities the government should engage in. This may seem to make the system unduly vague and open-ended, especially when compared with the totalitarian and ultralibertarian programs at the ideological extremes. But the question of specific government functions ought to be secondary to the deeper ethical problems of personal rights and opportunities. And we should allow ourselves to reconsider the public-private boundaries as public and private demands, or technological possibilities, change. So no apologies are needed for our tentativeness in this regard. And if we stick to our **libegalitarian** principles, we must permit the contours of government to be constantly redrawn.

The Territorial Foundation. Governments, by definition, represent territories and the residents of those territories. It follows almost axiomatically that a government should look after the common interests of the citizens occupying the territory it represents. Conversely, it should stay out of the affairs of those groups or individuals whom it does not represent— i.e., individuals residing in other territories. And—one hastens to add—it should stay out of affairs that do not involve all the people residing within its territory or which cannot be effectively handled on a selective, decentralized basis.

The national government's natural function is consequently to protect and enhance the freedoms, rights and opportunities of the resident population, without preempting tasks that could be better performed by other entities. Its main job, as far as adults are concerned, should be to produce goods that benefit all citizens and which are worth their collective costs. In short, the national government should, first and foremost, produce national-collective goods.

The primary example of such a good is physical security. This means protection from attack, coercion, theft or other acts that can destroy or diminish material or human capital. As the potential threats to the security of each of us stem from similar sources, it tends to be practical and cost-effective to deal with those threats on a collective, and not an individual, basis. The commonality of many security threats makes the elimination or reduction of those threats a composite collective good; for if the threat is reduced for one person, it tends to be reduced as well for other persons in nearby locations or in similar circumstances. This view is widely held, not only among public-goods theoreticians but among analysts of almost all political persuasions (with the exception of the extreme libertarians).

When such threats are directed against the nation as a whole, there is a common national interest in restoring security through a national defense, diplomatically or militarily. Defense can thus, indeed, be a worthwhile productive activity, notwithstanding the common, naive assertion that defense in "unproductive."

Defense, in proper amounts and of the proper kinds, can definitely make us better off. This must, by definition, mean that its benefits outweigh its costs (however hard it is to measure the benefits). Having a cost-effective defense should mean that the remaining civilian resources can be put to better, safer use; they will yield us larger or safer benefits in the future—or the defense cost would not be justified.

National defense expenditures can best be regarded as a kind of property or capital insurance. They can enhance the citizens' lifetime income and consumption opportunities, even though they absorb resources that, viewed in isolation of security threats, could have been applied to creating such opportunities. In the absence of sufficient defense, we might lose part of our physical or human assets—limbs, homes, the ability to find buyers of our labor skills or just about anything else. These losses might outweigh the value of the resources used up in the defense effort.

Given the potential existence of unfriendly nations with dangerous weapons directed against us, the case for a national defense seems painfully obvious. This general observation is in no way contradicted by the recent cordiality between the superpower blocs, by particular disarmament deals or by signs of the Soviet Union's political disintegration. The risks may have declined; but they surely will never be zero (and eliminating security risks altogether could, in any case, rarely produce the proper cost-benefit balance).

Most ideologists agree on these points, except for the those on the anarcholibertarian right. The anarchists (such as Murray Rothbard) stick to a consistent antigovernment stand, and they have tried very hard to explain away the need for a national defense department and a tax-financed defense budget. In addition, they advocate a noninterventionist foreign policy—as if one could transpose the laissez-faire principle from the interpersonal to the international plane.

Unnecessary? Their arguments deserve a brief **libegalitarian** response. Perhaps there really is no external threat to the United States from the Soviet Union or other potential adversaries. Perhaps Mr. Gorbachev's interest in arms reductions and in better relations with the West has signaled an end to all military and territorial competition.

If this were the case, we could all agree to drastically scale down the entire U.S. defense apparatus. Except we would then have to assure ourselves that the threat was permanently absent or so small that it could be dealt with through private countermeasures. That assurance does not yet exist. And even if the war-fearing skeptics became a small minority, their security needs would also represent a need for a collective good.

Indeed, the **libegalitarian** position is not that a national defense will invariably, and under all circumstances, have to exist. It is rather that, if international conditions so indicate, such a defense may be needed and that it would be wasteful of the nation's resources not to provide one.

The **libegalitarian** government certainly cannot be considered militaristic; nor is it pacifist. It would be "protectionist" in the sense that it would shield our economy and capital against unnecessary destruction (though not in the traditional sense of keeping out commercial competitors). But it would not have any *a priori* position on the kind or extent of defense that might be called for now, or in different hypothetical future situations. It would not try to second-guess the territorial or ideological aspirations or capabilities of the Soviet Union or any other potential adversary. It consequently would not pretend to prescribe what American countermeasures might be worthwhile—just as it does not prescribe what amount of civilian public goods would best serve our varying national needs.

The **libegalitarian** government is also not interventionist, in the usual exploitative or meddlesome sense. But we should keep open the possibility of encouraging other nations to accept a similar constitutional system, for the long-run utopian goal of a **libegalitarian** world. An ideal world government would provide global collective goods, including world peace and security. Achieving this lofty goal would require a great deal of intervention in the affairs of foreign nations. But the intervention would be geared toward two constructive long-term objectives—ensuring unregulated global voluntary exchange ("free trade") and equalizing lifetime opportunities for all nationalities. On the other hand, exploiting other nations' resources, or hindering the foreign resource uses preferred by their owners, would be impermissible for a **libegalitarian** government.

Private Defense Organizations? But, some libertarians argue, whatever defense is needed could be provided adequately outside of government channels, i.e., via the private market. On this reasoning, anarcholibertarians have pushed the idea of "voluntary protective associations." These organizations are supposed to supply just the defense that we, in our individual capacities, actually want and are willing to pay for, without any need for governmental involvement in its organization or financing. They would be subject to the pressure of market competition. They would therefore be more cost-effective than the bloated, inefficient government bureaucracy now responsible for defense.[20]

Those who wanted defense protection could simply join one of these associations, much like a voluntary neighborhood organization—although preferably one that had committed itself to the types and amounts of defense that those persons preferred. Or a citizen could flip through the yellow pages in the phone directory, call up a defense service supplier and hire it to perform specific protective services, say, during a nuclear attack. Plausible? Not quite.

Better, cheaper defense will be possible if, as now, we pool the needed resources nationwide and maintain a shared defense system—a classic illustration of the collective-good argument. Hardly any individual today could afford the defense he might need. A missile in every backyard is not an economical proposition. Possibly, a few rich individuals or corporations could get together and set up a private defense force with some tactical nuclear weapons, bombers and an infantry militia, and with some deterrent or retaliatory capabilities. But the force would, by necessity, be either inadequate or too costly for the organizers relative to its benefits.

The basic weakness of voluntary protective associations is that they could not find a way to charge the costs of the needed national defense among all, or even most, of the beneficiaries. If groups of citizens organized themselves so as to finance a national defense of their own, the benefits would accrue also to many who did not contribute to the organization's efforts.

Such organizations could hardly have the right to force any citizens to make financial contributions to their private defense budgets, for doing so would blatantly contradict the voluntary exchange principle. Instead there would be freeloaders, who would be inadvertently subsidized by the defense organizations' members. And freeloading efforts could not reasonably be excluded from the list of citizen rights, as long as they didn't involve any coercion or any breach of contractual promises.

The Financing. If, contrariwise, all the beneficiaries of the defense effort can be required to take part in its financing, through the agency of government, more funds can naturally be made available. This improves the prospect that true defense needs can be fully met. Moreover, a broader sharing of the financing will lead to a reduced financial burden for those who would have considered supporting a voluntary defense agency.

So a more adequate defense can be achieved publicly, without violating anyone's cost-benefit requirements. This is partly a matter of economic efficiency, achieved through a better balance between the individual benefits and individual costs of a collective defense scheme. But it is partly a matter of equity, achieved by placing the financial burden on the actual beneficiaries and not allowing it to be concentrated on some of them.

The big defense question is not if, but how much and what kind, and who should pay how much of its costs. To fully answer these questions, we would have to leave the area of ideology and cross over into the field of defense technology. And we would have to make probabilistic estimates of our potential enemies' future moves—a tricky forecasting job. Luckily, as ideologists we ought not to be held responsible for this mind-boggling task. We should only have to supply some permanent socioethical ground rules, while referring the matter of appropriate defense techniques to military strategists and planners.

The **libegalitarian** ideology requires a defense effort that is worthwhile relative to its costs but does not leave any worthwhile incremental defense needs unmet. If the national benefits of one more aircraft carrier exceed its cost, let's build it with taxpayer money; if not, let's not. This principle will produce a defense effort that maximizes our national consumable income prospects (net of defense costs) and hence our true national capital.

To help finance the national defense, each individual should bear the portion of the total costs that corresponds to the resulting improvement in his consumable income prospects and hence in his true capital—or he will be unfairly exploiting his fellow citizens. Nobody else owes him that defense—except, ultimately, the potential attackers themselves (who we could not really charge anyway, unless we ultimately overtake them).

Given an external threat, an appropriate tax-financed defense will permit each individual to enjoy a net increase in his personal capital, as compared with conditions in a pacifist, publicly undefended society. These capital increases will be mutually sustainable, nonexploitative and equitable.

Unless there is contrary evidence, the defense benefits that each individual receives are likely to be roughly proportional to the size of his income or his socioeconomic activities; for the more he has, the more he has to lose. The case for proportional taxation to finance defense is therefore strong, at least as a first approximation. This seems intuitively correct, yet the proportionality principle has not generally been adopted, neither in the United States or elsewhere. In actuality, defense is, today, financed through general income tax revenues, mostly from individuals; and personal income taxes are progressive, not proportional. Substantial tax reforms would therefore be needed if we decided to set up a **libegalitarian** national defense.

Internal Security. Internal threats should be dealt with analogously, ideologically speaking. Terrorism, assault and theft are illegitimate deprivations of personal or community capital that cry out for prevention or compensation. The risk of their occurrence thus indicates a need for internal defense. In addition, their actuality requires reparations or compensations, whenever possible. Police and courts, consequently, are necessary ingredients of a free, efficient society—contrary to what the anarchists may tell us.

If a security threat is national in scope, it should be dealt with by the national government, the national territorial protector. If such threats are local, two procedural alternatives present themselves. The national government could provide the needed protection. It must then devise a method for making the local, protected residents pay all of the costs, most naturally through local tax assessments; or there will be an unwarranted redistribution of spendable income between benefiting and nonbenefiting residents. Or, alternatively, the protection task could be delegated to lower-level governments, whose jurisdictions encompass, or coincide with, the threatened territories. It will then be understood that these governments have the required tax authority over the protected residents.

But care must be taken not to assign the protection job to jurisdictions whose geographic scope is too limited. The defense effort would then be either too weak and ineffectual or financially too burdensome for the residents. The crooks might cross the county border and go into hiding elsewhere. If there is no police authority to pursue them, law enforcement will often fail. And if there is such an authority, but poor coordination with police work in other localities, the hunt and apprehension procedure will probably not be cost-effective.

In more general language, we need both local and national police forces—not really a surprising conclusion. Their national tasks should be nationally paid for; their local tasks, locally paid for. All Americans have a stake in physical protection from without and within and will be better off if protection is publicly financed.

Private protective services, without taxpayer backing, can never avoid creating freeloader problems, because the protective umbrella will gratuitously shield nonsubscribing neighborhoods or more-distant regions as well. New Yorkers should not have to pay for the apprehension of local petty thieves in Georgia. But they are presumably willing and eager to support efforts to stop national, or cross-border, theft operations. Yet they can, of course, supplement public security services with some of their own, so as to satisfy their own, extra risk-averse preferences or their particular protection needs. In other words, the public police does not necessarily obviate the need for private guards, private guns or private theft insurance.

This is not an area were the **libegalitarian** ideology would strike most readers, except the anarcholibertarians, as controversial. Yet our rules for distributing the financing burden are clearly at odds with established U.S. and foreign practice (under which there is little connection between personal benefit and tax contributions). And we have subordinated defense and security issues to more basic equity and efficiency concerns, instead of making them—as do law-and-order conservatives—a primary ideological matter.

PROPERTY, CRIME AND LAW ENFORCEMENT

The need for protection against external and internal aggression derives from a broader principle: our individual right to keep, use or liquidate all assets that we have legitimately acquired. Broadly defined, this is the basic property right—a fundamental tenet of every individualistic society. A nation that wants to honor this right will have to prevent or rectify infringements as much as possible, normally through the intermediation of government.

Internally, the rules about how society is to deal with involuntary encroachments on personal assets or capital belong mostly in criminal and civil law, and enforcement will be delegated to the police and the courts. These institutions will indeed be necessary also in a **libegalitarian** society. But their functions will have to be defined somewhat differently, consistent with that society's ideological premises.

As a general proposition, the law should be understood as a collectively adopted structure of individual and organizational rights, specifying their contents, their limits and the methods for their mutual reconciliation. Crimes and law breaking conversely are transgressions of these rights. They constitute attacks on the rights embodied in our lifetime capital positions, as do foreign invasions and foreign abuse of our shared global environment.

In the **libegalitarian** system, property rights violations can take two forms: one, a denial of an equitable initial capital endowment, and two, obstructions of the freedom to acquire, preserve, employ or dispose of that capital. Both rights are resource or property rights, extensively understood, and unsolicited destruction of other persons' property is the prototypical crime. The simplest popular concept that captures this notion is theft. It follows that anything that can ethically be described as theft should be outlawed; and if it nevertheless occurs, it should be rectified at the perpetrator's expense.

Redefining "Crime." But the concept of crime is a loaded one, and its meaning within a **libegalitarian** system needs to be carefully articulated. The term has both legal and moral connotations in the present-day vocabulary. If we want to retain it, some of those connotations will have to be scrapped. Alternatively we would have to discard the concept and replace it with something that better captures the revised meaning we wish to give it.

The main problem posed by the current notion of crime is its heavily moralistic overtones. When the law calls a transgression a crime—whether a felony or a misdemeanor—there is an extra dimension of intrinsic ethical wrongness, quite apart from the economic damage inflicted on the victim.

Crimes are generally subject to more severe formal sanctions than non-criminal rights and property infringements, i.e., actions that now might be described as torts or contract breaches. In the aggregate, those extra sanctions are largely offset by the greater difficulties in securing a legal verdict against the culprit. But this "offset" will mean little to those who are indeed found guilty of criminality. In addition, crimes usually carry a moral stigma, which compounds the total "price" that the perpetrator has to pay for his action.

The **libegalitarian** system, by itself, should be a logically complete code of public socioeconomic ethics. It should thus make no accommodation for additional public-ethic norms, however widely accepted these may be. Introducing such norms would not only mess up our neat ideological scheme; it would create ethical cross-purposes, conflicts and confusions that would have to be reconciled—perhaps through compromises of our mostly deeply held principles.

We therefore have to strip the term crime of all the moral connotations that separate it from other infringements of property rights, like those now calling only for civil sanctions. Moreover, the legal and ethical distinctions between crime, on the one hand, and tort or contract breach, on the other, are uncomfortably vague, and we cannot retain any such distinction within our general ideological context. Privately each individual can, of course, make his own value judgments and use whatever emotional—or cynical—terms he prefers; but private preferences should not be elevated to a normative public-policy status.

A "crime" should really be no more, or less, than a property infringement for which the public at large, or part of it, has been given a right to restitution. At most the crime designation ought to indicate that there is a multitude of victims, rather than that the total offense is of a particular financial magnitude; a crime might thus be thought of as a collective, or public, bad. But the number of victims is not, ethically speaking, something of overriding constitutional importance, and we might as well drop the crime concept altogether.

The need to correct property infringements stems from an ethical requirement that we mutually respect and preserve personal capital, not from an urge to publicly enunciate moral principles, per se. If we wish to fully abide by this rule, we will have to draw an unorthodox conclusion: The right to property protection and restitution for inflicted damage should have nothing to do with the motives underlying the perpetrator's behavior.

Conventional Judeo-Christian ethics has unfortunately persuaded the public and our lawmakers to give more lenient treatment to unintentional or nonnegligent property infringements. This practice undercuts the principle of restitution. It implies, absurdly, that the perpetrator's good intentions were a compensatory income item for the injured party. And as it plays a relatively bigger role in criminal, as opposed to civil, law, it introduces another dubious distinction between the criminal and civil branches of our legal system.[21] In reality, good intentions or good will are no good at all when it comes to property maintenance and capital accumulation. It deserves no constitutional sanction.

Individual rights should be coupled with individual responsibilities, or those rights can erode in almost any interpersonal conflict situation. From the victim's standpoint, the economic loss due to a car collision will be the same whether the other driver was out to kill or just did not pay attention. The sole criteria for culpability in an individualistic society should be damage and causation, not errant or hostile private thoughts. And the majority's view on the morality of the damaging act should be irrelevant; otherwise prosecution cannot be counted on to bring restitution.

Government Property Violations. These ideas about crime, property infringement and the law are sharply at odds with conventional thinking. They aim at "demoralizing" crime and subordinating it under general ideological rules about property rights. They mean to downplay the distinction between law enforcement and government programs for public spending, regulation or taxation; all of these programs entail a taking and a giving, and they should be so analyzed.

In all these public-policy areas, the authorities today have enormous powers to redistribute resources and to divert the use of those resources from the uses that their original, rightful owners would have preferred. In all of them, government ideally should comply with the same socioethical and legal standards that pertain to relations among individuals and private parties. Just as the government should correct resource and property infringements among private parties, so it should show the same respect for private resources and the associated socioeconomic opportunities. Governments, being the servants of the citizens, ought not to be allowed to operate under separate property rules. If a privately undertaken property infringement is considered illegal and calls for restitution, so does, in a justly organized society, any similar action by the government.

To be sure, we have today laws that protect us against malfeasance by public officials and other forms of official law breaking. In particular, there are laws prohibiting completely arbitrary asset expropriations and taxation rules that discriminate on a purely personal or ethnic basis (as opposed to discrimination by economic criteria). "Excessively" cruel punishment is also constitutionally forbidden.

But these protections are very vaguely and elastically formulated.[22] They are much too permissive of vast redistributive control and tax schemes. As a result, our government is nominally free to violate even well-accepted rights. And it is, unfortunately, free to violate many of the more stringently defined rights embodied in our **libegalitarian** system. These rights and property infringements have the general attributes of robbery or theft.

The inevitable conclusion is: Socioethically speaking, our government, as currently operating, is indeed a thief. This charge may sound hysterical to those who instinctively trust the fairness of our constitutional system and the rectitude of our political leaders. But this is the conclusion not just of the radical libertarians and other theoretical individualists but also, it seems, of a large portion of the general, ideologically unsophisticated American population.

Yet we have acknowledged that governments perform some positive functions, and all government claims on resources cannot therefore be called thefts. So we have to be a bit more discriminating in making the accusation. And we should take special pains to clarify some of the distinctions between **libegalitarianism**—which is essentially a limited-government scheme—and anarcholibertarianism—which is, enthusiastically, a zero-government movement.

Aspects of Government Theft. When the government fails to provide a young person with an adequate standard upbringing, it robs him of some of the personal capital due to him. It puts him on a lower potential life path of income, consumption and well-being than he deserves. It does so, in particular, by robbing him of future potential job opportunities that presuppose a better foundation of intellectual, psychological or physical capital.

If the child, despite the odds, nevertheless is to catch up and gain easy access to the job market, he will normally have to make exceptional sacrifices in the meantime. He may have to study harder and play less. Or he may have to take special steps to overcome or tolerate his physical or psychological handicaps, through unpleasant diets or costly trips to the doctor. Replacing missing start-up capital in these ways is costly, and it will leave almost anybody poorer than his better-endowed peers in the complete lifetime context.

One could easily give specific examples of how the American government engages in this kind of robbery, judging by our equal-opportunity standard. One could point to the inequities of the public-private school system or to children's unequal access to health facilities. One could recall to the fundamental arbitrariness of the nuclear family system, which allows parents excessive discretion in the transfer of resources to their offspring.

Contrariwise one might, in this respect, give some credit to governments that reduce such interchild inequities. Those governments have tended to be of a socialist or social-democratic persuasion. Russian, Chinese, Israeli and Scandinavian children thus seem to enjoy somewhat greater equality in their initial resource endowments, achieved through day-care centers, children's allowances and less parental control over children's upbringing. (It should be added, however, that the lifetime benefits of those resources to the recipients are greatly diminished by regulatory and tax impediments to subsequent resource use; capital redistribution is hence accompanied by capital destruction.)

Underendowment of social capital constitutes a major form of government theft in an equal-opportunity society. It is something we could not easily put a price tag on; yet there can be little doubt that its magnitude in America today is often very large. The victim groups include children growing up in poor, mismanaged homes with irresponsible parents, or attending overpopulated, understaffed and underdisciplined public schools, or not getting proper medical care. These children are victims of uncompensated educational or medical-care theft. They are victims of theft of potential development capital, and the theft constitutes grand public larceny.

In the adult world, the performance of government should be judged, in part, by its provision of public collective goods. Each of us should have the right to expect delivery of such goods as long as their usefulness outweighs their costs and we are, collectively, willing to pay for them. If the government fails in this regard, the losses we suffer can fairly be labeled theft—though theft by omission rather than commission.

If my house is bombed to pieces because the government failed to provide the necessary air or missile defense, I am effectively being robbed of my house through governmental negligence. Similarly, if the government is to oversee the enforcement of private contracts—which is a reasonable position—it should be liable for any failures to do so. For instance, if my customers do not pay me and the government fails to back my collection efforts, I will indirectly suffer a government-inflicted loss. Technically the government, through this intermediary responsibility, will become my robber.

Taxes and Regulations. Government theft occurs as well, and perhaps more clearly, through excessive taxation and regulatory controls. There is a long-held libertarian position that taxation—all taxation, regardless of the use of the tax revenues—is institutionalized robbery.[23] Libertarians schooled in the economics of regulation undoubtedly would feel the same way about government actions of this kind.

Those who acknowledge the merits of public goods cannot fully share the libertarian perspective. Government theft does not, meaningfully, occur when taxes pay for desired, worthwhile collective goods. But it does occur whenever they do not. An analogous distinction can be made with respect to regulations, although the potential cases of theft-free regulations will be few.

In the area of taxation, one technically has to link particular government expenditures to particular tax levies, even though such connections do not seem to exist in actuality. On top of that, one will have to weigh the benefits to each socioeconomic group of those expenditures, relative to the cost of the taxes paid—also a tough analytical task. Alternatively one could try to tally up the government benefits received and taxes paid by each such group. One might then be able to determine whether, overall, the group members are getting their money's worth, through the net impact on them of the government's budget. If they are not, they are indeed being governmentally robbed.

Tax theft, as defined here, has two aspects. One involves tax payments that are too large relative to the value of the activities they finance. If the armed forces are too large or too lavishly equipped, they must, logically, be too costly; this is the other side of benefit-cost comparison. The taxpayers are then deprived of some superior spending opportunities in non-defense areas (with a consequent loss of personal capital), even after allowing for the imputed value of the defense services received. This is an example of large-scale nationwide robbery, affecting the majority of individual taxpayers. It is not simply a zero-sum theft from ourselves; it is, from the aggregate national perspective, a case of self-imposed waste, inflicted through a malfunctioning political system that permits a misuse of national resources.

The other aspect of tax theft involves a maldistribution of the tax burden. If taxes are levied with insufficient regard to the distribution of the associated benefits, some taxpayers will have to foot tax bills that properly should have been sent to other addresses. If upper-bracket wage earners have to pay a disproportionate share of the total defense, or law-enforcement, costs, they are being robbed of income and capital. Whatever the tax structure, the theft favors those who are comparatively undertaxed; there is government-intermediated intergroup theft.

The step from taxation to government regulation is very short, and economists have learned to think of controls as hidden, implicit taxes. Those who find their activities unreasonably restricted because of regulatory controls are nearly in the same boat as those who pay excessive taxes; both groups suffer income, opportunity and capital losses. This is true of people who cannot pursue their preferred business ventures, be it private highway development or bordello management, even if they are ready to pay the resource costs of these ventures. It can also be true of those who would have wished to smoke cigars on government-regulated airplanes or to take an unapproved but beneficial medication, while willingly assuming the associated costs and risks.

These persons are implicit financiers of the production of the collective goods embodied in environmental protection, public order, consumer safety or other broadly sought benefits. But some of these persons would have been willing to pay the true costs of any collective damage they might impose on the rest of the public (e.g., through smoky air). The existing controls then overpenalize them, while robbing them of something that is, ethically speaking, due to them.

In short, controls tend to be wasteful and inequitable, in that they hit some people too strongly. That extra, uncalled-for penalty represents a net loss of opportunity and capital for the restricted parties, and often for the entire economy as well. If there is a public cost to be borne, the preferable method is taxes. This kind of public penalty will still allow the taxed activity to occur whenever it is worth its tax price; and it automatically raises the funds needed to defray that cost. Taxes are thus both more efficient and more fair than quantitative regulations or complete prohibitions. Effective regulations almost always constitute theft; fairly assessed taxes do not, contrary to what the laissez-faire anarchists have been telling us.

Private Property Infringements. Private property conflicts present similar issues, and their solutions are often simpler. We can easily agree that the unauthorized, noncontractual taking of another person's physical or financial assets should indeed be regarded as theft, subject to restitution. Such acts include physical assault, manslaughter and murder, for these actions clearly lessen the victim's physical capital and income-earning capacity.

But the conventional dividing line between criminal and civil transgressions has, as we have already noted, no firm ethical or ideological basis, apart from traditional moral prejudice. That dividing line will not exist in the **libegalitarian** system. Either a person is responsible, or he is not. The severity of transgressions should be fully reflected in the assessment of compensatory damages, and no additional social reprisal is warranted.

Consider a failure to pay off an unconditional debt or to deliver legitimately sold goods to the buyer. Either of these acts unquestionably constitutes an illegitimate deprivation of property and capital. These actions are therefore also examples of theft, even though our present legal system usually does not so classify them.

The contractual right to receive something of value is in itself an asset, often exceeding the price paid for it; nondelivery is clearly theft. That a seller has a right to collect the price of goods being delivered is equally obvious. These conclusions are broadly in accord with all modern legal systems; but their ethical underpinnings are rarely as strong as in the libertarian, and the **libegalitarian**, ideologies.

The general, noncontroversial rule is that all voluntary exchanges must be honored either through their execution or through full restitution by the delinquent party. We can add, for our own part, that the mutuality and equality requirements of the **libegalitarian** system would otherwise be violated.

The only qualification to be made in this respect is that individual agents must be free to make their contracts contingent on just about any conceivable circumstance. For instance, financial misfortune, like bankruptcy, might be stipulated in a contract as a permissible excuse for non-performance. Such contracts ought to be allowed—the general freedom of contract so requires. The bankrupt party that fails to deliver will then, technically, be in compliance with his obligations.

Note that current American law, by contrast, is more lenient toward those who go bankrupt: Courts can sometimes wipe out a bankrupt firm's debts without the full prior or subsequent consent of all its creditors, a provision meant to prevent large or interconnected business failures from disrupting commerce. This is another unfortunate example of disrespect for voluntary exchange and private contracts. Admittedly, avoiding bankruptcy-related interruptions of commerce might be a significant collective good, warranting an allocation of some societal resources. But the collective-good aspect could surely be handled better through clearer contract provisions, subject to full enforcement—perhaps with recourse to backup lines of bank credit or insurance policies covering possible default losses.

Similarly, most Western legal systems provide nonperforming contract parties with exonerating excuses in special disastrous circumstances, often attributed to some "force majeure." These legal excuses are highly questionable; and they ought to get much more attention among free-market advocates.

De facto, such legal rules absolve one party of his responsibility not to impoverish another—and they thus become a peculiar vehicle for income redistribution. They shift the onus of unforeseeable disasters from the original risk taker, rich or poor, over to his business partner, for no solid efficiency or equity reason. Instead the producer-seller ought to bear the full business risks of his delivery promises—unless he contracts them away (through appropriate contingency clauses, normally coupled with a reduction in his sales price). Earthquakes or plagues—which could, indeed, interrupt a production and delivery plan—are no legitimate reasons for a seller to leave his customer empty-handed. The cost of a "force majeure" ought to be borne by the party who was unfortunate enough to be hit by it—not by his business counterparts.

True Public Needs. In an efficient system of voluntary exchange, there is unquestionably a collective need for law enforcement. Legal recourse is certainly a collective good: Everybody depends on it, and it cannot be distributed through individual, personally selected channels without official policy power.

This is clearly a governmental task, especially since the markets in which exchanges occur usually have a territorial aspect and legal action against delinquent parties requires some territorial control. Private parties could not fully handle the job of tracking down and obtaining damages from the nonpaying parties, even though private security forces, collection agencies and mediators might able to do part of the job.

Even with substantial private collection efforts, there would have to be a last-resort authority resolving remaining contract and property conflicts between private business parties or their financial guarantors. Without government-backed procedures for resolving private contract disputes, commerce, financial planning and personal capital accumulation would suffer unnecessarily.

A system of contract law enforcement, geared to maintaining property rights, would not only meet basic requirements for economic equity. It would also act as a deterrent to potential transgressions of such rights, helping make the private exchange system more efficient. The risk of being caught lessens the incentive for self-interested individuals to steal, either in the traditional sense or via contract breaches or torts; and reduced risks of theft tend to encourage productive investment.

But public efforts to enforce contracts are, in some degree, costly—and these costs must be properly allocated. To whom? Of course, to the law or contract breaker. He causes the costs, and he is responsible for making good the losses he imposed on others. And the deterrent effect will be reinforced if we let the party at fault foot the entire bill, including collection expenses, accumulated interest and the costs of court proceedings. He should pay, or some other party—the seller, buyer or lender, or perhaps the general taxpayer—will unfairly have to put up the money.

Nevertheless there will be cases when collection efforts fail or when the risk of such failure will make additional legal efforts too costly. Some property loss may then remain uncovered, and the mutuality of the market system has been violated. While this is in itself an individual loss, the risk of its occurrence is to some extent a collective or public "bad," for the risk is inherent in the market system, and not individually created. It should be up to the government to balance this public risk against the potential payoff of further law enforcement efforts, so that the risk will be adequately minimized.

Thus, not even the **libegalitarian** society will be completely free of societal risk to personal property and capital. There will remain some risks that public-good functions, including law enforcement, will be imperfectly carried out, and these risks cannot always be perfectly differentiated from the ordinary commercial risks that everybody assumes through his market activities. Who, then, should ultimately bear the costs of these systemic failures?

A credible case can be made for assigning them to the general public. The government would then have to reimburse private parties for its failure fulfill its public-good functions in regard to law enforcement. The resulting taxpayer costs might be rationalized as part of the fee we have to pay for membership in the public-good-producing nation. The fee will allow us, among other things, access to the nation's not-quite-perfectible legal machinery. And some trial and error ought to be permitted also on the governmental plane. The "costs" incurred through imperfect law enforcement (or imperfect national security, etc.) could even become useful collective investment in a longer-term societal learning process that might gradually permit better government.

BENEFIT-BASED TAXATION

All taxes are evil because they rob us of spendable income and potential personal welfare; taxation, by definition, constitutes theft, since it is involuntary. No, some taxes are necessary to help finance government activities; while the overall level of taxes today may or may not be too high, they are imposed in an unfair, inefficient manner, with too little attention to their effects on particular taxpayers and on the whole economy. No, again; if we are honest about it, American taxes are really too low, for there are large unmet needs for government services and transfers that the taxpayers should pay for.

These are three types of criticisms made against the current American system of taxes—their overall rationale, their incidence and their macroeconomic consequences. The attitude one takes can be a matter of ethics or efficiency, or simple expediency. For those who subscribe to a general economic-political ideology, the answer to the tax problem should flow from that ideology; for if we have decided what, precisely, the purposes of government should be, we can almost automatically deduce what taxation system is appropriate for its financing. Those who don't have a comprehensive ideology will, ethically, be groping in the dark; they will have to be content to look for ad hoc tax-evaluation criteria.

Prevalent Views. The libertarian anarchist rejects all taxes on account of their coerciveness and the lack of any need to finance the nonexistent government. To him, the institution of perfectly private enterprise is more important than the possibility, which he may deny anyway, that its productive capabilities may be defective in some collective-goods areas. To him, the income saved through the abolition of government could be better used for purchases of private goods, including subscriptions to "voluntary protective associations" and his favorite private criminal court.

At the opposite end, the perfectly socialist system need not bother to collect any taxes at all, since the state controls the distribution of all national income in the first place. Wages, whether in cash or in kind, are then merely a type of privilege or bonus, benevolently offered by the omnipotent state to its worker-subjects. And whether these wages are subject to charges for certain public services or offered on a "net" basis is a trivial accounting matter. The whole notion of "taxes" becomes ambiguous in this kind of society.[24]

Mainstream American attitudes fall somewhere in the gray, ill-defined middle. With their lack of ideological awareness, Americans tend to display an inarticulate blend of three attitudes: a permanent set of antitax gut feelings, a grudging sense of taxation's inevitability and a strong suspicion about the system's fairness. Opinion surveys tell us little more, except that most nonideological individuals share a self-centered, self-serving mentality: They themselves are paying too much, while most others pay too little.

The traditional American conservative wants taxes to be no higher than necessary to finance the government's few, well-defined functions, though perhaps including some support for the poverty-stricken and elderly. He is concerned about the distortive consequences of taxes on private activity. He may also believe in the message of the "supply-siders," popularized during the Reagan years, about the negative effects of heavy taxation on the incentives to work and invest. He may even subscribe to their claim that raising income tax rates could, through the added disincentive to work and save, make tax revenues smaller, rather than—as conventionally believed—larger.

The social liberal sees taxes both as the necessary payments for public goods and as a means for income and wealth redistribution in an ostensibly egalitarian direction. To him, taxes should be levied on those who can best afford them, i.e., those who, at the moment, earn high incomes or possess large wealth. He subscribes to the "ability-to-pay" principle of taxation. His egalitarianism on this score implies a sharp distinction between what we earn in the private sector and what we "earn" (and may keep) in a fuller, socioethical sense. In particular, when our incomes reach higher-than-average levels, the extra earnings are to be partially disqualified, through progressive income taxes.

Most of today's centrists straddle the conservative-libertarian and liberal-socialist positions. They are usually willing to seek a trade-off between equity, as defined by liberal "time-slice" standards, and overall national economic efficiency. They will try to expand the socioeconomic pie, up to a point, even if this means that the disposable-income slices going to different socioeconomic groups will have to be noticeably unequal. They are wary of imposing such high taxes on business that private investment, technological progress and job creation will slow and thereby jeopardize future living standards.

A Fairer System. Our proposed **libegalitarian** system of taxation will be substantially different from those just outlined. It establishes a definite principle for the determination of tax liabilities, thereby eliminating the ambiguities that characterize other taxation approaches. And it effectively makes taxes noncoercive—not just in a collective, majoritarian sense but, more important, from an individual taxpayer perspective.

In the **libegalitarian** system, taxes will not serve any redistributive purposes at all. Since the basic equity problem will be resolved outside the realm of taxes—through an equalization of debt-financed initial capital endowments—the tax structure will not need any equity-restorative provisions. It can therefore be tailored entirely to the needs of efficient, nondiscriminatory exchanges (tax-paid public-good provisions) between the private and the public sectors.

A **libegalitarian** tax will invariably be an implicit payment for goods, or for the benefits embodied in goods, received from the government. It will simulate an individual's payments for goods that he is voluntarily buying in the market: Everybody pays for what he gets. This is the "benefit" approach to taxation. The term was coined by neoclassical economists, who have been attracted by the prospects of removing the efficiency-reducing effects of taxes through a market-simulative taxation approach.[25]

The benefit approach is a pay-as-you-go method, or, better, a pay-as-you-get method. It achieves the same superior efficiency in the financing of public goods as the competitive private market does in regard to nonpublic goods. It avoids the hypocrisy of accepting two irreconcilable notions of "earnings" at the same time—one being private (gross) and another being social (net of redistributively imposed taxes). Instead the benefit principle recognizes that what is privately earned will be also be socially, and legitimately, earned.

Translating the benefit principle into an actual tax program will entail three steps. First, the beneficiaries of government activities must be identified. Second, the magnitudes of these benefits must be estimated, ideally on an individual basis. And, third, practicable, low-cost methods will have to be devised for collecting the indicated tax payments. These matters are not entirely of an ideological nature, but we nevertheless ought to be able to indicate the directions in which tax reform technicians will have to proceed.

Identifying the Beneficiaries. If the government devotes itself exclusively to producing national collective goods, the entire nation, by definition, will benefit. If it engages in collective-goods production of more limited scope, it should already have ascertained who the beneficiary groups are or how they are to be identified. Otherwise, this activity will not qualify as belonging to the governmental sphere. It will then belong in the

94

private sector (if anywhere), which will have to attract financing directly from private buyer-beneficiaries or other supporters.

With respect to national collective-goods production, the mere fact that a person resides, and engages in economic activity, within the nation, will indicate a potential tax liability; residence points to public-good benefits. Simply put, residents should pay for residence-related benefits. In the case of more limited collective goods, additional circumstances must be invoked if tax liability is to be established—circumstances that demonstrate actual benefit, or participation in socioeconomic groups that benefit.

In some situations, it is easy to see who these beneficiaries, and the targeted taxpayers, are. Residents of particular coastal areas, and visitors to them, ought to pay the taxes needed to finance coastal beautification—to the extent they want such beautification. If a U.S. foreign aid program for Central America really is warranted, business firms trading with that region might possibly be asked to pay part of the cost of that program (while private philanthropies might also wish to contribute). Asthmatics, in theory, ought to pay a disproportionate share of the taxes needed to keep the air clean, since their clean-air benefits are larger than those of the rest of us. And so on.

Yet such taxes might better be construed as user fees, with the government acting as the custodian of particular national resources and spokesman for related national interests. It will then seem perfectly natural that the government should collect payments from the user-beneficiaries of these resources (beaches, air, etc.) and other interested parties so as to cover its benefit-production or benefit-maintenance costs. The semantic distinction between taxes and fees will then be trivial; both sources of government revenue should meet the same cost-effectiveness and benefit distribution tests.[26]

By far the biggest portion of **libegalitarian** taxes will, in practice, be those which finance easily identifiable, broadly shared collective goods. We can be sure of this because the national government, in particular, isn't very good at handling smaller collective-good jobs with differentiated beneficiaries, and the private sector usually will have to assume these tasks. The central question, therefore, is how to tax-finance the production of the major, readily observable national collective goods: external and internal national security, property protection, contract fulfillment and the preservation of nationwide natural resources.

Recall that defense or security is a kind of property or wealth insurance. The benefits connected with a given amount of security will normally be proportional to the insured person's wealth, including both tangible and intangible aspects; the more is at stake, the more the risk reduction will be worth. As income is essentially the return on wealth, either wealth itself or the income return on it can thus serve as a reasonable base on which to calculate this tax liability. (But, of course, the tax rates needed to generate a certain amount of tax revenue would be much lower if the base were wealth instead of income.)

However, there is also a timing question. To ensure that the taxes will be paid by the true beneficiaries of the associated government spending, the taxes will have to be due when the benefits occur, and not necessarily when the government makes the outlays. Government outlays today that will produce benefits only in, say, five years ought not to be financed by today's taxpayers. If the latter's economic circumstances change, they might not be in a position to gain a substantial share of the ultimate benefits; or they might not even be around at that time. This implies that if government spending is of a delayed-benefit (i.e., investment) nature, it should be debt-financed. And the debt should be retired concurrently as the benefits emerge, through the use of funds obtained through tax collections at that time.

What about the costs of public health care and income support to poor grown-ups or of Social Security? In the **libegalitarian** society, these programs will no longer be part of the national government budget. If they are to be continued, it will have to be done on an entirely voluntary basis, and the programs will then be self-supporting.

What about aid to college education, subsidies to tobacco farmers or grants to performing-arts organizations? Such items also will not likely appear in the budget of the **libegalitarian** government. All education for grown-ups will, in our ideal society, be privately financed, through drawdowns of private savings or through private borrowings. Agriculture will have to be self-sustaining, like all private business. And the performing arts will have to try to make a go of it in the marketplace, or seek private charity, if they cannot demonstrate cost-efficient contributions to the education of children (in which case they could deserve support from the national educational budget). So there will be no need to pinpoint the beneficiaries, for the sake of distributing the tax burden.

Tax Base and Tax Rate. An individual's tax liabilities are normally determined by two variables: the tax base and the applicable tax rate. This is the way it ought to be, whenever tax obligations are to reflect some measurable aspects of his economic behavior or circumstances—aspects that can then be captured by a well-defined tax base.

In selecting the appropriate base for a particular tax, one ought to identify the best available indicator of the distribution of benefits from the particular, tax-financed government activity. That indicator, or a closely correlated economic variable, can then serve as the tax base; in effect, it becomes a proxy for the relative magnitude of the benefits received.

Setting the right tax rate then becomes a simple matter. In many cases, the tax rate can be made uniform for all taxpayers, especially if there is no clear evidence that the benefits are not proportional to that tax base. It will then equal the percentage relationship between the cost of the government activity and the aggregate tax base.

Most of the benefits an individual will derive from government in a **libegalitarian** society will be closely linked to his own socioeconomic activity or to the resources he employs in it. The general tax base ought to be defined accordingly—as a measure of activity or of resources.

The best summary index of economic activity is a person's income, broadly defined, whether obtained in cash or accrued.[27] The best measure of a person's resources—the resources that government activity, properly restructured, will enhance and make more valuable—is a person's tangible and intangible wealth. Thus a personal wealth tax is, in theory, a logical alternative to a personal income tax. But wealth should then be defined very broadly; it should represent the sum total of all income-producing resources (assets minus liabilities), which include personal skills and useful education. Measuring this variable will generally be more difficult than measuring the resulting annual income. So practical considerations will favor using personal income as the general tax base. (And if income is taken to include both distributed and undistributed profits from business firms, there will be no reason to tax businesses at all.)

Deductions and Exemptions. One kind of individual income tax deduction, exemption or credit against the personal income tax seems very much in order, given our ideological premises. Its purpose will be to achieve a truer, more relevant definition of income, not to extend special tax favors in contravention of general taxation principles.

Part of each person's gross income (especially his income from labor) is generally used for the purpose of sustaining his capacity to earn that income or similar income in the near future. That part of his income ought not to be subject to income tax, but should be deducted before his tax is computed.

He should thus not have to pay tax on that income which is necessary just to survive and work, because that portion of his income will be absorbed in the income-generating process. The deduction should correspond to his costs of shelter, food, clothing, transportation to work and basic health care, estimated at the lowest generally acceptable levels. This will essentially be a deduction for "maintenance costs" for the individual worker. (Incidentally this would be a much larger deduction than permitted today in the form of personal exemptions.) What remains is his "net" (pretax) income—a more reasonable income tax base. As a result of these provisions, low-skilled wage earners without significant income-producing savings would pay very little, if any, tax, whereas today they often do.

At the other end of the income scale, the **libegalitarian** tax system would give no tax preference to those who make substantial contributions to private charities and claim large deductions for them; the tax subsidy of private philanthropy would end. So would many other opportunities for tax escape that now exist, through tax shelters and "loopholes" that have no relation to the taxpayer's contributions to public-good production.

Combining a basic living-cost deduction with a flat general income tax rate may give the appearance of a progressive overall income tax structure. After all, the share of tax payments in gross income will increase with income. But this would be a superficial, false conclusion. Tax obligations will in reality be proportional—to net income, that is. So this is how one ought to characterize the **libegalitarian** tax system—a simplified flat-rate system.[28]

But how high should that rate be? Unfortunately one cannot make a precise estimate, since there would be a wholesale reform of the public sector in the **libegalitarian** society. One cannot predetermine the extent and cost of the various government functions that ought to remain or be introduced. But with much more limited government functions, the overall tax burden would clearly be much lower than today, in the United States or in almost any other country.

The **libegalitarian** tax would be like a territorial club fee, payable for services rendered and when truly received. It would not be a penalty for hard work, diligent saving or luck. Nor would it be a scheme for redistributing earnings or pressuring businesses to alter the scale or direction of their productive activities. Instead it would be an instrument for financing the public services that individuals need to maximize the value of their spendable personal incomes and their socioeconomic opportunities.

Chapter V
IMPROPER GOVERNMENT FUNCTIONS

PRIVATE-PUBLIC BOUNDARIES

Government—good government—can promote or expand individual freedom or opportunities without adverse consequences for anybody. But, unfortunately, it can also diminish the freedoms and opportunities of some, if not all, of us. The two situations will have to be differentiated if we are to define the scope of government in our idealized, **libegalitarian** society. Only in this way can we draw the proper boundary line between the private and the public sector.

At first this may seem like a forbiddingly difficult exercise. It would seem to require that we identify and measure all the various freedoms and opportunities that either government or private organizations and individuals could potentially create; how else could we restore what government now takes away or fails to deliver? It would seem to require an analysis of the relative productivities of the public and private sectors and, in addition, a judgment on the public sector's ability to identify and properly charge the beneficiaries of its activities. Obviously this would be impossible, even in our computerized age. And our ideology might then seem fuzzy and unrealistic.

Fortunately the task is not quite that big. In particular we do not need, and should not even try, to determine what individual goods ought to be produced. This should be a private responsibility altogether, based on private initiative, private resources and private negotiation in the marketplace. Ultimately what individual goods are to be produced, and how they are to be distributed, should be decided by the individual consumers. Mutual interactions between consumers and producers will produce the most efficient production and distribution of such goods, and there is no case for government involvement—or for prejudging the results.

Consumer sovereignty should prevail over the selection of all private goods, and free, voluntary exchange transactions will allow workers, investors and entrepreneurs to produce and deliver the goods the consumers select. An effort by government to predetermine this selection would be distributionally inefficient, as well as totalitarian. And government would have no competitive advantages in mobilizing the most cost-effective resources, or in applying the best technologies, for the goods' production.

Much the same conclusion holds for many goods that we consider collective. It holds for goods that produce widely but erratically distributed benefits, not tied to well-defined geographic areas or to other reliable socioeconomic groupings. Since government then cannot easily identify the types and quantities of goods needed, and since it usually has no practical way of charging the true beneficiaries, it should leave these tasks to the private sector. So in this situation, too, the market will normally make the best production and distribution decisions.

But the collective-good consumers will have to organize themselves so as to secure sufficient financing for the desired volume of production. Otherwise they will run the risk of seeing some of their demand unmet or having to pay the costs of supplying freeloaders as well as themselves. This is an inherent problem in all nonpublic collective-good provision.

There might, however, sometimes be an alternative: provide enough credible information on the distribution of the benefits so that a government agency might begin to take over the job and tax-finance it accordingly. Even a **libegalitarian** government should allow this possibility, as long as it can efficiently organize the production of the nonpublic goods and is ready to charge the actual beneficiaries. As an example, one can envision a neighborhood association transferring a local security job to the city police, with an appropriately structured local tax introduced to finance the costs.

All remaining potential goods are in the public-goods category. By definition the market does not work well enough to be allowed to single-handedly take care of such activity. That is why government will have to step in; otherwise too little will be produced (and freeloaders will enjoy some of the benefits). This is, then, where the private-public border line should be drawn. And since the public sector's performance is everybody's concern, its functions need to be publicly, and constitutionally, clarified.

Public-good theory establishes the basic principles, even though it does not yield specific, quantitative norms for public-sector activity, or for government expenditure and taxation. This theory provides the conceptual model after which legislators and public administrators ought to structure the public sector in a **libegalitarian** society. It should be reflected in a national constitution that authorizes government to establish a system of cost-effective public-good production and to raise the necessary tax money in an equitable manner.

This constitution should force government to eliminate or redesign those government activities that do not fit the definition of taxworthy national collective goods. It should require that the tax system be so restructured that tax liabilities will match the pattern of benefit receipts across the population. And it should create a mechanism for continuous public review of the government's record, with procedures for correcting government mismanagement—a matter of "consumer sovereignty" at the public-good level.

The Information Argument. Much of the private-versus-public choice depends on the possible flow of consumer-to-producer information and on producers' ability to respond through cost-sensitive supply changes. Producers need to be able to predict how much consumers will demand and what prices they are willing to pay. They also need to be aware of how costly their production will be, depending on the prices of labor, material, machinery, technology and capital. Without adequate information about buyer demand and resource supplies (or resource prices), the right production and distribution decisions cannot be made—and the economy will suffer.

If government knew both what goods are worth producing and how to distribute them to the user-consumers who want them, its functions might, in theory, seem completely open-ended. If it had access to perfect low-cost information both about each individual's desires and about available productive resources, it could thus, hypothetically, take over the whole national production job. And with this knowledge, it would know automatically who should pay the production costs—these same individuals. Basic consumer rights could then be perfectly fulfilled, it seems. The only missing rights and opportunities in such a system would consist of those connected with private entrepreneurship and equity ownership per se.

But such information about consumer preferences and resource availabilities is, in fact, scarce and costly, and government possesses no superior capability for acquiring it. Instead the market is generally the best-known device for exchanging information among the economically interested parties on both the producer and the consumer side. Most benefit and cost data are of a narrowly private nature, subject to constant shifts in each geographic and commodity segment of the market. Those data are not broadly uniform across the national economy, but individualized, localized and variable.

As a rule, the market provides timely, low-cost signals about preferences, wants, technologies and relative resource scarcities—the signals needed for efficient production and distribution decisions. A centralized government agency will be at a competitive disadvantage in the information area if it tries to enter a private-good activity.

Cheap, ready information makes the market's price mechanism function much more smoothly and responsively. New information about the strength of demand translates into changing price pressure in the final-product market, and the pressure is in due course transmitted to the markets for labor, raw material and other requisite resources. At the other side of the process, data on changing resource availabilities translate into newly estimated production costs and acceptable supply prices. Demand and supply shifts will create mutual feedbacks, back and forth. The market is the ideal mechanism for coordinating decisions with respect to all individual-good production. In particular, the permits efficient decentralized dissemination of information, and it systematically reveals both resource scarcities and consumer preferences.[29] True, consumers and producers act not so much on the ways things really are, but on the ways things seem to be. Yet the closer they are to the market process, the more accurate their perceptions will tend to be, and the more nearly they will be able to satisfy their economic goals.

The private market also can be used for collecting the preference information required for the organization of private collective-good production, although this can be a more difficult job. Choosing the proper technique for exploring the strength of demand, or for soliciting contributions to the desired activity, is in itself a quasimarket task. It is exemplified by the work of neighborhood associations, arts guilds, philanthropies and special-interest clubs—or much of the "not-for-profit" industry.

When collective goods have a strong geographic base—that is, when they benefit the residents of particular regions—the information question tends to be simpler. The geographic affiliation itself becomes a critical, low-cost datum, one that can solve most of the consumer identification problem: Barring evidence to the contrary, the area's residents (perhaps including visitors) can be presumed to be the beneficiaries of the collective-good activity; and their benefits usually accrue in some proportion to their incomes or spending. Residence may thus obviate the need for detailed data on consumer preferences. The private market will then have no particular advantage in this respect. The government's special ability to collect taxes on a territorial basis may then clinch the case for governmentally organized production.

Costs of Misgovernment. There will, even in the idealized **libegalitarian** world, always be a gray border area between the public and the private sector. Indeed there will be scope for constitutional innovation and potential intersectoral reassignments of productive functions.

All the same, society needs constitutional safeguards that protect well-established sectoral boundaries that remain valid while preventing costly, uncalled-for changes in public-sector functions. Such changes can pose severe threats to socioeconomic rights.

Government in some cases produces too few of the collective goods we actually want; this is a matter of undergovernment. In other cases, it produces the right quantities and qualities of goods, given our wants, but its methods for allocating the production costs among the beneficiaries are inequitable; this is a matter of financial (tax) misgovernment. Or lastly, the government can be guilty of overgovernment, either because it wrongly assumes a market function, or because it extends a governmental activity beyond its proper, cost-determined boundaries.

In any of these situations, individual rights, as seen from the **libegalitarian** perspective, will be violated, and some individual opportunities will be destroyed. Some individuals will be worse off than they would be in a fairer, more efficient society, perhaps devastatingly so. And while government activities may confer some extra, unearned benefits to others, this is no excuse. If we were to allow such excuses, we would implicitly tolerate government-intermediated theft.

SELECTIVE SERVICE

Production of defense requires manpower. Despite spectacular advances in military technology, the military still depends on labor. An unmanned, or undermanned, military would surely be inefficient and overly costly in terms of nonlabor resources. Somebody has to pull the triggers, push the buttons and program our next potential defense moves. And since we all benefit from the defense of our country, we should all contribute to the national defense effort and to the provision of military manpower.

This reasoning might seem to suggest that we all have a basic, presumptive obligation to offer our labor services to the military, even in the new, post-cold-war climate. It might seem to justify a system of general military conscription. Of course, it also appeals to sentimental traditionalist notions of patriotism and honor.

However we feel about patriotic duty, isn't it in everybody's individual interest to support our national defense effort by accepting military service obligations, especially if these are to be shared by all? Besides, the military draft seems to be a cheap, effective way of raising manpower, to the benefit of all the taxpayers. And if some find honor in serving, they will receive an extra, nonpecuniary wage bonus, at no public cost; this should be just fine.

Costs and Inequities. But these kinds of prodraft arguments are fallacious. And since they are likely to be raised anew—when global conflicts again are heightened or if nuclear disarmament leads to a reemphasis on conventional, labor-intensive defense forces—the arguments need to be dealt with.

Everything considered, the draft method is not cost-effective. It is also not at all equitable, either as between the two sexes, or among different men (or, hypothetically, women) at a draftable age.

Accept the uncontroversial premise that each person owns a complex, individualized stock of personal capital, including a variety of human-capital items. For each person, this capital has distinct preferred uses, with different productivities in different lines of work. It is easy to see that the draft fails to respect these distinctions. It leads to a large-scale, unevenly distributed confiscation of personal capital, including vast amounts of manpower, leisure and consumption opportunities. The remuneration offered does not nearly compensate for the service obligations it imposes; this is always a key feature of a draft. In short, the draft is an involuntary, coercive exchange transaction, and the balance of costs and benefits will look very different for different individuals.

To some draftees, the financial and room-and-board compensation is sufficient to offset the costs. These draftees suffer no real net loss. In their case, the compulsoriness of the draft is happily ineffective, and we need feel no ideological compassion for them. Other draftees—typically, the majority—do suffer net capital losses. These losses can be approximated by their forgone opportunities for higher civilian earnings and more enjoyable leisure, i.e., by the extent to which their military real income falls short of their alternative civilian well-being.

The draft is akin to a tax, clumsily levied with little regard for the draftees' incomes, professional preferences or other personal circumstances. It implies a uniquely punitive taxation norm in that those with the greatest civilian skills, or the greatest reluctance to serve, will be hit the most; their forgone opportunities will be especially large. Conversely, those at the lower end of the income spectrum, or those who would have voluntarily served at the prevailing draftee compensation level, escape that tax.

And the presumed national cost saving due to the use of low-cost labor is wholly illusory. Some might define that "saving" as if it referred only to the financial position of the government, as shown in its annual budget, and not to the nation as a whole; they then get a false perspective. If, instead, one looks also at the personal costs of the draftees, one can easily see the true costs of the draft—and the national waste that results from this institution. Specific, credible dollar numbers are hard to come up with; but there can be little doubt that the costs are huge.

The Vietnam war opposition, whatever else it wrought, helped sharpen the public awareness of the inequities of the draft. The post-Vietnam public reservations about the draft were well-founded and ideologically welcome. They clearly helped bring about the end of the formal draft, by the Nixon administration, in the early 1970s. Clearly, the introduction of volunteer armed forces in that decade was a big step in the right direction.[30] Conversely, the Carter administration in 1980 took an ominous step backwards by reinstating draft registration, and the Reagan administration declined to reverse this decision despite its broad commitment to voluntarism and free markets.

The possibility of actual conscription in the future remains a serious threat to our liberties—including our occupational freedom, freedom of residence, freedom not to wear uniforms and all the socioeconomic freedoms connected with a preferred, better-paying job. The threat might seem remote today, unless the unresolved Middle East conflicts should assume much broader geopolitical dimensions. But one would hope that a permanent national commitment could be made not to revive the draft and to phase out all draft registration. This could best be done through a constitutional amendment banning all compulsory employment, whether it is called slavery or selective service.

Some defense planners like to observe that our military manpower needs might suddenly escalate in an unexpected global crisis. To them, the draft is an expedient mechanism for quick mobilization, or a national manpower-insurance policy. The answer to these concerns is not even a "standby draft" but a system of "standby service contracts"—voluntary contractual commitments of reserve personnel to report for duty on short notice, in exchange for up-front fees as well promises of adequate service pay.[31]

Antiminority? Liberals have raised another concern. They have noted the large proportion of black men and other ethnic minority groups, usually with below-average education, in our present volunteer armed forces; this pattern was particularly strong in the early years of the volunteer system.

Thus, aren't minority groups unfairly assuming an extra defense burden on behalf of better educated, more prosperous, predominant middle-class whites? Isn't this "exploitation" a sign that we should go back to the fairness of a color-blind draft, with no exceptions for white college kids?

Hardly. The volunteering minority representatives are now benefiting from the added job opportunities created through the market recruitment process. They are overwhelmingly better off because of the voluntary army. And they should be allowed to respond to these opportunities as they see fit. It is no disgrace for them to choose this or any other profession. Note the irony: What used to be called an honor, is now, by liberal supporters of the draft, considered a disgraceful handicap. Neither attitude deserves any public sanction.

However, army, navy and air force recruitment does have some disturbing ethnic aspects. The relative attractiveness of the armed services for blacks surely reflects gaps in their educational backgrounds—in their initial social capital endowments—relative to those typical of whites. More equal schooling and family environments would have made the composition of the military applicant pool resemble the overall population more closely.

But this is no valid argument against the voluntary army. On the contrary, the services' ethnic imbalances are a healthy, though incomplete, correction of more basic inequities in our socioeconomic system—inequities that ought to be remedied more directly, more thoroughly and more permanently in other ways.

A National Youth Service? Many of the same reservations must be made, on a smaller scale, against proposals for some kind of "national youth service," performed in a public-sector capacity. Under various proposals, young men and women would be invited to sign up for either military or civilian work, for instance, in health care, education or social services. Some compensation would be offered, but part of the inducements for participation would take noncash forms.

For instance, Congress has been looking at a plan to tie such service to vouchers for college tuition credit, on top of small cash stipends. This plan would attempt to stimulate college attendance by facilitating its financing. It thus has a dual purpose in that it would promote both the designated public-service sectors and higher education, at very low costs.

But one should suspect that there is no "free, two-course lunch" of this kind. Outside of the military, the services to be performed will mostly involve what actually are private, not public, goods. So any new programs pushing resources into these activities are likely to be counterproductive: They will aggravate the inefficiencies that already exist because of over-

106

government. The taxpayer dollars to be spent on these activities could have been better, and more equitably, spent privately, in accordance with competitive market criteria.

Subsidizing higher education in this roundabout way also seems unwise. Normally, higher education ought to be financed privately, through access to capital markets, and each potential student ought to assess his own educational prospects and desires and plan accordingly. Educational subsidies to those who enjoy certain types of social-service work would tilt private career choices and induce some young persons to take over college slots that should, for both efficiency and equity reasons, belong to others. And, again, the taxpayers will be stuck with extra bills, rarely connected with benefit received.[32]

Admittedly voluntarism is ethically preferable to conscription. As it helps attract those whose services are most readily available, and who therefore command the lowest market price for their labor, it is less costly to the taxpayers and the nation at large; and the inequities tend be milder. But the voluntarism is of an incomplete, and publicly biased, variety, because it forcibly involves the taxpayer and distorts resource allocation among industries.

The whole idea of inducing young men and women to demonstrate their patriotic commitment by taking jobs in the existing public sector is offensive. It points toward additional unwarranted "entitlements," with new unhealthy dependencies on the taxpayer. It is also, in most circumstances, economically ineffective: If the public-sector jobs need to be done, they should be filled regardless of any special youth service; if not, the pay they offer will be a waste of taxpayer money; and to the extent that the purpose is educational, the real problem is to ensure equitable, cost-effective access to educational facilities irrespective of public-service needs.

PUNITIVE LEGAL SANCTIONS

The purposes of a law should be threefold. It should inform the citizens about the boundaries of their rights. It should establish rules for how transgressions of the boundaries are to be identified, measured and evaluated. And it should prescribe sanctions for such transgressions. In all three respects, the law should reflect the ethical values of the national constitution and the underlying ideology; otherwise it may contradict those values and thwart their realization.

Law and Ideology. Most political analysts probably do not regard the law as an important, clear-cut expression of the prevailing economic-political ideology. College courses in comparative social systems do not devote much time to different notions of contract breach or criminality or to parallels between criminal sanctions and taxes.

Capital punishment is a special, value-laden exception, usually connected with conservative ideology. So is, vaguely, an emphasis on law and order. Almost everybody might realize that, at bottom, the national constitution is an ideological document; and there is a small group of economic-theoretic scholars (mostly connected with the University of Chicago) who specialize in the economics of the law.

Beyond these occasional connecting points, the inherent nexus between ideology, economics, and law is poorly appreciated. The Supreme Court has not been very helpful in clarifying the economic ramifications of its decisions. No wonder most people draw an artificial line between the issues of economic rights and opportunities (for law-abiding citizens) and the questions of legality and legal recourse.

But, of course, even lawbreakers must normally also have some rights. And if we regard both ideology and the law as, ultimately, matters of ethics, the connections become even clearer. Whatever general system of ethics we adopt, it must have implications for appeals procedures, prison conditions and statutes of limitations—as well as for liquor taxes, waste disposal and Federal Reserve policy.

One related idea is that the law should embody and articulate the prevailing popular ethics. As ethics change over time, the law needs to change, too, so that it becomes a "living document"; and it will then help to consolidate society's overall value system. But the idea conflicts with the notion that the constitution should be a nearly permanent set of political rules based on the nation's deepest socioethical values and subject only to slow, evolutionary change.

If we believe in a permanent set of individual rights, immune to majority pressure and to demands for political accommodation, we cannot treat the law (let alone the constitution) relativistically. The law must corroborate and validate our rights, securely and permanently. We cannot allow individual rights and opportunities to be wantonly destroyed or redistributed in accordance with shifting popular ethics or legal-professional fashions. If we stick to our ideological principles, there can be no room for compromises with shifting popular ethical perceptions, neither in legislation nor in law enforcement. At most we might concede that there will transitional problems of implementation: Just as political and economic reforms may take time, so will the required changes in the nation's legal framework.

Still, the ethical principles embodied in the **libegalitarian** ideology will leave room for different sets of private ethics. Any values that do not infringe on our constitutional principles can be accommodated as matters of personal preference. But they should then remain private. No legal sanctions should be especially stiff just because popular morality sharply condemns the illegal act—say, for crimes such as rape, sexual molestation and drug-related activities.

Appropriate Sanctions. From a **libegalitarian** standpoint, there is a lot to criticize in the current American system of law. In fact, one cannot detect any consistent ideological point of view, despite all the Constitutional references to rights and liberty.

The law is vague, contradictory and constantly shifting; the latitude of judges and jurors is wide; and there is no firm rights structure to refer to, despite the many rights ostensibly embedded in the Constitution or in federal and local statutes. Sanctions vary arbitrarily from state to state; and they depend on irrelevant, trivial circumstances, such as the composition of juries, the location of the court proceedings or the predilections of justices. It follows that, by our ideological standards, many sanctions must be inequitable.

If we tried to sketch a more ideologically credibly system, what rules would govern the use of legal sanctions? Of course, the rules should flow from our overall view of crime, contract breach, and other deprivations of other persons' property. Each person should be treated as if he has a right to full respect for his property—and an obligation to honor that same right on behalf of every person he somehow comes into contact with. This is the basis for the imposition of all legal sanctions, whether they are now called damages, fines or something else.

Accordingly, legal sanctions should always, as much as possible, be restorative. They should repair, rather than punish per se. Each sanction should be no stronger, and no weaker, than necessary for complete restoration of the damage done. It should make the party at fault compensate fully, but no more than fully, for the losses he has inflicted on others.

This rule creates a strong preference for relying on monetary compensation, whether they are called damages or fines. By contrast, imprisonment is not economically restorative (though some may think it morally restorative). Instead, it imposes additional costs on the taxpayer, on top of any losses incurred through the criminal act itself. Thus it should be used only as a last resort, not as a standard sanction on lawbreakers who are capable of full monetary restitution. Imprisonment may satisfy primitive demands for revenge, as well a more civilized desire for protection against repeated crimes. But a **libegalitarian** society would give every convicted person the option of paying off his associated debt, in cash or whatever payment instrument feasible.

Lawbreaking will then, de facto, carry specific, limited costs, including primarily the cost of restitution. Illegal acts will resemble purchases, made at prices that correspond to the value of the victims' losses or the costs of filling the resulting gaps in the victims' net assets. This may seem like a cynical view, especially with respect to crimes against persons. Yet there is no system that would strike a fairer balance between the interests of the two parties.

The **libegalitarian** approach outlined here would help erase the artificial distinction now made between crimes and noncriminal transgressions (contract breaches, torts). It would let everybody retain his basic constitutional rights and basic property protection, despite any property transgressions that he might have committed. Conviction should not imply a suspension of these rights, once restitution has been made. Excessively harsh punishment, including imprisonment of persons prepared to make good financially, is a form of government theft that should not be tolerated.

It is impossible to make a fair generalization about the severity of all the types of criminal and noncriminal sanctions imposed on Americans today. For one thing, no comprehensive statistics of this kind exists. Yet some impressions are unavoidable. Surely many sanctions turn out to be too mild, especially when the incompleteness of factual proof lets the culprit off the hook altogether. Some members of the public will then be cheated out of some of the corrective or protective benefits of the law, with an unjust property loss. Meanwhile, many sanctions are undoubtedly too strong, especially when they are based on crude public prejudices largely unrelated to actual damage to the plaintiffs. The lawbreaker will then suffer a loss of rights, opportunity and capital to which he is still, despite his transgression, entitled.

In particular, the current practice of exacting double or triple damages in civil suits intuitively appears wrong. By definition, they overcompensate, so that they end up being confiscatory rather than merely restorative. The usual justification for the practice is that there is a strong public interest in discouraging a type of behavior that might otherwise easily be repeated. It then becomes tempting for legislators, juries and judges to set strong, conspicuous examples of what sanctions are in store for potential future offenders.

For instance, banks have recently been forced to pay triple damages for overcharges of interest on consumer loans. So have companies responsible for chemical spills. And so have producers of drugs, food items and other consumer goods deemed "unsafe," even without any evidence of actual harm to their buyers.[33]

The legal principles that the courts have relied on in reaching these verdicts are varied and without a consistent ideological foundation. But the severe judgments exemplify the expansive application of tort law and the punitive fines that long have been allowed in tort cases. Excessive judgments also have been meted out in cases when the law stipulates joint liability even for parties who play only a subsidiary role in the harmful acts. This has led to many "deep pocket" suits against well-heeled businesses, insurance companies and government agencies who have had to pick up the whole, punitively inflated tabs.

Moreover, the courts now have a tendency to hold manufacturers and other businesses strictly liable for damage attributable to use of their products, without any clear evidence of negligence on their part (let alone malicious intent). Many of the current critics of the American tort system question both the common-law validity and the economic justice of applying strict liability in these cases.[34]

But the real problem seems to lie elsewhere—in the flimsy presumption of an underlying contractual promise that a product will be perfectly "safe" or "effective." If a manufacturer sells a product without any guarantee whatsoever, he ought not to be liable for anything, except the product's delivery. If he does promise certain product characteristics, and some of these characteristics prove absent to the detriment of the buyer, he should be fully—strictly—liable. At present the law is unfairly biased in favor of the buyer-consumer, who gets an unearned distributional bonus and a misplaced signal to relax his own precautions.

Fortunately, these anomalies and injustices have lately begun to attract public attention. Many observers now rightly claim that we have a "tort crisis," and there have been signs that the Supreme Court will soon take a critical look at the problem. In fact, some of the big awards might already be unconstitutional: They might be construed as violations both of the Eighth Amendment's prohibition of "excessive fines" and also, because of the lack of clear statutes in this regard, of the 14th Amendment's insistence on "due process of law."[35]

On more pragmatic grounds, legal-economic scholars now widely realize that grossly punitive damage awards can be detrimental to innovation, entrepreneurship and business planning, and thus to longer-term macroeconomic efficiency.[36] The mere threat of severe penalties for a malfunctioning commercial product can sharply restrict the incentives of business firms to develop new, potentially very useful products. The emergence of new and better products will thereby be delayed, and all those third parties who could otherwise have benefited from the potential products will be worse off. This raises equity, as well as efficiency, concerns, especially from a **libegalitarian** perspective.[37]

Deterrence? But legal tradition has long favored sanctions that frequently go way beyond restitution, especially in criminal cases. The tradition suggests that punishments are not just restitutions to the victims but something more severe—an extra punishment for the violation of the legal or socioethical code itself.

It is often felt that convicted lawbreakers should be punished with extra severity just because many other lawbreakers, and probable lawbreakers, are going scot-free. In fact, many sociologists and economists believe that this is actually the ideal combination of results. According to them, extra heavy penalties on the convicted should make up for the lack of penalties on those who slipped through the net of the law. This, it is believed, will produce approximately the right expectation in the minds of potential criminals who ponder both the probability of apprehension and conviction and the likely severity of punishment, before they undertake their criminal acts. The risk of stiff fines or long prison terms will, in this reasoning, defer a sufficient number of them from going ahead with their criminal plans.[38]

And while penalties could be reduced if law enforcement efforts were strengthened, these extra efforts may be unnecessarily costly to society. So the apprehended criminals will, as a result, have to pay the price for society's poor law enforcement mechanism. The price will vary arbitrarily with the size of Justice Department and FBI budgets. The additional penalty is an ethically arbitrary tax, inimical to individual freedom and equal opportunity.

Deterrence, for the sake of deterrence, should be recognized for what it is—essentially a coercive exploitation of the criminal's rights. Deterrence means that the apprehended lawbreaker is held responsible for a societal prevention and insurance program. Indeed, lawbreakers become martyrs for the common good—in this case, the public good of reduced police and court costs.

To be sure, deterrence may be a helpful side effect of sanctions, and threats of sanctions may help maintain the individual rights of law-abiding citizens in the future. Deterrence is in this sense a collective good. Yet this circumstance cannot justify the destruction of the lawbreaker's rights, net of his obligation to correct his misdeed. The cost of that collective good ought to be borne by the general public and not passed on to a small, vulnerable minority. Lawbreakers should have the same rights as anybody else once they have corrected the damage they inflicted on others, for they will then have paid their dues.

The Issue of Murder. Murder poses special problems for criminological ethicists and ideologists. It is, of course, both extremely severe and irreversible; it is utterly destructive of the capital that has been built up in the victims. The principle of corrective compensation to the affected individuals therefore is not directly applicable. How, then, should we resolve the well-known dilemma of compensating for the incompensable, with a minimum sacrifice of individual rights?

There would seem to be two possible, though very different, answers. The impossibility of restitution might suggest that we scrap any sanctions purporting to have that purpose alone. Sanctions based on pure deterrence, meanwhile, should always be out of the question. The only remaining acceptable rationale for sanctions will then be compensation to third parties, arising from unfulfilled contractual obligations by the murder victim. This would primarily amount to support of surviving dependent family members, roommates and other associates. But murdering old and lonely never-marrieds might then become almost costless—which could seem discriminatory and unfair.

The other extreme alternative is, of course, to force killers to "pay" with their own lives. Such reciprocal "murder" by the government will produce a neat analogy with tit-for-tat exchange in the marketplace. But of course no true compensation will then occur, only a matching loss for the killer. Fair and balanced—or uselessly destructive, not to say vindictive? This is a truly vexing question, even within a socioethical system that purports to be very comprehensive and nearly exhaustive.

On the one hand, letting any murderer escape severe social sanction would be blatantly disrespectful of the life and person of the victim. On the other, capital punishment may represent excessive retribution, if the victim, had he been consulted, would not have wished such retribution to be exacted.

The answer? Let each individual, as a potential murder victim, decide for himself how this is to be resolved, but with an initial presumption of capital punishment. In other words, each individual could be given the right to waive the capital punishment otherwise imposed on his potential future killer—an idea that is occasionally advanced within libertarian circles. This could be done through a contractional arrangement with society (via the U.S. Department of Justice) to that effect, and the waiver could be made conditional on specific, mitigating circumstances defined by the potential murder victim. Such an optional capital punishment would sufficiently honor the individual's right to life, while at the same time allowing the individual the right to forgive the debt of life owed to him.

Motive. Conventionally a great deal of ethical and legal importance is given to the motive of the accused. Recall, for example, that current American law draws a distinction between involuntary manslaughter, punishable by jail, and murder, in most states punishable by death. This implies that the added circumstance of intention may put the culprit in the electric chair. Intention thus becomes an incremental circumstance that can tip the scale and bring death—which seems ethically obscene.

113

Our general compensation principle suggests that whether the murder was intentional or accidental ought to be legally immaterial. It seems absurd to execute people for their motives. This is especially so in a society that takes great pride in honoring the freedom of thought and speech. Nasty motives are hardly worse than nasty thoughts or nasty speech—which we generally permit, without criminal implications. Instead, motive should generally be irrelevant to the determination of responsibility. Otherwise, we will discourage the thought processes through which motives are developed. We will encourage people not to think but to act on sheer, thoughtless instinct, so as to qualify for greater leniency—a perverse result of a humanitarian-sounding principle and another example of moral hazard.

There is no reason to accept the current ethical folklore on this score. Motive ought not to be a legally aggravating circumstance within our constitutional system. Rather responsibility should depend simply on causation, even in murder cases.

Nor should there be legal penalties on attempts at crime that have no criminal results. Harmless attempts to commit what seem like potential crimes, even if evidenced by actual preparations, should be free from restrictions of any kind. Unrealized hypothetical acts (the potential number of which is truly infinite) are nonevents that cannot reasonably be considered illegal—except by those who are willing to let deterrence considerations wipe out basic human rights. To punish such plans or preparations is to create additional martyrs for the collective good, thereby violating the rights of a truly innocent minority.

Risk-Producing Behavior. But what about the danger of damage to others? Isn't danger, and risk, in itself a damage to the threatened party or, perhaps, to society as a whole? Shouldn't society punish a person or corporation that endangers other people's health or property—say, through unsanitary living or working conditions or through sloppy maintenance of a building or a private road? Or should risk production be criminal?

Admittedly, risk is sometimes an actual cost item—this has to be acknowledged. Risk—potential, uncertain damage, contrary to contractual arrangements or to general market expectations—can be considered a cost when we are looking ahead and try to evaluate our opportunities and our implicit capital. Most of us are risk averse and would be willing to pay some price to avoid risks of particular concern to us. Conversely, risk elimination can be an individual, or sometimes a public, good, whenever it restores some of our individual or national income prospects. It can be a matter of reinforcing a physical structure, reducing the amount of harmful chemicals in drinking water or altering traffic regulations. Or it could be a matter of educating children so as to reduce their potential criminal tendencies.

Each such risky situation will require its own solution, and society needs rules about who will bear the costs. Most risks occur entirely within what ought to be the private arena, and they should be privately dealt with. In the absence of contractual obligations, they will normally have to be treated as potential violations of property rights. Some are broad enough to have "public-bad" elements that might justify publicly financed protection—or public recourse to compensation from risk-producing private parties.

In very few cases will it be possible or advisable for society to eliminate the risk, or its source, completely; that would usually be too costly in terms of lost resources or forgone opportunities for other pursuits. And remember that the cost of risk is only a temporary, *ex ante* matter. It is the final outcome that ultimately matters; many risks do not materialize, and some losses will be offset by better-than-expected outcomes in other situations.

What role, then, should risk considerations play in the definition of crime or in legal sanctions? A few basic principles can be derived from our ideological premises. Equal weight must be given to the two sides, whether one or both is a public agency, and whether individual or collective interests are at stake; threatening the public can, qualitatively, be no worse than threatening individuals. Risky thoughts should of course be freely allowed; no thought can be so evil that it really invades anybody's property, at least not if society has a well-functioning mechanism for correcting actual property infringements. Outright prohibitions of risky behavior will hardly ever be justified, except as voluntarily agreed within private organizations.

One especially problematic situation is the case in which the value of potential damage exceeds the financial capability of the potential lawbreaker or property transgressor. Voluntary exchange principles, or ordinary legal restitution rules, then could be inadequate. One possible solution: Those exposed to such dangers might then be allowed to demand some kind of "safety deposit" or "liability insurance" from the latter—for instance, from a neighbor playing with heavy explosives in the backyard. Possibly there is a localized public-good function here, justifying some form of governmental damage insurance, covering both criminal and civil matters.

Similarly, actions that impose immediate, risk-related costs on society at large might call for precautionary measures of some kind. There is a case for asking nuclear power facilities, for instance, to insure themselves against potentially devastating accidents. Without some fall-back arrangements of these kinds, the public might be unfairly exposed to risk-prone private behavior for which full compensations could not conceivably be made.

Victimless Crimes. The unfairness of punishing harmless acts should be obvious. It makes the law a net destroyer of rights and opportunities, rather than a situational equalizer and restorer, between culprit and victim. It is a practice more generally associated with totalitarian regimes, especially on the right but sometimes on the left.

In an equal-opportunity society, there can be no victimless crimes, because if there were, the victimless "criminal" would then be put at a special disadvantage. If no individual victims can be found, there also cannot be any victimization of society as a whole; there is no such societal entity, separate from the individuals who constitute it. So the notion of "crime against society" is a murky, deceptive one.

This reasoning has major implications for how the **libegalitarian** society would respond to various currently punishable acts. For example, it would stop the practice of arresting and locking up drunken drivers merely because of their drunken driving. And it would not declare drug manufacture or drug dealing in themselves illegal.

In short, neither of these acts does any direct, actual harm. Additional circumstances must be present before any harm can be demonstrated. And the circumstances may depend on interconnected acts by others—for example, careless driving by another person, or actual drug consumption by a person tempted by the drug dealer's sales offer. The possibility that such behavior as drunken driving or drug sales might in due course lead to actual damage is ethically not enough.

Needless to say, payment of damages is wholly appropriate if drunken—or sober—drivers single-handedly cause accidents; and if voluntary payment does not come forth, a legal judgment that forces payment is entirely appropriate. The same applies if a drug seller violates his contractual obligation to deliver goods of a certain quality, with the result of health damage or other reasons for customer disappointment. In the former situation, drunkenness should be viewed as no more than an incidental circumstance without any criminal implications. And also in the case of the drug sale, no societal sanction is justified, provided the deal was fairly agreed to and honorably executed. Neither drunken driving nor drug use should become a matter of legal concern until it causes damage to other parties.

But how, then, will the public be able to protect itself against the potentially destructive consequences of irresponsible behavior of these kinds? The answer should depend on whatever contractual or constitutional obligations exist between the individual and those who claim to suffer from his behavior. And, to be sure, these obligations might have to be clarified in a fundamentally reformed society.

For the safety-on-the-road problem, the preferable solution will be found in the private market, which is always the best arbiter of clashing private claims. If allowed to function freely, the market would set the "price" of drunken driving at the right level. This will be the level where the two sides' interests balance and both enjoy an improvement in their overall driving opportunities.

How, exactly? If roads are privately owned and managed—as they ought to be—different roads will have different safety features and different driving rules, which the road users contractually have to accept. Road-owning companies may then establish differentiated access fees and access rules for each road facility in accordance with the demands of the drivers, just as the typical firm adjusts its product qualities and prices to the requirements of its customers. Some driver-customers may prefer that everybody take a sobriety test, while others may not; some might require "safety deposits" against potential damage claims; and others might insist on insurance policies—while some will prefer to operate virtually without rules.

One way or the other, drunken drivers will then have to pay for their risky and, statistically speaking, damaging behavior over the long haul—either through actual damage assessments or through extra insurance premiums or access charges. It is quite possible that most highways would be a bit riskier under these private-market arrangements. But if this were the case, it would merely reflect a fairer division of benefits, costs and risks among the parties involved. It would also mean that there is today a suboptimal level of risk on the road—a conclusion that most observers, unfortunately, would not have the courage to draw.

The current political approach to the "drug problem" painfully illustrates the same repressive, illibertarian mentality, with gross disrespect for individual rights and little desire for equitable conflict resolutions. The scared, badly informed public tries to find "crimes" where—by normal, democratic or individualistic standards—none exist. Drug trade between consenting adults is construed as a serious assault on the public at large, and respect for privacy counts for little. Even many avowed free-market conservatives—including the Bush administration's "drug czar"—are pushing for severe penalties for innocent market transactions in the name of better public health, easier criminal prosecutions and reduced claims for public assistance in drug-afflicted communities. Frankly, the political establishment seems to be embarked on a big retreat into prohibitionism and totalitarianism.

We should hasten to acknowledge that, given current health-care, education and income-support programs, the drug problem does have definite "public-bad" aspects. Drug dependency obviously imposes costs on taxpayers when it leads to additional claims for Medicare services, unemployment benefits or AFDC money. The costs can also include losses of income tax receipts and public expenses for imprisonment of drug offenders.

However, most of these costs are publicly self-inflicted: They are the result of government involvement in private affairs, based on overcollectivization, a blurring of the private-public border and a lack of respect for private choice. The sad fact is that by assuming such vast social-welfare functions, government has felt forced to expand its control over many private activities that are causally linked to social-welfare claims.

In the meantime, as every big-city resident now knows, attempts to stop importation and sales of drugs have produced an enormous black-market drug industry with its own crime culture. Thus the official criminalization of drugs has had a big, perverse multiplier effect on the totality of drug-related crimes.

It is hard to think of any major drug-related "public bads" that would remain if the government confined itself to true public-good functions. That is, almost all of the negative public budgetary effects of the "drug problem" would disappear if government stopped underwriting the health of grown-ups (as through Medicaid and special drug rehabilitation centers) and if it did not provide them with income assistance (as through Federal food stamps and many local welfare programs); whether easier drug availability would lead to fewer or more true property crimes is an open question. Altogether, the "drug war" is shaping up as one of the all-time biggest U.S. policy disasters, judged by its ineffectiveness, public monetary costs and unnecessary loss of individual rights.

In the long run, drugs should clearly be legal, like everything else the costs of which can be equitably allocated. Decriminalization is the only lasting solution to the "drug problem," along with private dissemination of relevant information and publicly supported education of the young. The costs of drugs to health and happiness among the adult population should be individually borne, unless they are contractually transferred, at negotiated prices, to insurance companies or other collective bodies. These costs would produce the appropriate disincentives toward drug use. And legalization would free government from the costly, impossible and inhumane drug-abolition job that it now taken on. This is also the solution recommended by most libertarians.[39]

JOBS AND UNEMPLOYMENT BENEFITS

To most of us, employment is the largest and most beneficial type of exchange transaction in our grown-up lives. Our welfare depends overwhelmingly on our success in finding and retaining pleasant, well-paid employment or in shifting into better and better jobs. Employment and job opportunities are clearly central socioeconomic issues, and they deserve a great deal of ideological attention.

Conflicting Views. Contemporary opinion on how jobs and employment can best be provided is ambivalent. On the one hand, most Americans regard career choice, job selection and the terms of employment as essentially private matters, to be resolved through personal efforts to exploit available labor market opportunities.

Free-market economists will add that the private labor market is generally the superior mechanism for allocating jobs to workers and workers to jobs. Wages, salaries, fringe benefits and other job features seem to adjust over time so as to reflect the productivity and job preferences of workers. They thereby induce employers and employees to seek out the right contract partners among each other. In this view, remunerative jobs are essentially individual goods to the workers who occupy and perform them; and productive workers are private (if not, in the corporate context, individual) goods to their employers.

On the other hand, social-liberal economists and government planners like to claim that the overall availability of adequate job opportunities is a collective national responsibility. In this view, every man and woman deserves the right to gainful employment under humane work conditions and with adequate pay.

If such jobs cannot be immediately provided by the private labor market, the government accordingly ought to step in, with public jobs programs, financial assistance or appropriate regulatory measures. At a minimum, there seems—in this view—to be a need for regulations such that workers will be protected against powerful, ruthless or insensitive corporate managers. Beyond that, government may have to establish incentives for private business to hire more workers or to force them to offer better pay or larger fringe benefits.

These two sets of attitudes are of course mutually incompatible. As a consequence, policymakers have vacillated between the two—between labor-market laissez-faire and labor-market control. In particular, there has been a long-standing controversy about what to do about unemployment. When this, in the 1980s, stopped being a general nationwide phenomenon, the controversy cooled off a bit. But the debate refocused on the remaining "hard core" of unemployed minority and female workers and on the relative labor market access for different ethnic groups. Without a clear ideological yardstick, it is natural that the steps taken or proposed should be inconsistent and irrational.

Results of Government Policies. Most government interventions in the labor market in the United States and elsewhere are ostensibly proworker.

They tend to favor particular worker groups, or low-skills workers, over employers and business owners. Occasionally, they purport to favor nearly all workers; but given the limitations of the total wage or income pie, such an ambitious policy goal will usually be unattainable.

One official purpose of U.S. labor market interference is to prevent ethnic or sexual job discrimination. Another is to raise the wages paid to the least-skilled, least-productive workers, especially through "minimum wage" legislation. Yet another is to protect workers against unhealthy or hazardous working conditions. In addition, the federal government has a Constitutional mandate to try to establish "full employment," for the hoped-for benefit of the entire labor force and the national economy.

In most of these cases, the government is trying to promote certain freedoms or opportunities of certain workers, individually or collectively. The apparent beneficiaries include those who are only marginally employable, except through the assistance of legislation. They include some low-skilled workers who might be able to retain their minimum-wage jobs despite their failure to consistently produce commensurate revenues for their employers. They also include the minority worker who is hired primarily so that the employer can meet an antidiscrimination hiring quota.

Among other, less conspicuous beneficiaries of U.S. labor laws are those who are not aggressive enough to evaluate their own prospective working conditions in available jobs. They benefit from the fact that the government performs this task for them, for instance, in regard to safety and sanitation. It might be retorted that few corporations, in any case, would allow job applicants to inspect premises, safety records or other pertinent sources of data on actual job conditions. Yet the unavailing corporate attitude may very well be the result of preemptive legislation or inadequate initiative on the part of organized workers. An unregulated labor market would obviously allow workers and unions to negotiate for whatever job and plant inspections they wish; and if they persisted, they would prevail.

For most workers today, the government is acting as an insurer that claims to offer certain approximate guarantees regarding working conditions in private factories and offices; and the insurance policy seems to be gratis. Having that insurance policy saves workers the trouble of inquiring into these matters themselves. Whether there are offsetting side effects in the form of reduced or distorted job prospects might not immediately occur to them.

Redistributive Effects. The beneficiaries of labor legislation almost certainly include workers whose personal preferences with respect to working conditions or compensation resemble the priorities of the legislators.

The government then becomes a welcome, zero-cost stand-in for them in the market. This will be especially well-illustrated if current proposals for mandatory employer-financed health insurance are enacted: Some workers will be pleased to get pretty much the kind of health insurance they would want anyhow, especially if federal tax support reduces the net cost to them (in the form of reduced wages). These workers could probably not have done quite so well in free labor and health-insurance markets.

But such legislative measures leave many other worker groups or many other worker freedoms out of consideration. They essentially rearrange job opportunities among different worker groups, with disadvantageous consequences for those who don't achieve specific, desired protection. More or better jobs for some will mean fewer or worse jobs for others, as employers try to economize on their resources or to recoup some of the costs that government regulation imposes. Some workers will be unemployed or not as well-employed as otherwise possible.

For example, if employers are forced to hire more minority workers, they will normally hire fewer nonminority workers; this has become painfully obvious through corroborated cases of "reverse discrimination." If an employer is pressured to install a new health-care facility, he will typically have to cut back on other fringe benefits; and the healthy workers who barely need that new facility will suffer.

These examples illustrate that government interventions in job markets, as in other markets, are almost always redistributive. They create extra opportunities for some, at the expense of others. The results are not compatible with a principle of generalized worker or labor-market freedom. Conceivably, some of those market interferences might have other justifications, based on equal-opportunity requirements—they could, perhaps, offer remedial on-the-job training. But it is very unlikely that unequal basic schooling can be efficiently compensated for through compulsory preferential treatment by particular employers. And so it will be better to look for other policy solutions to the educational problem.

Moreover, most of these market interventions unjustifiably tilt the balance of economic power between workers and their employers. The government, in effect, tries to pressure employers to hire workers with submarginal qualifications or on better terms than the workers could have achieved themselves. Very often this is a main purpose of populist and egalitarian labor legislation (such as minimum-wage and health-insurance provisions): Such legislation often, openly or secretly, hopes to lessen the freedoms and opportunities of corporate management or owners, who are perceived to be unduly powerful, greedy or rich.

Yet the employer-corporation is usually not completely defenseless but can take steps to mitigate his inconvenience or earnings losses. Sometimes he will be able to compensate for the cost of legally required fringe benefits by reducing wage rates, or he will be able to cut back on hiring so as to afford to pay the minimum wage. In the latter case, part of the cost of the minimum-wage provision will be borne by those who are squeezed out of the labor market altogether, a high cost indeed for these job seekers. That this actually occurs on a significant scale has been amply demonstrated in econometric labor-market studies.[40]

But the employer-manager usually cannot unload the entire costs of labor-law compliance on other workers. He will instead try to pass on some of the costs to the buyers of his products by charging higher prices; or he might try to shift the added costs to his suppliers by lowering the prices he is willing to pay for parts or raw materials. Failing this, the corporation's owners, the stockholders, will have to absorb the labor-regulatory costs.

In any of these cases, the government will have transferred income from consumers, suppliers or stockholders to the favored workers, in contravention of free bargaining and contract making. There is thus a violation of the disfavored groups' right to unrestricted labor market access— another example of governmental theft.

Unemployment Compensation. Public programs for unemployment assistance, such as those in the United States, ostensibly compensate job seekers for temporary declines in the market's demand for particular worker categories. The programs could perhaps be considered as corrections of labor market failures or inefficiencies for which individual workers have no responsibility. They have some appeals for egalitarians, who believe every able-bodied adult should have a chance to earn a steady income. They may also have some appeal to those who view the program as a national insurance policy and generally support the insurance principle. And they are particularly appealing to those who regard them as "free."

Superficially, most of the needed money is contributed by corporate employers, through payroll taxes. But it is a forgone conclusion that the ultimate costs of these taxes are shifted almost entirely to the employed workers through reduced wages. For workers who stay employed, the wage reductions diminish the returns on the educational and training capital that they have invested in themselves or which employers have invested in their employees. The workers' personal capital is then effectively diminished—unless and until they are laid off and begin to recoup their indirect contributions to the program.

Conversely, workers who are frequently laid off make offsetting gains. And some of them manage to become unemployed sufficiently often to end up with a net gain over time, because of job-market bad luck—or because of their ability to contrive frequent quasivoluntary layoffs. A rational career planner will naturally consider the pros and cons of various such strategies.

One might try to defend the wage losses of the steady workers as indirect payments for wage insurance, existing for the workers' own benefit. After all, almost anybody might want to collect benefits at some point, and most workers might prefer to be financially prepared for this eventuality. Many of them undoubtedly would have been willing to pay similar insurance premiums on their own if the public unemployment assistance program had not existed.

But other workers would surely not, because they make more optimistic assessments of their job prospects or because they have greater financial or psychological tolerance for the risk of temporary income shortfalls. Moreover, the insurance premiums that would exist in a private market would probably be set at different levels from those that are now, invisibly, embedded in the structure of worker compensation. The premiums would in all likelihood be differentiated so as to reflect the probabilities of different worker categories being laid off and failing to get comparable new jobs; this is what both insurance efficiency and insurance equity require. So many workers would have been better off with private job insurance.

Market-adjusted premiums for private employment insurance would also, like other private insurance premiums, help induce premium-reducing behavior within the labor force. Workers would have an extra incentive for more, and more work-related, schooling, and they should become more inclined to undertake serious job searches—for they could then soon qualify for reduced premiums. These would be some of the market responses that could reduce the moral hazard—and well-known reality— of workers taking advantage of the current, compulsory insurance system.

In short, the current payroll taxes have broad counterefficient, inequitable consequences. Prolonged or repeated unemployment benefits are, by and large, unearned gifts, unfairly extracted from the general labor force and the public at large. Private insurance would be the most cost-effective and fair method for alleviating the effects of temporary, employment-related declines in incomes.

Jobs Programs. Public jobs programs are, in effect, government makework arrangements justified by a public desire to provide employment. They also do not have much to recommend them. They are undeserved subsidies to the otherwise jobless, paid for through confiscatory tax levies.

Basically, public jobs, unrelated to the production of true, national collective goods, are not worth their costs in human effort and in the required absorption of cooperating resources. Moreover, such public jobs reduce incentives for the workers to search for really worthwhile jobs in the private sector—another sign of impaired job market efficiency.

If we don't need that public project (e.g., a highway or a Peace Corps venture), or if it is not worth its true execution costs, let's not undertake it. Besides, both the need and the costs usually can be better ascertained in the private market, through competition between alternative products and between alternative production or delivery technologies.

It is a fallacy to think that the unemployed workers recruited to do the make-work jobs are a zero-cost source of labor for the government. The workers could almost always have found jobs elsewhere if they had tried hard enough. The few who might not, or not very soon, will suffer losses of leisure and of opportunities for informal, worklike activities in their homes. These are costs too, although they are usually forgotten in the public policy debate, and they will further add to the overall costs of a public jobs program.

Granted, government policies in other areas might distort the labor market so as to make it difficult for some workers to find suitable jobs. The government might then seem justified in repairing some of the harm it has already done. For instance, a sudden tightening of credit by the Federal Reserve might at one point push up interest rates to such levels that construction firms (which tend to be especially sensitive to credit costs) will have to curtail their activities and lay off many workers. Does not the government then owe the laid-off workers other jobs? Possibly, as a limited, transitional arrangement. But the best solution would be to attack the underlying causes, not just its symptoms—ideally, by moving toward a society built on the **libegalitarian** model.

Is the Market Failing? Admittedly, the argument against government involvement in the provision of jobs presupposes a well-functioning labor market, in which everybody could find a job for himself. Such a market does not currently seem to exist.

Consider the official unemployment statistics. The unemployment rate was officially estimated at nearly 10 percent of the potentially active labor force during much of the 1970s. It began to drop in the 1980s, reaching what seemed like a rock-bottom rate of about 5 percent late in the decade (although the rates for nonwhites, especially black women, has remained much higher). Yet the statisticians admit that the numbers can be very misleading. In particular, the statistics are sharply affected by the number of willing workers who stop searching for jobs, and by the extent to which women move in and out of the labor force. So the picture is actually rather murky.

A superficial analysis suggests that there is an apparent labor market failure, though less so today than in the pre-Reagan era. That "failure" seems to undermine the case for a free, unsubsidized and uncontrolled labor market. Perhaps work is, after all, too important to be left to the vagaries of the private market.

But much of that "failure" is a misrepresentation of facts. There is a mistaken public perception that the availability of jobs at each particular moment is decided for us by that big, unresponsive labor market—primarily by large corporations with rigid, self-serving employment policies. In reality, jobs are a function of both employer-supply and employee-demand efforts. They are a matter of mutual, interactive accommodation, with repeated efforts to search out suitable contract parties and to define mutually acceptable contract terms.

Undoubtedly many individual firms may in the short run be rigid and unresponsive when it comes to defining their available jobs and the pay they will offer. A sudden change in hiring and production volume can be especially costly. But they do not generally collude in setting such employment conditions that there will be an overall shortage of vacancies. To do so would not be in their own self-interest. And the passage of time permits easier revisions in hiring and production plans.

At the other end of the bargaining table, and with countervailing bargaining power, are, of course, the labor unions. When they succeed in pushing up wage rates, something else will have to give. Some potential jobs may then have to be eliminated, at least in the short run.

The unions' power over wages and other employment matters has long been enhanced by a number a labor-supportive laws concerning union membership, compulsory union dues, bargaining practices and picketing rights. For example, workers have long been coerced, by the law, into paying union dues as a condition of employment. This obligation was recently restricted to dues used for collective bargaining, contract administration and grievance procedures. It thus exempts the portions of dues going to political or other job-unrelated purposes—a welcome weakening of a market interference that ought to be completely abolished.

Overall, unions do not any more play such a commanding role in the overall job market, nor do they receive the same favoritism in Congress as in previous eras. The growth of service industries and the relative decline of manufacturing—historically a union stronghold—has reduced their power and their membership. Today unions represent only some 15 percent of the American labor force, compared with nearly twice that level a couple of decades ago. As a consequence, the damage done by the unions, and by government support for them, has undoubtedly declined in recent years.

In a better future, unions would become purely private instruments, without public-policy support, for meeting collective worker needs at plants, at company headquarters or in industry-wide negotiations. This would be their ideal role, in which they would be subject to the full pressure of free market forces. It would allow the private bargaining process to fairly balance their members' interests against those of managers, stockholders and corporate customers.

Contrary to popular perception, the job market is actually quite flexible. One should remember that work at home is work too. It is self-employment. And work at home includes many activities, from painting one's house to raising children to learning new skills through private study, that mistakenly are left out of the gainful-employment picture. Counting these informal, extramarket job opportunities, the flexibility of the national job supply is even clearer.

But aren't many such self-made jobs usually wasteful, as well as inadequately remunerative? Not to the person who has carefully weighed the available opportunities and chosen such a job, especially not when his choice is unobstructed by government market interference.

One major reason why many skilled persons have job difficulties is their lack of multiple talents and an unwillingness to consider alternative professional paths. These handicaps have been aggravated by a popular view, reinforced by liberal policymakers, that jobs should be offered to us by society once we have picked our line of work. This attitude is both personally and socially costly. The individual ought to assume greater responsibility for his own job preparedness, once society has given him a normal educational foundation. His job search will then be a normal, fully acceptable exercise in self-help.

Over the longer run, employment prospects should be a matter of individual human-investment planning, for which we should take individual responsibility. If we fail to develop sufficient skills, we will be stuck in inferior jobs that reflect our poor professional capital endowments. And if we fail to search for jobs or to adjust ourselves to the locational, occupational or salary requirements of the job market, we may also end up with unsatisfactory jobs. But nobody else, including the government, could really do any better in planning our careers and fulfilling our job objectives without undue cost burdens on others.

Proper Government Role. The involvement of a **libegalitarian** government in labor matters would be much more limited than it is in America today. The labor market would be freed from all direct government interventions. This would mean no publicly financed unemployment assistance, no minimum-wage legislation, no regulations that upset the labor-management balance in bargaining, and no industrial or macroeconomic policies that distort the structure of labor demand.

The government definitely should not attempt to guarantee every citizen a job. Guaranteed employment would create a costly distortion of the labor market and impose a burden on the taxpayers who would have to finance all wages that were not justified by the workers' productivity. There is no clear ethical or economic basis for making the public compensate us for our inability, or unwillingness, to find work. Jobs are opportunities for service exchanges, best identified by labor-dependent producers and job-seeking individuals and not by public bureaucracies. The labor market, if allowed to function freely, will always provide some gainful job opportunity for every sane, healthy person, notwithstanding the conventional notion that large-scale involuntary unemployment can still exist. If we speak of "worker rights," these rights should consist of the freedom to seek whatever job one wants and can get without government obstruction.

But society should assume one large job-related responsibility: that of providing every young person with an equal basic educational capital endowment, designed to impart rudimentary skills and to facilitate professional training later on. Each person will then be as equally prepared for work as his natural personal qualities permit. After that, government should keep a hands-off attitude, for labor market freedom offers the most efficient and most ethical job conditions possible.

There will, in this ideal society, be a variety of public sector jobs, and these should be filled in a manner that will minimize the costs of getting the public-good production job done. The government should clearly not restrict access to these jobs for particular citizen groups, racial or sexual, yet there should also be no preference for any such group. Thus even foreign-born people ought to qualify for the national presidency.

Nor should the government force the private sector to adhere to racial or sexual quotas or to undertake "affirmative action" that gives preferential treatment to specific applicant categories. Rules such as these impose unfair disadvantages on other job seekers, as the notion of "reverse discrimination" has finally made clear to the general public. They are also not cost-effective and thus not conducive to maximizing individual opportunities.

SELECTIVE CIVIL RIGHTS

The term "civil rights" has a great deal of immediate ethical appeal. It suggests individual freedoms or opportunities that stem from citizenship and are acknowledged, perhaps grudgingly, by an otherwise powerful state. The rights referred to are usually understood to be guaranteed in law and not quickly revocable by temporary legislative majorities or administrations. Establishing and enforcing such long-lasting rights is, of course, a major objective of both democratic and laissez-faire ideologies.

But as actually used, the term is awfully vague, and its diffuseness invites multiple interpretations that suit particular, limited group interests. The term does not have a definite, accepted definition that corresponds to its literal, broad meaning. Nor is it generally linked to any clear socioethical principles. Instead a right often seems to become "civil" just because its spokesmen want to give it this ennobling label while cloaking their special interest in the idealistic guise of fundamental justice. Besides, we need to realize that whatever rights we have will ultimately have to be "civil," i.e., formally and explicitly associated with citizenship; otherwise they might not be sustainable.

What Rights? Civil rights used to be confined to political rights, especially the rights to voting, voter registration, free speech and general participation in the political process. In the 1960s and 1970s, the term was extended to include access to housing, public accommodations and employment. This suggested that perhaps there is no meaningful distinction between "political" and "economic" rights, at least not in terms of the underlying concerns for a basic minimum level of human well-being. After all, the exercise of political rights typically aims at economic betterment, and the attribute "political" should denote method (government) rather than purpose (economic benefit).

Yet it is remarkable that the public list of economic civil rights has been so short and so selective. Shelter and jobs—and to a lesser extent, restaurant meals, hotel rooms and public bathrooms—matter a awful lot to most of us. But there are so many other economic rights that most Americans also cherish: free consumption choice, overall; unrestricted opportunities to save, invest, and borrow; the right to run a business of our choice and so on. Why not include these too on the list of civil rights that are to be constitutionally protected? Why draw an artificial line between civil and other rights in the first place?

There seem to be two interrelated answers to these questions. Some desired rights and opportunities are considered more basic than others, because they are so valuable to so many, or because their existence is a prerequisite for so many other, derivative rights. If some people couldn't vote, they might not have any effective political spokesmen who could air their social grievances. If some people could not buy houses in their preferred neighborhoods, they might not be able to take advantage of their

128

preferred educational or cultural facilities, to the detriment of their children as well as themselves.

In addition, some claims to rights have greater social appeal or perceived merit than others. Labeling them "civil" can then simply be a way of exploiting broad public preferences or ethical biases, through a connotation of obvious moral rightness. The term then often acquires redistributionist, antielitist connotations. The right of the rich to champagne does not qualify as civil by most people's standards, but the poor's right to bread might; and proclaiming the latter right to be "civil" may easily suggest that everybody has a permanent right to a minimum standard of living.

None of these justifications for particular commodity-specific or group-specific rights is ethically acceptable. They make distinctions that do not fit into any comprehensive framework of general socioeconomic rights, available to all. Contemporary civil rights are thus much too selective; they have very objectionable discriminatory aspects. By contrast, the **libegalitarian** society would have no predetermined list of authorized civil rights at the exclusion of others. It would provide a general rights structure, based on broader ethical principles, and applied neutrally across the population.

U.S. Civil Rights Laws. In all fairness, some U.S. civil rights legislation has helped restore some valuable rights and lessened some unacceptable discrimination, not only by current U.S. Constitutional standards but by **libegalitarian** criteria as well. In particular, removing racial and sexual discrimination in government employment allowed formerly disenfranchised groups to expand their job opportunities—opportunities that they deserved. Of course, the previously favored workers, consisting mostly of white males, lost the advantage of racial preference. But this privilege was ethically unearned, and its removal has generally pushed them closer to the point of socioeconomic equity.

The reforms also helped expand the labor pool available to the public sector. Thereby the taxpayer has probably gained too, through better use of the tax dollars spent on publicly employed labor. Yet one should keep in mind that many government jobs ought not to exist in the first place. Eliminating job discrimination in government activities that encroach on private freedoms or exceed public-good requirements is of ambiguous merit. Sustaining such activities can produce an artificially inflated demand for particular labor services, which may be linked to particular ethnic or skills groups—a questionable victory for the overall cause of civil rights.

One clear-cut case of a constructive civil rights reform was the decision to allow women to enter the armed forces. Military-minded women thereby gained opportunities that a private armed-services labor market also would have offered them. Another, less clear-cut case was that of eliminating racially biased restrictions on voter registrations.

Why less clear-cut? Because our entire system of voting, political representation and democratic government is ethically and ideologically so defective. It is therefore unclear whether the added voting rights will have beneficial or detrimental consequences; what really matters is their use, not their sheer existence.

It was certainly unfair not to permit poor, uneducated blacks to register to vote some decades ago; apart from the removal of an ugly symbol of official racism, it helped them air true and deep grievances. But it is also unfair to subject all of us to the rights abuses permitted by our political system, in which voters, legislators and officeholders can allow special-interest groups to take discriminatory, rights-destructive actions against any of us.

To participate in the political process is to participate, in ever so small ways, in the injustices perpetrated by the officeholders we have voted for. Voter rights have become rights not only to speak up against official injustice or innate economic disadvantage, but also to deprive others of rights and opportunities that they ought to keep. Expansions of voting rights have thus cut many difference ways, some constructive and others destructive.

It is precisely because of the abuses of democratic majority powers that we need to firm up our constitutional protection of individual rights. If we accomplish this, the functions of balloting will, by necessity, have to be reduced and narrowed considerably.

In a functioning **libegalitarian** system, voter rights would mean much less than they do today. Rights would not generally depend on ballot results, but be firmly embedded in permanent constitutional law. At most, voter rights would involve regular opportunities to express personal preferences regarding the kinds or amount of public goods that are to be produced. They would not offer possibilities to block private exchange transactions or to forcibly reallocate legitimate personal wealth. Political rights could not be employed for purely redistributive purposes.

Minorities and Women. In the 1970s and 1980s, much of the focus of U.S. civil rights activism was actually on privilege, in the false name of greater equality. This view would have been called callous and bigoted fifteen years ago, but the well-informed public finally started to see through the fog of the civil-rights rhetoric. In particular, the debate over minority quotas in private employment slowly brought home the unfairness of all private-market quota systems. It gave birth to the idea of reverse discrimination, thereby highlighting some of the redistributive consequences of civil-rights law.

Minority quotas are now seen, perhaps by a majority of Americans, as unfair competitive barriers to nonminority workers, and the same holds for quotas for women. "Affirmative action" and hiring "goals" have come to suggest a milder, more subtle form of quotas, yet their distortive effects on labor market conditions and worker rights are also fairly well recognized. The arrangements are implicit job subsidies, usually paid for by the nonminority male workers who are thereby squeezed out of their desired, deserved jobs. The same holds for "set-asides" of contracts to minority-owned businesses, as sometimes required by law; set-asides act like racial quotas that span jobs, entrepreneurship and corporate capital all at once.

Sure, many minority workers have suffered educational disadvantages in the past, and favored access to jobs now can give them some compensatory on-the-job training or some extra cash in lieu of the missing human capital. But the actual quotas and hiring goals established in accordance with federal law have never been so defined as to single out individuals with such handicaps; and this would not have been practical. Rather, there has been an across-the-board suggestion that racial groups, as such, suffer from inherent, generally shared incapacities—both an untrue and an ethically repugnant supposition.[41] Understandably, many Americans now view racial quotas as perversely racist.

It is also not surprising that the Supreme Court should have great difficulty in reconciling existing civil-rights laws with broader American legal traditions, including the Constitution's equal-protection clause. In recent Court decisions, minority preferences have been accepted as remedies for "old patterns of segregation" by individual employers, demonstrated primarily through a statistical underrepresentation of minorities in the work force. The key statute, Title VII of the 1964 Civil Rights Act, has survived, even though its call for reverse discrimination is constitutionally suspect. For now it seems that prominority discrimination is mandated by federal law; but the Rehnquist Supreme Court has raised hopes that some of the worst reverse civil-rights offenses will be curbed.[42]

Women's liberationists have insisted for some time that the pay scales of women be adjusted so that they will conform to those of men. Women's pay ought accordingly to be based on "comparable worth," i.e., the salary levels for jobs, held by men, with similar educational requirements and working conditions. Perhaps a laundry worker—so far, usually a woman—should be paid as much as a truck driver, and an experienced secretary as much as an electrician, if their skill requirements and job conditions indeed are, somehow, "comparable."

It has been shown that, very often, pay scales differ despite such apparent equivalence. The average pay gap between "comparable" jobs has been estimated at about 20 percent, even though all such comparisons are known to be fraught with statistical difficulties. Does not the pervasive pattern of pay differentials suggest a market deficiency that deserves to be governmentally corrected? Would not the "comparable worth" principle be especially applicable in public-sector employment?

Not really. The ideal standard of comparability is not a scientific proportionality formula but the edict of the competitive market. If one finds a clear difference between male and female pay scales for jobs with seemingly similar requirements, the observed pay difference should be taken as *de facto* evidence that the job categories, in actuality, are not comparable, everything considered. There must thus be some hidden factor that favors one sex over the other—perhaps innate physical suitability, customer acceptance or the likelihood of long-run availability for employment.

Equal pay, enforced by law, would then create subsidies for the lower-valued sex, whichever sex that happens to be (and it would reduce the number of jobs that the employers can afford to offer). This cannot be a desirable consequence. Market preferences ought to be honored. And if the market exhibits certain sexual preferences, translated into pay differentials, these preferences should be accepted even in the public sector.[43] The impersonal, nonsexist market might, in fact, produce a special "mommy track" with different productivity expectations and different compensation rules—yet allow the ambitious individual worker the chance to transfer to other tracks.

Doesn't this mean that the government, in its hiring practices, would be endorsing publicly illegitimate prejudices? No, not so long as the public sector does not suppress its demand for female workers by making gender a separate, noneconomic hiring criterion. The government should merely be following the least-cost principle in satisfying its labor needs, and costs are best determined by the private market. Not following this principle would be unfair to the taxpayers. Judging resource costs, including labor's "worth," is not a government function, and imposing separate public-sector pay standards would create inefficiencies in the private-public allocation of resources.[44]

Handicapped and Homosexuals. The successes of the black and female civil rights movements have alerted other groups to the possibilities of gaining similar legislative support for their interests. In effect, those successes have encouraged people to form alliances with others who seem to share certain disadvantages, or to invent new, previously unheard-of special-interest groups with claims for public-policy assistance.

The trick seems to be not just to point to some socioeconomic failing, but to link it to a shared physical or social characteristic that might elicit public sympathy or compassion. A combined appeal to compassion and egalitarianism can then produce broad support for civil-rights reform. The group might then achieve a "certified victim status"—a big public asset.[45]

The physically and mentally handicapped are a special case—one whose disadvantages are honestly and painfully obvious. There is clearly a strong public desire to improve their situation. They, and their professional spokesmen, can easily pull at the public heartstrings and assert a special need for compensatory favors from the government or the private sector, such as protected access to jobs and special transportation facilities. They have indeed been relatively successful in these efforts. Can we really question that the handicapped deserve this kind of treatment?

Taking a position "against" the handicapped on any public issue is not a popular thing to do. But our personal sympathies and emotions should not be allowed to cloud our ideological judgment. And not all unfortunate circumstances could possibly warrant governmental consideration. There is also a charity "market," in which anybody can directly take his case to the public without the assistance of government.

Some handicaps are obviously inborn and have thus not been caused by society. There is then no *prima facie* societal responsibility for correcting or compensating for them; government cannot credibly pretend that nature is a manageable department under its jurisdiction. On this basis, natural inborn handicaps will have to be referred to the private sector for its voluntary, compassionate consideration.[46]

Other handicaps—preventable permanent illness, in particular—are as obviously due to poor care during childhood. In these cases, society can be said to be guilty of initial neglect—of failing to give the victims adequate societal capital endowments during their formative years. Some belated compensation may then very well be in order. Longer term, neglect should of course be prevented in the first place so that there will be no question of remedial compensation. Since this outcome might be practically impossible to attain, an extra remedy may be necessary: Each person could be offered, at birth, a public insurance policy that covers the costs of permanent physical or mental impairment caused by substandard child care. Yet if his parents or guardians, or child-care centers, are demonstrably at fault, the insurance fund should be able to seek reimbursement for its payout from these parties.

Other handicaps are surely self-inflicted in the sense that responsible individual actions could have prevented them or provided adequate private remedies. This describes a grown-up who has lost a leg swimming in shark-infested waters or become afflicted with syphilis-related blindness.

It also describes physical impairment incurred through a car accident that could have been avoided or for which insurance was available.

Overall, handicaps need to be differentiated with regard to their nature and cause. They cannot be turned into an automatic source of governmental favors. Responsibility must first be ascertained—a rule that should permeate all governmental claims on private resources.

Since the mid-1980s, the list of serious health-related handicaps has also included AIDS and infection with the AIDS virus. These conditions have become major employment handicaps in that they can affect patients' productivity, their work environment and the costs of health and disability insurance. Amidst all the public concern and compassion, spokesmen for AIDS victims, and for the homosexual community, have pushed for laws protecting against "discrimination" against AIDS (and AIDS-virus) victims. Some states and localities have granted such legal favors—e.g., in the form of protection against AIDS-based job discrimination and of the right to refuse on-the-job blood testing.

Adults cannot normally claim that the conditions were forced upon them by society, without any cooperation from themselves. Among grown-ups, the handicaps, as far as we know, have nothing to do with substandard upbringing or early education. So they should deserve no special public attention in a society in which both health care and employment are private responsibilities.

Except in cases connected with medical malpractice or infection at birth from a drug-abusing mother, the economic responsibility for AIDS should generally lie with the victims, rather than government or community. It is hardly reasonable for representatives for AIDS victims to demand special governmental provisions favoring their clients—favors not accorded to many others who are "handicapped" by such conditions as a substandard native intelligence or a disagreeable appearance.

A free-market economy will have ample chances for competitively priced insurance against illness, job loss or other misfortunes. The insurance premiums will reflect the best available probabilistic assessments of potential payouts (plus administrative costs, etc.) as of the time of insurance. Therefore health insurance for people already infected with the AIDS virus naturally will be commensurately costlier—as it should be. This is no injustice and not discriminatory. It will be the fair result of private-market bargaining that neutrally evaluates the relevant insurance factors.

By contrast, government rules preventing insurance companies from differentiating their premium levels in this way will give AIDS-afflicted persons a special subsidy. The insurance companies will then have to charge other people more to make up for the undercharging of the high-risk AIDS group, something that reportedly is already happening in some areas.[47]

Long before the AIDS crisis, homosexuality had been claimed to be another "handicap" warranting compensatory government measures. By and large, that "handicap" has been in the form of moral and psychological barriers, erected by the heterosexual majority—barriers that it has had a right to erect on the private level. Many of the barriers seem to have been fallen in response to society's growing moral permissiveness and the pressure of the gay civil-rights movement. There have been a number of legislative changes in favor of the outwardly gay labor population, together with greater public tolerance of the homosexual life style—but at the price of increased violent confrontations in public places. "Gay rights" bills, enacted over the last ten years, now criminalize discrimination against gays in employment, housing, public accommodation and insurance in some parts of the United States.

How should we, ideologically, feel about these new laws? To start with, whether homosexuality is mostly hereditary or attributable to conditions in early childhood environment need not, and cannot, be resolved here. All that society ought to do, and can do, is to provide an adequate, standard upbringing suited to each child's genetic characteristics. Nature should run its course, if nature it is; but if misguided child care is to "blame," conceivably a case could be made for financial compensation for demonstrated suffering, paid by the parties at fault.

Then, do we need any civil rights laws for gays? And do gays deserve any protection whatsoever against the socioeconomic repercussions of majority disapproval of their life style and of their diminished role in perpetuating the human race?

They deserve such protection only if and to the extent an efficient use of public resources so requires. No public agency should be allowed to deny homosexuals employment purely on the ground of their sexual orientation; that would be both unfair and inefficient, a double offense. That is, government should not waste tax money by refusing to employ qualified gays in legitimate public activities and hiring less-qualified, or more-expensive, straights instead. And the judiciary should not waste any judge's or jury's time by trying any private morals cases, gay or straight. Private sex among consenting adults is none of the public's business. It is a legitimate exchange of services, undertaken for mutual benefit, and at the private risk of dissatisfaction or ill health.

But private parties should retain their full right to choose whom they wish to associate with. "Antidiscrimination" principles cannot be invoked to destroy the voluntary exchange system. Employers, landlords and businesses should retain the right to do business, or not to do business, with any group or person, regardless of race, creed, gender or sexual habits—just as each of us should be allowed to bargain for the best opportunities in the market for sex.

If we feel that bigoted people should be made to open their minds and hearts, this is a private concern. We can, of course, rely on private education or private advertising to seek that result. In particular, one could envision profit-conscious stockholders pressuring corporate managements to remove all discrimination against cost-effective job applicants (including, no doubt, some carriers of the AIDS virus). But this is, again, a question of private market tactics; it is not on a par with questions of ideology or public ethics.

If, contrariwise, gays were given special job quotas, why not do the same for people with an unattractive appearance or bad manners? Of course this would be nonsense. Private preferences, privately expressed, must be socioethically sacred—or we violate a basic tenet of an individualistic society.

In a **libegalitarian** world, "civil rights" should denote the whole cluster of constitutional rights. These ought to consist of the right to an equitable social capital endowment, the right to voluntary exchange and the right to satisfy public collective-goods needs through government.

Selective rights for particular groups are inherently discriminatory. Civil rights should be synonymous with "human rights"—a term that currently is applied in grossly restricted, and biased, ways. (All the rights we are concerned with are certainly "human," and not directed toward fauna or flora.) Civil rights, protected by an improved national constitution, should be generalized across the population and standardized across socioeconomic activities. They should not be pretentiously labeled subsidies to aggressive special-interest groups.[48]

SOCIAL SECURITY AND HEALTH

Governments in all modern societies give financial help to their older citizens, especially if these are judged needy. It is done through income support, free medical care or subsidized services. These programs are part of the "safety nets" that are supposed to guarantee retired persons an acceptable minimum standard of living and keep them from becoming a burden on dependents or private charities. They help satisfy popular feelings of compassion toward the old and weak. But their ideological and socioethical underpinnings are flimsy.

In the United States, the main old-age benefit program, Social Security, has a long, nearly sacred tradition. Access to it is commonly regarded as a basic right. But its growing costs have raised more and more questions about its proper purpose, its financing and its influence on the nation's overall economic performance. On the one hand, greater longevity tends to increase claims on the Social Security trust fund, and a rising national income would seem to make it possible to honor those claims. On the other, rising incomes permit individuals to save more on their own, so the need for income support actually ought to fall.

So far this conflict has been resolved in favor of relatively stable benefit levels (apart from cost-of-living adjustments) for each elderly person. This has led to a series of Social Security "crises," the most recent one in the early 1980s. As the number and amount of Social Security claims continued to swell, it became necessary to raise the taxes that finance the program (by raising the rates of employee and employer Social Security tax payments and by increasing the income base on which these rates are applied). Thereby the latest Social Security "crisis" was papered over.

Partly as a consequence of the reform, the trust fund is now projected to grow substantially for next couple of decades. But the basic issues of the system's soundness and fairness have certainly not been resolved.

What Is It? The concept behind Social Security has always been murky. The nature of individual citizens' rights to participate in it is subject to different interpretations. And the way it is financed has become entangled in the general debate over government finances and the federal budget.

In one sense, the system seems like a government-administered, obligatory scheme of individual pensions. We pay in money (out of our paychecks and through payroll taxes) during our productive years. We take out money when we have retired, i.e., when we may or may not have sufficient other means of support. In the meantime, the government is the custodian of our paid-in premiums, through its management of the trust fund (although we can never hope to know what it is doing with all that money).

In another sense, the Social Security system is a form of compulsory income support from active, young or middle-aged wage earners to inactive, old retirees. It is, in this sense, an intergenerational transfer scheme. There is hence no reason for the trust fund to have any substantial surplus, as long as current outpayments do not substantially, or permanently, exceed current receipts.

Yet the line between an intergenerational transfer system and an individual saving program may not seem terribly sharp. Most of us are at one time net financial contributors to the system, at another time net financial beneficiaries from it. If we represented the "average" person, we might even think that these roles somehow cancel out over time. The system might then look reasonably fair, as our early tax payments are balanced by government retirement income (presumably consisting of principal plus interest) later on. It might seem like a long-term cash management program, or an honest-to-goodness pension program, for such a person.

But we are not, individually, "average." The "average" person is a blurry, abstract concept of little value in socioethical analysis. For "nonaverage" individuals, there is not such a neat correspondence between tax payments and the value of their old-age benefits. Moreover, frequent reforms of the entire system have tended to further weaken the links between the payment and the receipt side.

Therefore we have to be concerned about how different groups of individuals fare under the system. One will then find that, as a pension program, it is grossly unfair to a large portion of the population. And as a pure welfare program, it has even less to recommend it.

Distributional Effects. Building up pension rights is an act of saving, or a deferral of spending power until a relatively distant future (depending on the payer's age). In the private-market context, this is an intertemporal exchange decision—often the biggest one in our lives and deserving careful personal planning.

A lot of potential freedom is at stake. The freedom to choose, or not to choose, a pension program of one's own should be a major aspect of the freedom to save. But the current Social Security system severely reduces that freedom. It forces us, when employed, to give up a substantial fraction of our incomes—currently, several thousand dollars a year for a middle-class worker. Escaping from this obligation is not impossible, but it is usually extremely costly: One may have to drastically change career plans so as to fall into one of the few exempt professional categories (e.g., free-lance artist) or to join the underground economy, thereby risking penalties for tax evasion. Almost all of us are stuck with Social Security tax obligations.

What can we expect to get in return for these contributions? Contractually, nothing. There is no formal government liability to repay us. No financial rights are earmarked for those who pay in, and there is no systematic proportionality between contributions and benefits. The rules may change again, and so we can't know in advance who will qualify and for how much. And the whole system could conceivably be restructured or even abolished.

Private pension plans, of course, also contain elements of chance and risk. They certainly do no preclude the risk of premature death and an inability to collect the full anticipated pension, or of a few insurance companies going broke some day. But private pensions usually provide ample death benefits to the deceased plan member's estate. And they can be tailored to the individual's preferences and circumstances.

It is foreseeable that recent increases in Social Security taxes will create a growing "surplus" for the trust fund, which will give it a small resemblance of a true pension program; the surplus (placed in U.S. Treasury securities) is projected to peak at about $12 trillion in the 2010s. But this figure actually refers to the fund's gross financial assets, not (as one might think) to the difference between these assets and the value of projected future liabilities for outpayments. In fact the present value of benefit liabilities (calculated in accordance with current law) grossly exceeds current paid-in assets (although by how much has not been reliably demonstrated).

Actuarially, the system is hence exceedingly underfunded, despite the temporarily growing "surplus." The bulk of the benefits to be paid out as far as the eye can see will still have to be financed through simultaneously collected Social Security taxes, not through drawdowns of built-up assets. Either future beneficiaries will then have to give up a major portion of their benefit claims or the future tax-paying population will have to make up the difference.

The official presumption is that taxpayers will indeed pick up the extra tab, in part through future tax increases already built into the current law. If, however, Congress should backtrack and cut future Social Security taxes, the trust fund would presumably be bailed out by general tax revenues; and some of these taxes would probably be taken out of the Social Security checks.[49] The necessity to draw financial assistance, one way or other, from retirees and other taxpayers underscores the system's lack of soundness and negates any concept of a pension fund.[50]

Moreover, the implications for individual retirees will vary greatly. Relatively best off will be those who will retire with no or little other income, live long and leave long-surviving spouses. These persons are already favored under current provisions, and they would almost certainly still get the highest priority in any reformed Social Security system. The biggest losers will be those who have other sources of income and therefore will shoulder larger tax obligations—as well as those whose innate health problems predestine them to an early death. These are hardly equitable results. By free-market pension standards, they imply gross, systematic theft.

A Better System. To restore equity in the pension and saving area, we will have to dismantle the entire Social Security system (including its provisions for Medicare). This could allow each individual to establish his own old-age financing plan, in accordance with his own intertemporal consumption preferences.

The individual could then decide for himself if he prefers to take relatively large, or small, risks in the search for maximum future returns. He would then no longer be pushed into subsidizing those who currently can take advantage of the system by paying in disproportionately little but accepting full benefits. He would also not become a financial burden on the next generation of productive workers. Aggregate pension assets could then be put to better use, for the benefit of a growing national opportunity pie.

Actually, the idea of privatizing Social Security no longer seems that radical. Note the privatization steps taken in so many other government areas during the last ten years, in the United States and abroad (especially in the United Kingdom, but also in other industrial countries).

A number of proposals for desocializing and privatizing the U.S. Social Security system have been put forth. Typically, privatization proponents have argued that the accumulated assets could be better employed if they were invested in private industry, rather than, as now, in federal government activities or redistribution schemes. Proponents believe that each individual be allowed to leave the system so as to be able to select his own old-age saving and pension-asset plan.[51]

However, there are concerns that many individuals will not be sufficiently savvy or resourceful to save enough by themselves. These individuals might then, after all, need the helping hand of government, so as not to fall into abject poverty (or go without medical care). For their benefit, perhaps a scaled-down Social Security system ought still to be available. This would remain part of the federal "safety net," to be financed from continued payroll taxes. As a long-run proposition, this would clearly be inequitable; and it would be conducive to exploitation of the taxpayers by the unproductive and spendthrift (a major societal moral hazard). Yet as a transitional stopgap for those who have been economically handicapped since childhood, it might deserve consideration.

Libegalitarian principles provide the permanent answer: Society should fulfill its general obligation to each one of us by giving us an equitable capital endowment at our start in life. If this were done, neither "need," nor age, nor sickness would be a sufficient reason for additional government support. Those who failed to save enought for old-age needs would, as a last resort, have to seek assistance from dependents or private charity organizations. The very absence of special government old-age support ought, in fact, to expand the supply of such facilities. If it did not, this would be the uncoerced consensus decision of a free, fair society. As such, it would be ethically unassailable.

Health Care. Health is a major aspect of personal capital. This follows from the simple fact that it contributes very importantly to our present and future productivity and income-generating capacity. That it provides immediate physical and psychological satisfaction gives it the extra functions of direct consumption support. Additional future income, satisfaction and comfort are the main dividends we receive from investments in health care and expenditures on health maintenance.

Some of the investments require money expenditure—this is the case with most curative medical care. Others involve behavior modification or other preventive measures. These are exemplified by the avoidance of unhealthy eating, drinking or drug habits, or a failure to engage in at least a minimum of exercise—typically at the cost of immediate gratification or leisure.

Individually and collectively, maximum health certainly seems like a highly worthwhile goal, generally near the top of both personal and social priorities. But since health is also in various ways costly, the economic question is one of optimality, not maximality, to be achieved through a balancing of costs and benefits. And of equal social importance is the financing question: How should the costs of health care be distributed across the population?

It would be terribly naive to reason that the importance of health—or its social ramifications or costs—will automatically make it a governmental matter. A bit of reflection reveals that many unquestionably important matters (eating, etc.) are best left to individual decision makers. And most of the social aspects of health are localized within families, neighborhoods, employment facilities or local communities—societal spheres not usually controlled by government.

The costs will, of course, have to be paid one way or other, and transferring them to the taxpayers obviously will not, in itself, make them any smaller. On the contrary, providing services publicly, rather than privately, often means that they will, overall, cost more, because of the public sector's relative inefficiency. So the case for nationalized or socialized health care is certainly not obvious. In fact, health care provides a big, complex test of the merits of different economic-political ideologies. Is there a persuasive case for **libegalitarianism**?

A Public Matter? The basic public-policy question should, instead, be whether there exists any health-related national public goods. If the answer is yes, there will be a second question about how these goods can be produced and then a third one about how the public health-care costs can be equitably allocated. If the initial answer is no, we can bring the public-policy debate to a conclusion much more quickly.

One will find that, yes, health care does have certain public aspects, in extreme cases even on the national plane. If there is a clear threat of illness stemming from one source and affecting the entire nation, the threat will constitute a clear-cut public "bad," and eliminating it would constitute a bona-fide national public good. A theoretical case in point: contamination of the entire atmosphere with disease-producing bacteria. By con-

141

trast, actual disease is, almost invariably, a purely individual "bad," because the community and the general public is usually unaffected (unless government has already stepped in and cavalierly made individual health a public concern).

In most realistic cases, however, the threat of disease will not pervade the whole nation but, at the most, particular communities or regions and in sharply varying degress. Recall various flu epidemics. The national public-good aspect of disease prevention is then very small and ambiguous. It will not compare with the large individual or private-collective benefits that can potentially be obtained by those particular social subgroups that are especially vulnerable (e.g., the elderly, coworkers or family members). Broad-scale national prevention measures will then not meet the standard public-good test.

Yet in the rare cases in which a public "bad" can be demonstrated, it is appropriate to ask whether cost-effective government techniques exists for preventing or eliminating that "bad." If the technology exists (perhaps in the form of a public vaccination program) and the cost is low enough, government involvment may well be appropriate; if not, the private sector should still retain the job. Similarly the government may have a credible health-related public-good justification for certain environmental control programs (e.g., tax disincentives for the disposal of unhealthy wastes into the ocean). By contrast, an individual's illness is hardly ever a major collective-good (let alone a public-good) concern.

Almost all steps to maintain or improve personal health belong in the private sphere, usually at the individual level (or within the family or workplace). By far most of the benefits are purely individual, and those with collective spillover effects typically remain well localized. And "externalities" in the form of potential contamination, failure to perform one's job or impositions on family members can usually be adequately handled through private contract clauses or informal understandings.

The individual almost always has superior access to the relevant facts, perhaps in consultation with his physician or psychiatrist. Each of us knows approximately when he or she is ill; we have some basic knowledge of medical care and prevention of illness; and beyond that, we can seek doctor's advice and access to hospital facilities—and none of these services are normally in the public-good division. Almost all aspects of health care are therefore perfectly suited for voluntary exchange in a free, competitive market. Health care ought predominantly to be a private matter.

Consider the job aspects. If my employer wants his staff to live up to certain physical productivity standards, he can, of course, ask for contractual assurances or behavorial guarantees that his employees will meet those standards (unless the government, unwisely, intrudes upon this right). In so doing, he will tend to reduce the potential pool of acceptable job candidates, and he may have to raise his wage offers. He will then weigh the added costs against the benefit of greater worker productivity, and he might reconsider and modify those standards. Conversely, job seekers can weigh the benefits to themselves of working in a healthier, higher-productivity environment against the possible cost of having to modify their health-related behavior. This is how private markets work; this is how employment-connected health questions ought to be answered— through negotiation, accommodation and price adjustment.

Choosing the private-market solution is, in part, an efficiency matter: Private health "production" costs less than any conceivable government arrangement for such "production." Centralized, governmental control over health-care decisions will almost invariably be less cost-effective. It will produce resource misallocations that ultimately reduce national and individual income.

But it is also a matter of equity. There is normally very little reason for the taxpayer to bear the cost of other individuals' medical expenses. Such a shifting of costs only reduces individuals' incentives to lead healthy lives or to economize on available medical facilities (another moral hazard for the taxpaying public). It constitutes implicit income redistribution, not based on any acceptable notion of fairness.

The Question of Nationalization. Nevertheless it might be instructive to briefly consider some contrary arguments. American health care is already a huge, mixed private-public undertaking, with large societal commitments by federal and local governments, corporate employers, insurance companies and charities. There is, at the same time, widespread public dissatisfaction with the results, and a confused search for better alternatives is under way. Health care is now placed high on the list of certified national public-policy crises.

The idea of a compulsory national insurance plan is getting more and more attention from the political left and center and from the socially hyperconscious media. The AIDS epidemic has over the last decade raised additional questions about governmental versus private responsibilities. Do we therefore need to reconsider our faith in the private market? Is the private health-care market inherently inadequate? Are there new or unavoidable social "externality" problems that cry out for social remedies?

Full-fledged medical-care socialism would require a complete system of government physicians and hospitals that was financed through general tax revenues. Such a system would make it possible to standardize all treatments for specific predefined conditions, so that nobody could boast of having undergone superior surgery or more up-to-date psychoanalysis.

Such a system would ostensibly be costless to the individual patient (as opposed to the taxpayer). As such it would naturally encourage frequent overuse; zero prices would have zero restraining effects on demand (as demonstrated by the long queues of untreated patients in countries with nationalized medical care). But whereas suppressed prices can create additional opportunities for care, the added care is generally not worth its costs in terms of the forgone opportunities hidden elsewhere in the economy.

Recent American experience is instructive. Zero or very low medical-care costs for individual patients have inflated care demand. Care suppliers have been able to satisfy that demand by shifting most of the costs to third parties without providing much evidence of improved national health. Most hospital costs are now covered by the government (through Medicare and Medicaid) or by private insurance policies rather than by the individual patients; and the costs of private insurance is borne mostly by corporations (and, ultimately, their multiple constituents) and the taxpayers (through tax deductions for paid-in premiums). There is thus no mechanism for item-by-item cost and quality control (the kind we have in all normal market situations).

The U.S. Congress has lately legislated a number of public cost-control measures that force hospitals and physicians to exercise some discipline over their choice of procedures, equipment and facilities. In itself, this effort is a health economy step of some merit; but it will inevitably reduce the system's ability to accommodate real patient needs. Rationing by decree, rather than through individual price-sensitive negotiation, can never be cost-effective.

The Necessary Rationing. The same problem afflicts, on a larger scale, all plans for nationalized health care. Government bureaucrats (perhaps in physician's garb) would have to ration that demand, deciding which illnesses deserve what treatment (and which are fake or too insignificant to warrant care). There would be tricky, judgmental cost-benefit problems. Should heavy colds be allowed to run their course? Is a costly kidney replacement on a 100-year-old warranted? Does this aging actress really need a new, surgically installed face?

Most current U.S. national-health care proposals (emanating mostly from liberals and Democrats) do not go nearly that far. They concentrate on the financing side, allowing a continued mix of private and public hospitals and physicians. The plans typically call for standardized insurance programs that would tend to equalize individual costs regardless of the extent of care received. They derive much of their inspiration from the national health plans already in existence in Britain, Canada and Scandinavia.[52]

The main popular appeal of these plans lies in their ostensible humanitarianism: Everybody "deserves" decent health care, regardless of income; we should all be samaritans; and health care can often be much too costly for private pocketbooks. This is, on the surface, an egalitarian argument. Moreover, a national health system could more easily provide preventive care for everybody, thereby lessening the future public-sector costs of caring for the sickly poor and reducing the loss of tax revenue from medically disabled workers. This is a public-investment argument.

The egalitarian argument suggests a special form of income redistribution, from the healthy toward the unhealthy. It is a call for subsidies for the sick—and for those who don't bother to take illness-preventive steps of their own. If the argument was squarely and honestly addressed in this fashion, most people would reject it and insist that redistribution questions be dealt with separately, as a general equity matter; whatever egalitarian goals people subscribe to, they tend to supersede questions of access to particular service categories. In defense, spokesmen for national health programs might say that nobody deliberately, or out of sheer carelessness, allows himself to become ill. But this claim flies in the face of all economic-behavioral experience. It also contradicts all the professional advice about how each of us should practice preventive health care in his own daily life.

In all fairness, some illnesses are inborn or linked to genetic or childhood circumstances; and the redistributionist argument then has some validity. But there is a better, fairer way of dealing with these situations: by providing adequate health care to all children and youngsters but giving each adult full responsibility for his own health. Such mandated children's health care might include an insurance policy covering health problems acquired either at birth or during the years of upbringing, either because of accidents or the negligence of guardians. These provisions would establish true equity in the health area.

The public-investment argument could very well make sense within its own context, i.e., on the assumption that the government will in any case be partly responsible for our future health. But note how sinister the implications can be of such an argument: If health-care costs are to be charged to the taxpaying public, the taxpayers will of course feel that they have a right to exercise some cost and productivity control over this government budget item.

The U.S. Congress, representing the taxpayers, will then have an almost automatic right to insist that we all obey the "correct" health-care rules, so that we will not "abuse" any public investment in our health by

145

incurring excessive medical-care costs. That right could easily be justified as just another instance of normal Congressional oversight. After all, spending *by* the people ought also to be *for* the people. Public health care will turn our bodies into quasigovernment property, the control of which will have to be shared among those financially responsible for them. Of course, those assumptions and implications are intolerable.

Lately, the notion of "catastrophic" illness has prominently entered the public health-care debate (and it figured in the recent expansion of the Medicare program). Perhaps government, at a minimum, ought to protect us against the financial catastrophes connected with severe, prolonged illnesses requiring especially costly treatments? Again the answer appears to be negative. Where do we draw the line between catastrophe and mere accident (or gross carelessness)? And why should the taxpayer have a separate obligation to protect others against catastrophes?

It is in the nature of most catastrophes that they are unpredictable. As such they are especially well suited for insurance coverage. In any case, one can see no reason for distributing the costs of catastrophes differently from those of other accidents. Unless the government has failed to provide adequate public-good protection (e.g., through national defense or environmental safeguards), such unfortunate events should be dealt with as individual accidental responsibilities.

The same analysis applied to the early phase of the AIDS crisis, before information existed on the ways in which the illness spreads and can be avoided: Infection was in the nature of a natural catastrophe for which the unfortunate victim, rather than the equally innocent taxpayers, should bear the consequences. After that phase, the ethical case for personal accountability should be even less controversial.

Private Insurance. In the long run, the solution to the problem of financing health care lies in the private sphere: Individuals ought to make their own cost-benefit analyses and their own choices, balancing the costs of continuous preventive health care and insurance (and occasional medications) against the potential costs of future hospital or therapeutic care, reduced income, reduced well-being and a shortened life. That is the **libegalitarian** prescription. There is no way for public authorities to make the right choices for us while showing sufficient sensitivity to our individual physical and psychological needs. This applies both to questions of prevention and treatment and to the question of appropriate insurance policy.

Of course, insurance companies must be allowed to evaluate all the pertinent risk factors and to price them accordingly (when structuring their premiums); otherwise some of the costs will be shifted to other parties. They should thus be allowed to charge higher premiums of people who smoke, carry the AIDS virus or have very large cholesterol counts. And they must be allowed to test any policy applicant for the presence of such conditions. They are not charity organizations and should not become involuntary organs for income redistribution.

In terms of dollar numbers, health care is probably one of the most mismanaged sectors of the American economy today. It is estimated that health care consumes over 10 percent of the American gross national product each year, a partial indication of what is at stake. It is also one of the biggest sources of inequality in the claims different individuals now can make on the public purse.

The national health-care debate has, fortunately, led to somewhat greater professional and public understanding of these issues. There has been some useful short-term reform efforts—to impose better cost controls, in particular. In 1989–90, a growing consensus seemed to be developing in favor of mandatory standardized health insurance for all employees of large and medium-sized businesses. Such a system would avoid full-scale health-care socialism. Yet it would introduce a new form of regulation that would interfere with private bargaining and reduce worker choice among potential benefits packages.

No such measures will possibly make our nation's health care more cost-effective or more equitable. Rather, they will reduce incentives for private health maintenance and expand demand for medical services even further. They will thereby either overburden public budgets and taxpayers or push the authorities to set up complicated rationing systems—forcing people into long, counterproductive queues at doctors' offices and hospitals. Only a combination of private choice and private responsibility at all levels could give us an efficient, equitable health-care system. The failure of our political leaders to recognize this threatens to take us a big step backward.[53]

Chapter VI
OTHER IMPROPER GOVERNMENT FUNCTIONS

CONSUMER PROTECTION

The national government is usually viewed as a protector of the public welfare. That "welfare" is, of course, not a well-defined commodity. But most people would feel that it includes a big element of physical and economic security or protection against general, pervasive dangers to our well-being.

The **libegalitarian** ideology presented here does not assign nearly that large and amorphous a role to government. But it does prescribe certain protective functions to it—especially in regard to national security, property protection and some aspects of the nation's physical environment. Why stop there? We are threatened not just by missiles, muggers and swindlers, but by irresponsible manufacturers, sales clerks and repair men whose practices or products can harm us.

We need protection also against shoddy, dangerous merchandise—either by having it removed from the market or by being properly forewarned about those deficiencies. At least up to a point, such protection can improve our living standards. Protection against mistakes and misfortunes can enhance our socioeconomic opportunities by preserving our personal capital. In addition, it can reduce the sheer anxiety we tend to feel about excessive risk and uncertainty, thereby giving us an extra, psychic source of intangible capital. To reject protective services out of hand would be to invite discomfort, danger and potential harm, foolishly and unnecessarily.

These perceptions lead many people to the conclusion that society, through government, ought to play a large protective role in almost all facets of our lives. Since consumption is the ultimate economic key to our personal well-being, it might then seem almost a foregone conclusion that government should protect this area of our socioeconomic existence. At a minimum, government ought to help reduce the many hazards that seem to afflict our daily economic activities—primarily because of substandard consumer items that could damage our health, our diets or our productivity. Or so it might seem.

There might even be a parallel with national defense. If we agree that the government should be our chief defender against external and internal aggressors, should not a similar defense be established at the personal consumption level?

This line of reasoning seems unfortunately to underlie much of the prevailing view of "consumer protection." Most people do not realize what the alternatives are, including private steps that provide protection or remedies. And people tend to overlook the hidden costs, to themselves and others, of government interference with private consumption choice and consumption-related economic activity.

Medication. Consider, first, current U.S. regulations on medication. Taking medicine is, in itself, a kind of consumption activity, akin to maintenance (of body or mind). It can sustain and promote the kinds of consumption that are truly enjoyable, in the present and in the future. Aspirin tablets, cough suppressants and antibiotics can all be "productive" inputs into our activities on the job and at home—activities through which we try to maximize our consumption benefits, today and tomorrow. That applies whether we are taking those medicines for curative or preventive purposes. By stretching the "medication" concept a bit, we can let the term apply also to vitamins, genuine "health food" and exercise equipment.

Most health-related consumer products in the United States must be approved by the Food and Drug Administration before they can be sold to the public. If the FDA does not find them both safe and effective (in curing or preventing specific health problems), they will generally not be made available—except, possibly, through black market channels. The FDA thereby protects us against medicines that might damage our bodies or minds, create birth defects in our children or simply turn out to be useless. And we don't even seem to have to pay for this protection. So why complain? Because a sharper look at these regulations will yield a very different conclusion.

The intuitive case for regulations on drug quality might seem strong.

For one thing, the benefits of regulation appear to be widespread and, in most cases, uncontroversial. For another, quality control requires a great deal of technical expertise, so it will need to be done by highly specialized organizations—or perhaps through a monopolistic government agency. In addition, the regulatory costs will be partly "reimbursed" when improved public health reduces claims on publicly funded or tax-subsidized health care.

But these arguments do not quite solve the matter. Many of the regulatory "goods" actually have very different benefit implications for different persons. Vulnerabilities to different substances and activities vary between old and young, between the constitutionally strong and weak, or among people with different life styles—suggesting that the "goods" have large individual elements. Expertise can of course be employed in either the public or private sector; on this score, private entrepreneurship actually tends to outdo government. And the reimbursement argument will collapse once we learn how to reinstate personal accountability in all individual health matters.

The case for regulation rests largely on a belief that drug quality is a simple, one-dimensional matter, not to be placed in the unreliable, unpredictable hands of individual drug companies. But there is no generally accepted way of qualitatively classifying drugs—or food, for that matter. Very few drugs are universally good, bad, harmless or harmful, either relatively or absolutely. Some drugs are useless to some people while useful—or harmful—to others. Not many drugs are always useful or never harmful. And few are always harmful or never harmless; timing matters, too.

We can rarely, with confidence, make such generalized evaluations and apply them to almost everybody almost all the time. So we have to take the agnostic view: Any existing or prospective substance might be useful, or harmful, to some people, somewhere, some of the time. And the average opinion about a substance's merits should not be given much weight either. For if we respect each individual's needs and desires, we cannot be swayed by average (or majority) opinions or experiences.

Another complication arises from the fact that many medicines can have multiple effects on our health, some predictable, others not. When we consider taking a medication, we are faced with probabilities, not definite outcomes, involving both its good and potentially bad aspects. So rational individuals, if given the opportunity, will evaluate a drug on the basis of its likely remedial health effect and its likely side effects along with its monetary costs; and the evaluation will have a large subjective element, related to individual health perceptions and risk tolerance.

Good drug quality is a matter of high, and highly probable, effectiveness and a low risk of undesirable, but preferably minor, side effects. To make the evaluation, the public needs information about the quality of each available drug, ideally complemented by knowledge of their bodies' and minds' likely reactions to it. Only in this way can people—or their doctors—make educated decisions about whether to use the drug or not. But again these are fundamentally individual matters requiring individualized prescriptions.

Drug-quality information is generally a mixed individual collective good. Some information is broadly relevant and useful, especially among persons in similar physical, occupational and habitual circumstances. A particular health warning may then have the same relevance to their well-being and carry approximately the same weight in their decisions. But collective elements are rarely well-defined enough to indicate the presence of a true national public good; and rounding up those who share a definite collective interest in a particular drug's quality (e.g., those with specific blood, heart, kidney or skin characteristics) would not be easy or economical. And much information has strictly personal implications. So the informational goods do not qualify for national production and distribution.

The government has no superior access to the needed scientific data (unless it, coercively, keeps data away from the private sector). It has no superior means for communicating the related drug quality assessments to its potential users. And it has no practical way of fairly distributing the costs of research, evaluation and public information. The government can, of course, appropriate these functions, force-feed the informational output to the public, control the availability of medication accordingly and charge the general taxpayer for the direct costs of these activities. But the result will usually be overgeneralized information and excessively restricted drug availability.

The job could be better carried out in the private sector, which has access to the same, or even better, technical data and data-distribution channels. Individuals could then make better decisions about their own health care. The quality information and screening that the market wants can normally be supplied by the market itself, without the heavy-handed intermediation of government. If demand for such services is there, it will find outlets partly in the buying of drugstore products equipped with such attributes, partly in market pressure for separate information services, e.g., new medical or health-related advisory publications and consultations.

That is, abolishing regulatory warnings will not necessarily, and not likely, mean that such warnings will not be available. But they will better reflect true individual needs. And flexible personal choice will replace the rigidly negative choice that the FDA now makes when it prohibits distribution of a useful drug.

"Regulation" will then be a private activity subject to the efficiency-improving pressures of market competition. The practical result is likely to be a mixture of self-regulation by individual consumer patients and purchases of regulatory—i.e., advisory—services from private health-care specialists. Private regulators will normally be more cost and quality conscious, since they have to accommodate public demands while also turning a profit. Since they lack police power, they will not be able to obstruct private choice—a major benefit of privatizing health regulations.

In the longer run, a free drug market would stimulate the development of new and better drugs—an incentive that the FDA bureaucrats now are suppressing. This is a problem that has become painfully obvious during the AIDS crisis. Fortunately, the FDA has now begun to respond to public and professional pressure by liberalizing its approval rules and allowing some new drugs, not quite certified as "effective," to be marketed. This is an indirect admission of the failure of the whole U.S. drug regulatory system.

Admittedly, individuals in such a free market would have to apply more personal judgment. But this is both their privilege and their responsibility in an individualistic society—until they voluntarily transfer that responsibility to their chosen spokesmen. Medical freedom ought to be recognized as an important aspect of liberty, as well as an engine of innovation and technological progress. At present, it is not, generally, so recognized.

Smoking. Tobacco smoking was until the last couple of decades considered a relatively benign phenomenon—at most a minor social vice. By and large, tobacco smoke was regarded as only a small annoyance to nonsmokers in the smoker's immediate vicinity, along with some vaguely perceived health risks to the smokers themselves. But the celebrated Surgeon General report on the apparent cancer risks in the 1960s began to produce a great deal of new public antitobacco sentiment. The new public pressure led to a number of legal restrictions on smoking in public places and private offices in the 1980s.

As a result, there is a new prohibitionist morality in this area. Antismoking advocates want to achieve three things: one, help smokers realize what damage they might be doing to their lungs and save them from that damage; two, spare others the environmental nuisance of tobacco smoke and the accompanying, though slight, risks to their lungs; and three, reduce the costs of smoking-related medical care to the government's health budget and to the national economy. Aren't these reasonable demands?

As expressions of personal interests, fairly commonly shared by large segments of the population, yes; as guides for general legislation or other public policy actions, no. Obviously, other interests are also at work—the interests of those who genuinely prefer to smoke, never mind the health risks, and of people and organizations that have devoted resources toward accommodating the smoker community. These groups include not only tobacco consumers but tobacco farmers, cigarette manufacturers, many advertising firms, billboard makers, advertising-dependent magazines and physicians specializing in lung cancer treatment.

As long as anybody really wants to smoke, and is willing to pay the free-market costs of this habit, smoking has social merit; it adds to the well-being of socially interacting individuals. So do all the ancillary economic activities that facilitate or accommodate this habit. And so does both pro- and antismoking advocacy—as long as it is carried out in the free marketplace of ideas, at private cost.

It is hence impossible to share the restrictive mentality of the antismoking forces. That attitude is an affront to individual rights and personal consumption freedom. The Surgeon General recently called for a completely smoke-free America—and that was, bluntly put, a gross expression of fascist puritanism.[54]

Needless to say, many other personal habits can be detrimental to ourselves or to our immediate associates, and they might add to the medical care bill now covered by government. Eating and exercise habits are two broad areas where demands for similar restrictions could accordingly be raised. How far should we go in taking care of people in these ways?

The **libegalitarian** answer is clear. Everybody should have the right to judge his or her own health requirements and even to abuse his own body if he or she so chooses. The individual should not have to curb his habits just because others find them offensive. He should not have to pay penalty taxes for any personal habit (as through excise taxes on cigarettes).

Ideally, the medical aspects should also be handled privately, so that cancer-prone smokers will not be able to shift some of their health costs over to others. Conversely, smokers should not be asked to bear more than the health-care costs they themselves are responsible for.[55] But private insurance companies should, of course, be free to differentiate the premiums they charge smokers and nonsmokers (and any other categories of the public). Higher premiums will then become part of social smoking costs that, appropriately, become "internalized" among the smokers themselves.

But smokers tend to foul the air, a resource that we all depend on and which is sometimes scarce. Is not this a collective "bad" worth removing, just as clean air is a collective good? Yes, if it can be done cost-effectively and equitably. But the collective element is, territorially, very limited. Not even the foulest cigar could affect air quality outside a very small area or with community-wide repercussions. Smoking is thus not a matter suited for control by any existing political unit. It is, rather, something to be accommodated within the private market segments or organizations in which air quality conflicts arise.

Ideally, our property rights system would specify who are the responsible owners of the air or of particular air spaces. And the air owners would have the final say on what can, and cannot, be done with and to that air. The system we have now is severely incomplete. It provides for a great deal of "air control" within private homes and offices, which is unobjectionable. But it complicates rational private decisions by imposing compulsory rules on how firms should behave and by regulating smoking in public places in a heavy-handed way.

Under more perfect property arrangements, the right to use air could be better negotiated and priced in accordance with air scarcity and air use interests. This ought to apply to both private and public property. Whoever is the air's owner, everybody should have the opportunity to take advantage of the existing air as long as he pays for any damage he might inflict on it.

A generous host may accept some temporary damage to the air in his home as one of the costs of entertaining; or he might rather pay the cost of missing the presence of his smoker friends in exchange for a more pristine atmosphere. A private business ought similarly to be allowed to accommodate its employees as it sees fit. Government offices ought to be able to do the same, with a blend of tolerance and concern all around.

Nonsmoking sections on air planes might be needed if passenger demands are to be met. But probably most air owners would personally find few occasions in which smoking restrictions are warranted, outside small, well-populated and poorly ventilated areas; and the cost of enforcement would usually be too high to allow restrictions in marginal cases. These types of market, or market-simulative, solutions point toward mutual tolerance—without the absolute dominance of either majority or minority wishes.

Addictive Drugs. How far should we stretch the notion of freedom in the marketplace and the related concept of "consumer sovereignty"? Does it apply to addictive drugs as well—i.e., to the production, distribution and use of heroin, cocaine, crack and other dangerous substances? Or are these drugs fundamentally different from tobacco, coffee and chocolate bars, in kind and not just in degree? Do they produce such collective national health-care and security threats that they merit a national protection system?

Once we sort things out, the answers will largely be negative. True, widespread drug availability has broad public policy ramifications. Such drugs create large demands on public health facilities; and they lead to costly patterns of crime and absenteeism on the job, to the detriment of national productivity.

But those problems are mostly of the government's own making—especially as it affects government-financed medical care and public income assistance. If the government better understood its overall responsibilities, it would no longer have to be in the drug fix in which it now finds itself. The "bads" connected with drug abuse would remain private, and the case for government intervention would largely evaporate. And the private sector would develop its own disincentives, through higher insurance premiums, for instance. Besides, no ideological system or political program can eliminate dangerous substances in nature.

The laissez-faire argument against massive government antidrug policies is clear and valid enough. If there is one soul who wants to buy the stuff at its true production costs, he must have that right. But then there will also be no public responsibility for treating any resulting health problems—no responsibility for instituting antidependency programs or for making up for lost family income. This points to full decriminalization and legalization, along with extensive reforms of health-care and income assistance programs.

The ideal, **libegalitarian** world would give people access to both drugs and information about their consequences—at market-determined costs, of course. There would be no drug-related border controls and no compulsory drug testing in private business. Smuggling and black market profiteering would disappear, while making room for legal profits and legal employment in the heavy drug industry.

Standardized schooling would give all children the information they need to make educated choices as adults. Those individuals who are now deterred from heavy drug use by inflated black-market prices would have to apply more judgment of their own as the price barriers came down. But that is a responsibility they ought to have, just as do those who can afford regular drug habits even today.

Consumerism. On the surface, the term "consumerism" seems to suggest a movement to make life better for the consumer—to help him satisfy his various demands and requirements. It would seem to endorse consumer rights, broadly and without blatant selectivity. But unfortunately that is not what is usually meant. There is no generally accepted notion of what "consumer rights" consist of. The message of the consumer movement is muddled; yet what message there is, is not very comforting.

The typical 1970s or 1980s consumer advocates—led by Ralph Nader—have shown a special concern about food, drugs and automobiles. They have spoken up for changes in product design, prohibitions against products they find overly dangerous and added labeling requirements. Their main cause has, ostensibly, been consumer safety, together with ease and accuracy of information. These product characteristics have undoubtedly appealed to many consumers—yet they have often been attained at the expense of product experimentation and innovation, probably hindering the long-run development of safer products.[56]

Precautionary labels (e.g., on electrical appliances or medicines) can of course benefit the consumer who otherwise would not have known how best to proceed; they represent informational goods. Yet if they are overly severe for a particular consumer's circumstances, they might scare and mislead him to not use the most appropriate product available—until he learns to disregard the warning and readjusts his eating or medication habits. In turn, restrictive labeling and design rules discourage the marketing of useful new products (e.g., drugs, food products, toys) that consumers would, because of those very rules, have found unattractive. Mandatory seat belts—and, potentially, air bags—limit certain types of leisure activity, while adding to the costs of the automobile; the evidence is clear.

There has been a lot of debate over sweeteners and food additives and the extent of danger that they might pose. The scare of Alar-sprayed apples created a stir in 1989. The surrounding controversies were healthy in that they signaled some public resistance to excessive food regulation. But by focusing on the degree of risk, they helped perpetuate a notion that greater health danger would have made the controls more justifiable; and this was economically unhealthy.

In New York City and other metropolitan centers, the most blatant encroachment on consumer rights is the rent control system (including the controls euphemistically differentiated as "rent stabilization"). As well documented, the system removes a large portion of the existing apartments from the voluntary exchange market by inducing rent-controlled tenants—housing consumers—to hang on to their cheap units much longer than economically warranted.

As a consequence, new arrivals in the city, and those wanting to move to different types of housing, have much greater difficulty in meeting their housing needs. To overcome this difficulty, they have to agree to pay exorbitant rents for uncontrolled apartments or to strike black-market deals with rent-controlled tenants. These detrimental results have at last become so obvious that even many egalitarian-prone liberals have begun criticizing those controls and searching for better housing policies.[57]

To be sure, some consumption restrictions may be quite innocuous, or they may reflect market preferences so closely that very few people will suffer from their existence. Some of the affected goods or consumer activities have close substitutes that are readily available at comparable costs. And in some cases, a consumer product restriction turns out to anticipate the private market's spontaneous requirement. This can occur, for instance, when the government outlaws a poisonous food item whose appeal in the end would have been too limited (or nonexistent) to make its production worthwhile. But this is a judgment that ought to have been left to the market, not to government bureaucrats, for the market's easy give-and-take increases chances that most product changes will be the desired ones.

Generally, the self-styled consumer advocate will speak for specific consumer-group interests and try to tilt the balance of rights away from other consumers or producers (e.g., through profit-reducing restraints on production methods, packaging or marketing). The legislative result: public discrimination among consumers of different goods, through ostensibly proconsumer government regulations. Every consumption restriction is a dent in the real income of the frustrated, well-informed consumer. It is confiscatory, and it unnecessarily lessens the personal welfare opportunities embodied in his income and wealth.

In a **libegalitarian** society, there would exist a general, unquestioned consumer right, side by side with producer and investor rights, to be exercised through voluntary exchange at market-determined prices. In addition, there ought to be a right to participate in the collective consumption of tax-paid public goods of proven cost-effective value to each tax payer. These two constitutional provisions would ensure a true "consumerist" culture.

ENVIRONMENTAL PROHIBITIONS

Equal opportunity implies mutuality—in the sharing of freedom and in rights to resources. Otherwise, one person's right will become another's nonright, or one person's resource gain would be at another's expense. There has to be individual accountability for the losses of resources or opportunities that our actions might impose on others. This is an intrinsic aspect of **libegalitarianism**.

In the context of market transactions, mutuality is, of course, satisfied through the freedom and voluntariness of exchange. Private negotiation and bargaining, unobstructed by government regulation, ensures that each transactor can ask for adequate compensation for his deliveries and adequate deliveries for his payments.

In the public-sector context, mutual accountability is, more indirectly, satisfied through the application of public-good theory and benefit taxation: Everybody pays, equally, for what he gets, so nobody will be relatively favored or disfavored. If particular resources are to be in public hands, access to the resources will also be mutually shared, and individual claims on public resources will have to be compensated for.

To put these rules into practice, we will need to determine what resources belong in which sector. If a resource belongs wholly to the private sector, very little will remain for us to worry about. Mutuality will be automatically ensured if society does not interfere with market exchanges, except by enforcing private contracts and generally protecting private property. By contrast, additional public policy arrangements must be made if a resource cannot be privately distributed and privately owned. Their pervasive character or undefinable location might preclude both individual and private-collective ownership, management or use.

What resources fall into this category? Basically, some—but by no means all—of the resources needed to produce public goods. Many public goods in the defense and law-enforcement areas can be produced through use of predominantly private resources. To start, all the human capital resources will be entirely private. In addition, many physical resources—machinery, structures, fuel, etc.—can best be purchased from the private sector.

Different questions come up when the needed resources are natural or environmental. Such resources pose special challenges for economic and political analysis, and for planners and managers. We often lump them together and distinguish them from machinery and human capital. But they are a very heterogeneous category: Some natural resources are easily divisible, others not; some are renewable, others not; and some have a definite economic scarcity value, while others are abundant and almost costless.

Some aspects of the physical environment lend themselves easily to private ownership. There will then be ready opportunities for ownership transfers through private exchanges in the resource markets—prominently the real estate market. But other aspects of the environment are not suited for such arrangements; they may be a source of public goods.

But this does not mean that we can, once and for all, classify all natural resources into the private and public categories. We do not have sufficient information about the physical properties of all resources and the technological possibilities for distributing and managing them to differentiate them so sharply. Future information or technological breakthroughs could, anyhow, force us to redraw the border line. So we need to be a bit flexible in suggesting the best policy approaches in this area.

Full resource privatization will hardly ever become practical or economical; it would actually destroy some of the opportunities we are trying to maximize. At the same time, private organizations might play a role in managing public resources located either in particular communities or in the nation at large; the public sector should often be encouraged to sub-contract to the private sector. And an ideology should not stand or fall on its treatment of particular asset types, such as police uniforms, missile hangars or lighthouses (although the question of lighthouse management has been hotly debated in some libertarian circles).

Land, Air and Water. Land can in most cases be easily divided and kept in individual parcels. It then conforms to the standard private-good model: Each lot can easily be traded separately in the market, without any sig-nificant "neighborhood effects" on other landowners and without major consequences for the general public.

But the situation can get more complicated if there is a large oil well underneath a group of properties. This is because drilling by one owner can then infringe on the prospects of the others and reduce their property values. Some collective property arrangement will then be in order, with common rules about drilling rights and the sharing of oil sale proceeds. Other problems will arise if the property borders are destroyed by ear-thquakes or other natural catastrophes.

Ideally, such contingencies can be dealt with through mutual contrac-tual arrangements among the adjacent property owners, as through for-mulas for resolving border disputes or provisions for arbitration proce-dures. In none of these cases is there any strong reason for government ownership or government control. At most, there might be a need for keeping public records of the contours and ownership status of each piece of real estate—much like those already kept in most civilized coun-tries.

Streams and rivers, by contrast, have almost always had an indivisible quality. Obviously, their flowing water makes different segments physically interconnected, and adjacent properties will be economically interdepen-dent (unless the stream is small enough to readily fit inside a private piece of land). Upstream property owners have a built-in power to control water supply for downstream owners—until a system of mutual water rights and obligations are established. The commonality of our ocean shores is perhaps even more obvious. For instance, moving water can easily transport waste material from one beach to another, with little prac-tical opportunity for stopping that flow.

Mountains and islands aren't really that different, economically and ideologically speaking. Occasionally, they might be located within com-mercial resorts or large recreation homes affordable by the rich. There is then no reason to question the economic status of such property: It is part of a purely private environment, at the full disposal of its legitimate owner—it is a 100 percent private good.

In the opposite case—when the area is subject to multiple ownership—some collective resource sharing can make economic sense. Efficient irrigation or cultivation might require joint planning and coordinated action. Such cooperation might easily be achieved through a private organization of land owners. Or a government unit could step in and apply the market-simulative rules of public goods (for benefit sharing) and "benefit taxation" (for the financing of shared maintenance or development costs). The choice will mainly hinge on the property owners' willingness to cooperate, instead of extracting freeloader benefits from their neighbors.

The air falls even more clearly into the category of indivisible natural resources, locally, nationally and internationally. So air, and its positive contributions to health and human life, will largely have to be treated as a vast collective good, with an elastic, expansive territorial base. All who breathe are *de facto* members of the global air-interest group. They—we—all have a mutual obligation to keep it breathable and usable for mankind's collective benefit. But only up to a point: it would not be economical to preserve or improve the air beyond the marginal break-even point, where added costs have caught up with added benefits.

This implies a careful balancing of different air uses and air-maintenance activities—industrial, governmental and personal. He who pays shall have the right to use and foul the air—while he who keeps it clean or restores it shall be tax-exempt or commensurately rewarded. Air demands and supplies will then, as much as possible, be subject to the cost and price pressures typical of the competitive market.

It thus seems that, for the foreseeable future, air will normally have to remain a public collective resource, to be managed by governments at various levels. All members of the public should of course retain access to it, but only on the condition that they pay for having destroyed or damaged it. This is the preferable approach to the whole air-pollution question.

The obligation to compensate for air pollution will have several socially beneficial effects. It will discourage unnecessary or low-utility air use that threatens to cause significant pollution; such air use will be too expensive. Moreover, a compensation obligation will induce some air polluters to take antipollutant steps, thereby reducing their pollution fees (or "penalties"). Lastly, the fees that are nevertheless collected can help finance the air's maintenance and purification, so that third parties—the rest of the public—will not suffer.

Existing pollution controls on industrial plants or automobiles already help preserve the quality of American air through prohibitions, fines and obligations for the polluters to pay damages. They seem to protect the general public, as they modify air-use behavior and induce some clean-up. Isn't this the right way to go?

Not entirely. There is a tricky question of how to balance the collective benefits of a cleaner environment and the individual benefits of air use (that happens to pollute). There is a conflict of interest centered on the choice between clean air and the various industrial and consumer benefits obtainable through the absorption of clean air.

In a democratic-individualistic society, we should not take a prejudicial stand in favor of either side. Both types of interest are legitimate, and it is up to government—if it wants to be humanly neutral—to fairly weigh them and strike a cost-effective balance.

The present public-policy approach is much too selective and too punitive. Too little effort is made to assess the general public's air preferences and demands, apart from a glib presumption that everybody wants the air to be as clean as possible. The merits of those demands ought to be compared with those of the added industrial products that could be available through more liberal air pollution rules and milder pollution penalties. The best evidence of clean-air merits would lie in the hypothetical prices that the public would be willing to pay for varying air qualities, and those prices ought to be compared with the price reductions that would otherwise be possible on industrial products that now threaten the air.

Recent U.S. legislation has not generally followed this prescription, and the actions of the Environmental Protection Agency have not either. Instead, selected industrial polluters, including sulfur-emitting coal- or oil-burning power plants, have been forced to pay disproportionately large fines, grossly exceeding the true value of the used-up resources. The approach is pretty much the same one as that prevailing in our entire criminal jurisprudence: Since we can't catch all of the sinners, let's punish those we do catch so much harder. The policy attitude is punitive rather than, as it should be, balancing and accommodative.

Some progress has, however, been made lately in the direction of more cost-effective pollution policies. The federal government is now showing a bit more sensitivity toward the problems created by overzealous environmentalism, and there is more awareness of the costs to the nation.

The Bush administration in 1989 offered a new clean-air bill that, among other things, wants to allow industrial polluters to sell their pollution rights (specified in the law) to other firms. The latter firms will tend to be those with stronger, more economically valid needs for polluting, air-using activities. This would be a welcome reform in that market-based price criteria could be applied in the use of legally "free" air (air without any penalties on its use); air allocation among firms ought therefore to improve.[58]

A similar method has for some time been used in allocating and exchanging air rights among real estate developers in certain urban areas. One developer can purchase high-rise construction rights from another—one with lower skyscraper ambitions—for their mutual benefit. In both cases, the result is a partial privatization of a public resource (air), so that the allocative effects of the private market can be simulated.

Unfortunately, the same approach has not been taken in the regulation of auto emissions: New cars will have to meet rigid emission standards, and manufacturers may have to develop vehicles that use "alternative" fuels (rather than gasoline). Why not allow car buyers to pick and choose among both cars and fuels while paying for the air damage they cause?

A Better, Cost-Effective Approach. To achieve reasonably clean air without distorting the allocation of air resources, the responsible government agencies would have to assess the public's air needs and estimate the cost of air maintenance. They would, in effect, have to determine the fair market "price" of air, as if air was an individual marketable good. That price would then serve to regulate the extent of air consumption, by individual parties and by the nation as a whole.

If the nation, as a whole, should desire cleaner air than existing previously, the estimated air price will have to be adjusted upward. This will discourage uncorrected pollution and restore the missing access to clean air, though at additional industrial costs to the nation. Conversely, greater tolerance of moderate pollution would call for a reduction of that price.

Polluters of scarce clean air (or public ocean water, rivers, etc.) should thus pay fees or taxes that are sufficient to restore the air to its prior state or to compensate the public for its clean air loss, whichever is cheaper. Outright prohibitions of air use should not exist, since they would inflict unnecessary harm on those with the strongest air needs. For example, smokestack industries could offer cash compensation (which many might use for health insurance policies) to the residents of smoke-affected areas. And if they can afford to do this adequately, they should certainly be allowed to continue to operate.

By the same token, perhaps each American should be endowed with a certain amount of initial air rights, measured in cubic feet of air of standardized quality. That right would entitle each one of us to foul a small amount of public air. But it should be matched by an equally shared liability to contribute to public air maintenance. The air right (or "air asset") could then be sold to air-needy and air-using firms, and the proceeds of the sale would be available for free private use.

By separating air assets from air liabilities in this way, the former could be more efficiently allocated among air users. In particular, pollution-prone firms would be able to operate at socially optimal levels, instead of being confined by a rigid antipollution rule or by a rigid air right quota.[59] In turn, air liabilities could be adjusted at regular intervals so that, in the aggregate, their value would match the cost of maintaining the overall quality at the level that the public overall finds cost-effective. They would be raised if the consensus was in favor of cleaner air and lowered in the opposite case.

Public policy should aim at bringing the market value of air assets into equality with publicly assessed liabilities, through more or less air purification efforts. When the right level is reached, an air liability would equal an air asset, thereby squaring the nation's air balance sheet.

The Global Environment. The 1980s saw a great deal of new concern about the quality of the global environment—in particular, the interrelated aspects of the atmosphere, climate and vegetation.

Correcting deficiencies in the physical global environment is now high on the agenda of many industrial-country governments, not to mention the "green" parties that have sprung up all over Western Europe. Many fear that coal burning and chlorofluorocarbon emissions will produce a "greenhouse" effect, especially if the large forests in the southern hemisphere are not saved and allowed to neutralize those emissions. Others note the effects of acid rain, attributed to power plants and autos, on lakes and fish populations.

These concerns should not be snickered at. There is credible evidence of large negative effects on crops, trees, animals, lungs and the esthetic appearance of nature. Some of the effects involve conventional aspects of production, income and wealth; others involve esthetic or sentimental factors (and also deserve a hearing). And the international spillovers and interdependencies are indisputable.

Pollution thus has international dimensions, connected with globally indivisible aspects of the physical environment. This suggests global collective goods that need to be globally maintained or supplied. Yet building international organizations with real clout is notoriously difficult, and economic-political solutions to global environmental problems are difficult to devise.

The scope of the problems is so large that we cannot rely entirely on international private initiative; instead we have to seek better intergovernmental arrangements than have existed so far. When the environmental goods are as extensive and pervasive as the global atmosphere, or much of the earth's ocean water, they are truly in the nature of global public goods. Such goods are, in most of the cited cases, insufficiently provided for. One can therefore recommend that new or existing international agencies be given adequate power to supply the missing goods and to impose the necessary financing charges. One can do so without necessarily falling into a trap of global physical socialism or overcollectivized cross-border environmental management.

But great care would have to be taken so that the new global antipollution measures did not become heavy-handed, rigid and insensitive to true public interests. Excessive controls could do more damage than no controls at all. So far, the record of international policy cooperation and global regulation has not inspired much confidence. The United Nations, with its prevailing anticapitalist proclivities, seems an especially unlikely instrument for global programs built on the **libegalitarian** model.

The possibility for a rational solution is better when the pollution problem is confined to two adjacent countries that are willing to negotiate and bargain with each other. Acid rain is demonstrably traveling across international borders, including the U.S.-Canadian one. It is inflicting substantial environmental damage of a still unmeasurable magnitude. It deserves a policy response, and the two governments have fortunately begun to talk.

Whatever the geographic dimension, the first step—a difficult one—should be to assess the physical properties of the threatened resource, the technological possibilities of maintenance and replenishment, and the market value of each unit (cubic meter, etc.) of the resource to industry or individuals. Most of this work will belong with physicists, biologists and engineers—not with ideologists or economists. So let them proceed (in a cost-effective manner, of course).

The second step should involve an estimate of the true cost to the public of losing access to the resource (or, rather, its different costs in different locations and circumstances)—a kind of opportunity cost. The cost estimate should be based on the resource's aggregate value to the entire public today—ideally, the summation of the values that different individuals put on each unit of the resource.

The third step ought to be an evaluation of the costs of the resource's maintenance and replenishment (normally the private costs of, say, air purification or waste disposal). These private replacement costs could then be compared with the estimated public opportunity cost and the industrial user value. In a true, competitive market situation, all three cost and value measures would coincide, and each party will bear his own cost. This would be the normal equilibrium situation and indicative of perfect resource allocation.

In the fourth step, the responsible international agency ought to determine what steps are needed to assign all the pollution costs to the polluters and to press them to make good, through replenishment or cash compensation to the public. In this way, the air-user beneficiaries will be forced to acknowledge their resource demand and pay the resource's scarcity price (i.e., its opportunity cost) to the public.

Thus power companies and automobile drivers would no longer be allowed to pay a zero air price while the public at large (the bird watchers, the health-conscious breathers) loses full access to a valued public resource. The mispricing would end; cost and price equality, at both the public and the private level, would ensure that just enough of the resource would be used up or would remain for use in the future—just as in a purely private resource market. And public users would then have no reason to object to the remaining, paid-for resource use by utilities or drivers.

Going a step further, one might even look forward to a time when global weather management can become part of the serious international political agenda. After all, good weather is a broad public good with clear international aspects. One can fantasize about each world citizen having certain inborn weather rights that he might wish to trade off for a cost- and value-based market price—for instance, to steel mills, farmers or skiers. Many tough questions would, however, remain: Who should "pay" for hurricanes? What is the proper price of a full solar eclipse? For now let's confine ourselves to somewhat more traditional government policy issues.

Animals. Our natural environment includes animals, plants and various nonliving substances (as well as humans). It is thus almost unavoidable that environmentalists should be concerned about the preservation of animals. And the beauty, or quasihuman qualities, of some animals make it so much easier to mobilize public sympathy for the cause.

There is now a long list of species for which environmental protection is actively sought. The list extends from bald eagles to rhinoceroses, elephants and white pandas to the sea bass in the Hudson River (a critical factor in the long battle over a proposed multilane highway in New York City). Many of them have been given the preferred official status of endangered species. Animal protection has become a fashionable activist cause, with its own priorities and its own political agenda.

What, if any, is the underlying ideological principle behind these concerns? Does nature, as a whole or in part, have rights, to be shared with mankind? Are the rights on a par with human rights, or are they of a lower caliber? Or is a concern for animals simply a selfish expression of interest in special types of public property?

It is hard to find any principled discussions of these questions in the economic-political literature or in the contemporary political debate. Simply asserting that animals have rights, too, is not enough; it begs too many questions about the nature and status of those rights, especially as they are bound to conflict with various human rights. And emotional appeals to our love for cuddly pets or handsome safari creatures will also not substitute for an explanation of the underlying value system, or its public-policy applications.

Animal lovers will of course disagree. Understandably, they will try to translate their special interests into a deeper ethical principle, perhaps turning it into an axiom that is impervious to counterargument. Some of them might even try to formally extend their ethical systems so as to accord a quasihuman status to some or all animals. Or they might be content to push for selective prohibitions.

For instance, the Animal Liberation Front advocates strict vegetarianism, denounces the use of animals for scientific experiments and opposes the wearing of wool clothes. The Swedish government has gone a bit further: It recently adopted an animal bill of rights, with protective provisions for cattle, pigs and chickens. It is hard not to detect an element of egalitarian-progressive policy parody in this action.

The animal rightists ought to be reminded of the scarcity of resources and the unavoidable conflicts that will arise. If we preserve animals for their own sake, we will automatically sacrifice some human rights—for instance, the right to wear baby seal coats, or to eat whale meat, or to decorate our homes with stuffed giraffe heads. We then sacrifice the sovereignty of the human consumer.

And the animal rightists ought to show more appreciation for the baffling questions confronting the ideological theoretician. Which animals should be constitutionally protected? How should the relative interests of hunters, merchants and gourmets be weighed against those of elephants, swans and pigs? What animals may I kill to protect my vegetable garden?

Instead, we might prefer to protect certain animal species as special aspects of man's property, without conceding any primary rights status to those animals (or to vegetables or minerals). Animals are, in many cases, valuable natural resources, not just because they might be commercially useful but simply because some people attach an esthetic or sentimental value to them. Had some people not felt that way, they would of course not have bothered to expend personal resources on advocating the animals' protection. Besides, many animals clearly have particular utility to scientists, as well as to zoo owners and ivory merchants.

Many attractive or exotic animals have both individual- and collective-good features. If they mainly produce public or collective goods, they are usually best kept on generally accessible property, owned by large private organizations (like giraffes in animal preserves) or the general public (like the eagle in the undivided sky). If they, practically, have to be publicly owned, they should be sustained, bred or allowed to multiply as long as the public is willing to pay the costs, via government intermediation. When this becomes too costly, the excess animals will have to be disposed of, in a profit-maximizing fashion.

However, when it is technologically possible to put particular animals in the exclusive hands of their human fans, they will, in effect, slip over into the private- or individual-good category. Such animals should consequently be sold to private parties as part and parcel of the lands where they roam and thrive or as separate pieces of property. Those who want to protect animals for whatever reason will then, individually or collectively, be able to translate this demand into pecuniary equivalents and buy the animals they want. It will then be up to the private owners to decide what to do with the animals—let them be sold commercially, be hunted or be preserved as inventories for future use. The profit-oriented owner-keepers will then be able to strike the best possible balance between conflicting animal-use interests, as expressed in the animal market. The merits of privatization will, again, be obvious.

For those who put people unequivocally first, there can be no special, *a priori* animal rights, for such rights would unfairly give animal lovers a privileged status in society. And to so restrict private use of a marketable resource would be to limit human opportunities.

INDUSTRIAL POLICY

According to both radical-left and much centrist thinking, the private sector of our economy needs considerable government guidance and control. In this view, the private sector is prone to inefficiency and failure, and it should be improved through government intervention. Without substantial government management, private industry is likely to end up producing the wrong mix of goods—"wrong" because the goods don't correspond to the citizens' needs, or perhaps because they could be more cheaply produced, as well as better distributed. Or the private sector in its entirety is producing too little, considering its use of capital and labor.

This line of argument suggests that there is a special kind of national collective good obtainable through government economic management. It would manifest itself through improved national productivity and a larger national product. Somehow this "good" would seem to derive from better national resource use—perhaps a fuller mobilization of managerial or technological expertise or a more efficient allocation of labor or capital among industries or regions. But what does this "good" really consist of, and where does it come from? Why it is not, or could it not be, available to the private sector as well?

Central Planning. The argument is sometimes presented as a case for "planning," sometimes as a case for a national "industrial policy." Both terms deceptively appeal to those with a strong basic faith in government.

Planning, wherever it is undertaken, denotes a deliberate, coordinated deployment of resources, in accordance with a given set of goals. But nothing in this definition, or in the act of planning, suggests that it has to be done by government or that government will perform it better. Planning can occur at any level of decision making, high or low, micro or macro; all it takes is a definition of purposes, some resources that can be used for these purposes and an intelligent application of these resources. Individuals plan; so do households; and so do business firms.

The real question thus cannot be whether governments should plan; everybody with any economic functions should, or he will tend to misuse his resources. The question is, rather, whether the federal government should extend its planning activities beyond the management of the particular public-sector activities assigned to its various departments and agencies—that is, whether it should plan for the private sector as well.

Outside of full-fledged socialist systems, these kinds of policies are, in their most ambitious form, exemplified by long-term government development plans, typically running for five-year periods. Many less-developed countries in Asia and Africa (as well as Eastern bloc countries) have operated under such plans, with elaborate sectoral output goals and programs through which these goals were to be achieved. Such plans were common in the 1950s, 1960s and 1970s, but then began to lose favor in countries that wanted to emulate the market-oriented policies of the leading industrial countries.

The hoped-for results have included a more rapid rate of overall income growth, changes in output composition and a more egalitarian distribution of currently available income. Some of the plan provisions have been imposed through direct operational guidelines on state-run enterprises or government agencies, while others have relied on taxes, regulations or incentives affecting private firms.

Among the many justifications that are offered for government economic planning is the need for broad, economy-wide information about available resources and public needs. Some planners claim that such comprehensive information can best be gathered and exploited through a central, public planning mechanism.

But this argument is fallacious. Information needs vary enormously, and decentralized private firms are actually in a better position to develop or acquire the particular information they need: They are more cost conscious and more selective as a result; and they are closer to the suppliers and customers whose market behavior they need to assess. Anyhow, if the government really possessed unique, useful data, it could sell those data to the private firms that needed them.

The question of central planning should be subordinated to the more general issue of public-good provision. In regard to public goods, the planning question answers itself, in the affirmative; in regard to private collective goods, the answer is largely negative; and in regard to purely individual goods, wholly negative.

More generally, a government that tries to escape the allocative prescriptions of the market mechanism, and the related public-goods rules, will impose efficiency costs on the national economy. If it is striving for particular redistributive results, it might be willing to tolerate those costs—although there will probably be more economical ways of achieving its distributional goals. Without ambitions of this nature, planning, as usually understood, is a mistaken strategy; it is wasteful, and it is distortive.

Ethically and ideologically, planning is incompatible with both the equalization and the maximization of socioeconomic opportunities. It tends to substitute the biased judgment of bureaucrats for the market-driven actions of private firms. Central planners tend to absorb or redirect resources that could be better, and more equitably, "controlled" by the invisible hand of the competitive market. Many individual opportunities will then be diminished or destroyed, both because of particular market interventions and because of planning-induced inefficiencies throughout the economy.

International Trade. One of the aims of contemporary planners is to improve the country's position in world markets. Many planners strive for greater national self-sufficiency, so as to lessen the country's dependence on imported goods and to protect local industries against the vagaries of unstable world markets. To this end, many governments subsidize import-competing industries or restrict the importation of foreign goods through high import tariffs or small import quotas.

Such commercial protectionism typically reflects a lack of confidence in the international market mechanism. It shows a failure to understand that the lost import opportunities will usually be costlier than the gains made through expanded import-competing activity at home. The policy is thus in conflict with opportunity maximization. Protectionists ignore the fact that the voluntary exchange principle is generally as valid internationally as domestically.

At times protectionism may involve a conscious pursuit of goals unrelated to economic efficiency. Perhaps the government wishes to penalize certain trade partners by excluding them from the domestic market or to help particular domestic producers or consumer groups with a great deal of political clout. In the latter cases, our objections should have a different slant: The underlying goals and values violate the principle of equal, non-discriminatory opportunity; they are thus inequitable.

Recent U.S. economic history is replete with examples of such interferences with international trade (although they have rarely been placed directly under the heading of "planning"). Today some of the most prominent, and most counterefficient, examples are the import quotas placed on many agricultural products, to the direct detriment of American consumers. They also include various agreements that our government has with foreign exporter countries to limit their sales to the United States. Thus, under the euphemistic label of "voluntary restraint agreements," American purchases of foreign automobiles, textiles and steel products have been artificially suppressed below their market-preferred levels.

Recent changes in international market conditions, including the huge export success of Japan, have produced a lot of additional public worry about American "competitiveness," with new calls for protection or industrial planning. Many have claimed that the key to competitiveness lies in research and development in high-tech industries, which are believed to become the dominant force in future global trade. High-definition television is a favored example of such industries. Can we "afford" to let the Japanese take the lead there, too?

To begin with, the whole concept of "competitiveness" among nations is very fuzzy. Nations with similar economic structures and production possibilities often compete for global market shares; that is true. But the dominant characteristic of a nation's trade relations with the rest of the world is complementarity (the opposite of competition), and most trade is based on differences (not similarities) in productive capabilities.

The most efficient international trading posture is that of exchanging the products we need the least for those we need the most. This can be done most easily by allowing our producers to make just those items that generate the greatest sales value and buying power for us abroad; this is the old, neoclassical principle of "comparative advantage." Accordingly, it is counterproductive to focus on competition per se—just to prove American competence and to try to "beat" the Japanese or the Germans.

As a nation, we should compete with ourselves by making the economy as efficient and productive as possible. As international traders, we should compete as both sellers and buyers. But this means not a maximum effort to export but an optimal effort to complement our own national output with products purchased from abroad. Optimality can be achieved only if we exploit our international comparative advantages, while readily importing products in which our trading partners have similar advantages. Market competition will normally reveal where those advantages lie—and market competition will allow them to be exploited, without the assist of central planners.

There is no evidence that American comparative advantages reside consistently or primarily in high-tech industries. That kind of evidence could be marshalled only through a detailed investigation of the relative costs of developing and producing high-tech products at home and abroad. These cost relations would have to be compared with similar cost relations in other industries, so that one could identify those industries in which we seem to enjoy the lowest opportunity costs (cost of forgone products of other kinds); and all cost estimates ideally should be corrected for the distortive influences of taxes and regulations. This would be a superhuman statistical job. It is better to let the competitive market sort out these things—while allowing its invisible hand to direct business investments into the most profitable product lines, whether for export or for home market distribution.

On the domestic side of the economy, the United States does not really have a history of ambitious central planning. But Franklin D. Roosevelt's "reconstruction" program in the 1930s meant a sharp policy turn toward such planning, following the previous laissez-faire tradition. Since then many left-leaning politicians and economists have tried to push further in that direction (although the term "industrial policy" is nowadays considered more respectable).

Actually, we have today, in the United States, a broad range of government policies and programs that serve a variety of purposes related to industrial development. Looked upon in isolation, they may seem helpful, rather than destructive, especially when they ostensibly subsidize particular industries. But there will always be a trade-off among conflicting interests, and ideologically we have no reason to take sides, among industries or among consumer groups.

The U.S. Farm Program. The most far-reaching set of industrial policies in the United States today are those connected with agriculture. These programs have, over the last decade, fortunately come under more public scrutiny. Recent administrations have tried to scale them down considerably, both because of growing awareness of their weaknesses and because of pressure to reduce the federal budget deficit. But little has come of these efforts.

The main features of the U.S. agricultural program have been price and income support, provided in various forms: subsidized government loans; government purchases of surplus production that cannot be sold at the official target prices; cash or in-kind subsidies to farmers who restrict their acreage under cultivation, and steep tariff or quota barriers against imported farm goods. The programs pertain primarily to grains, soybeans, dairy products, tobacco and sugar.

There is clear evidence that these policies have stimulated severe over-production, resulting in huge government stockpiles of surplus commodities. At the same time, they have reduced the incentives for inefficient farmers to shift into other crops, other farming methods or different, nonfarming pursuits.

The U.S. farm program indeed helps many farmers, especially in the short run. But it does so at a large, multibillion dollar cost to the taxpayers.[60] It is also a big, incalculable burden on the consumer, who has to pay inflated prices in the grocery store or may be deprived of his favorite varieties of imported cheese or meat as a result. The program is, economically and ideologically, a disgrace. It noticeably lessens the total American economic pie, while driving a wide and costly wedge between consumers and producers. It has no credible economic, nutritional or ethical rationale.[61]

In particular, the farm program lacks a solid collective-goods justification. One might possibly argue that we have to be able to feed ourselves without foreign help; we might therefore have to sustain an inflated farm sector that could fill our food needs even during the next world war. But existing support policies go much beyond any such international insurance requirements—which, anyhow, have not been clearly established. Realistically it could only be a matter of short-term emergency supplies. We would only need enough supplies to tide us over until the crisis has receded or domestic production has been adequately sped up. And it could comfortably be arranged through private inventories.

Especially in regard to grains and tobacco, U.S. farmers can boast of providing large export revenues to the nation. Yet this, too is a false indicator of benefits due to the farm program: The labor and capital used up in producing the exported commodities would probably have been able to produce more in other industries, for export or for domestic consumption. Allowing this to happen would require free, competitive trade, without costly subsidies or distortive controls.[62]

Autos. Auto manufacture is still one of the pillars of the traditional American assembly-line industry, and its international performance is often seen as a symbol of American competitiveness. But Japanese car makers have obviously been more adept at anticipating changing buyer preferences and reducing production costs, and they have sharply eroded the American dominance of the home market. Government policymakers have been called upon to set things straight.

As a result, the international auto market has been significantly distorted by foreign, as well as American, policies. The Japanese government has allowed itself to be pressured into imposing maximum quotas on auto shipments to the United States. By reducing the number of Japanese cars available to American buyers, it has, in effect, pushed up Japanese car prices in the United States very substantially. This means that a foreign government and the U.S. government have been conspiring with U.S. manufacturers to rob American car buyers of substantial wealth and well-being.

Conceivably, in the mid 1980s one could claim that the large American demand for foreign autos was largely the result of the inflated value of the U.S. dollar, which cheapened imports, and the high value of the dollar was, in turn, due to an excessive government budget deficit in the United States—a complex, but not implausible, explanation. If this reasoning is valid, the strong dollar could be said to have imposed a large collective "bad" on our import-competing industries, including autos.

The damage could possibly have been undone through an across-the-board compensatory import tariff, perhaps coupled with a matching ac-ross-the-board export subsidy—although this would have set a danger-ous international precedent. At best, this would have been a temporary, partial corrective while the dollar was out of line and subject to removal when the dollar strengthened later on. Even in the short run, the prefera-ble remedy would have been revision of U.S. budget policy that could have helped correct the value of the dollar, without interference with pri-vate trade transactions.

For the long term, the ideological norm should be to let the private sec-tor plan on its own and let private risk taking run its course, unobstructed by government intervention. Exceptions should be made only to the ex-tent required by the production of national collective goods (as for na-tional defense or environmental purposes). This is the **libegalitarian** ap-proach.

Industrial policy is a poor solution to "problems" that do not exist, ex-cept in the form of unavoidable scarcities, or that have been created by the government itself. It is usually a step in the wrong direction, toward more distortions in the productive efficiency of the private economy.[63]

MACROECONOMIC STABILIZATION

There is a fairly common perception that private market economies are inherently unstable. This is what many macroeconomic textbooks tell us. Most of the media seem to agree—or so it seems, judging from the exaggerated newspaper and television alarm over short-term swings in fi-nancial markets and in the performance of the national economy. The Oct-ober 1987 stock market crash might also be taken as partial proof of financial and economic fragility. The crash seemed like a heaven-sent anticapitalist argument until the steady, prolonged market recovery in 1988–89 suggested differently.

The market's instability allegedly manifests itself in large cyclical swings in the aggregate production level, the extend of unemployment and the rate of inflation. It leads to a pattern of boom, slowdown, depression and gradual recovery. Socially the most painful imbalance is severe unemployment, especially when it reaches depression or deep-recession proportions.

Moreover, because of cyclical downturns, the economy may grow much more slowly over time than it would if it followed a full-employment, full-capacity path. Living standards, and the opportunities connected with them, will therefore not improve as fast as should be possible. Granted, the amplitude of the business cycle seems to have been reduced over the last few decades, unemployment has fallen, and the number of persons holding jobs has increased markedly. But we have instead seen a permanent slowing of productivity growth—very possibly, the "price" of getting closer to full employment.

This is not just a Marxist caricature of the doomed capitalist system, but a summary of rather conventional views in western industrial societies. It does not, however, have a convincing basis in economic theory, nor has it been credibly verified by empirical studies. Rather, the perception of market instability and failure is mostly based on a careless reading of ambiguous evidence, spanning the Great Depression in the 1930s and the "stagflation" of the 1970s and early 1980s. But the case histories are replete with misguided government policy actions that very likely contributed to the observed economic problems.

The Case for Activism. The market failure theory has provided ready made arguments for corrective government actions, usually described as "stabilization policies." The government, it is felt, must step in to prevent or offset the worst imbalances in the private sector. It should smooth out the private business cycle, raising the levels of employment and capacity utilization in recession- or depression-prone periods.

Successful macroeconomic stabilization would promise both to reduce immediate human economic suffering and to raise the longer run growth in incomes, wealth and consumption opportunities. The government seems to have a large number of powerful policy tools at its disposal—fiscal and monetary tools, which might be supplemented by trade and regulatory tools. It would seem grossly wasteful not to use these tools, especially if the benefits of their use can be almost universally shared. Perhaps these benefits are in the nature of public goods?

A great deal of skepticism is in order and not just because the policy prescriptions may strike us as collectivist and statist. In fact, belief in the

U.S. macroeconomic management peaked in the 1960s and has declined steadily since—perhaps a sign of a collective learning process. Hardly anybody speaks of governmentally "fine-tuning" the economy any more; that would sound presumptuous.

Government action to change the course of the economy will almost by necessity have to be coercive to be effective. People will have to be nudged to engage in economic activities that they otherwise would have refrained from, through incentives and disincentives of some kinds. Some social critics may retort that this is exactly what is needed: Private businesses are often too ignorant or short sighted to know what to do, so perhaps they need a helping government hand. On the other hand, the government cannot easily tailor its macro policies to the shifting circumstances of firms, workers, investors or consumers; it does not possess any special expertise in performing such complex tasks.

Aggressive macroeconomic policy does not square with the freedom of voluntary exchange or with the efficiency rules for private- and public-good production. Many of the goods that macroeconomic policymakers want to create are in the nature of individual, not public, goods; and such goods (e.g., in the areas of health care, pensions and education) are best produced through private economic transactions, regardless of the state of the business cycle—in other words, at the micro level. Collective goods are of course another matter, especially if they are so broadly desired that they qualify as public.

Herein lies the crux of the macroeconomic policy problem: Can broad macroeconomic management be justified on public good grounds? Can it be justifiably argued that fiscal and monetary policies produce public goods in the form of higher overall incomes, more jobs or, in other circumstances, greater price stability?

Fiscal Policy. Take the case of an incipient recession, when the government is trying to pump up spending to increase jobs and incomes. The administration, with the assistance of Congress, initiates new spending programs, perhaps through more generous health-care or family assistance, or through weapons development or environmental protection measures; it may also lower tax rates. And the Federal Reserve, with a similar purpose in mind, may engineer an increase in available credit and in the existing supply of money.

In the first instance, the government may then create both some new public-sector jobs and thereby produce benefits to certain members of the public. Old-line Keynesian macroeconomists will regard these benefits as nearly costless, since most of the newly hired workers might otherwise have been unemployed; thus their opportunity cost will be zero. So the policy will seem effective and harmful to nobody.

175

But most contemporary economists will admit that there is a considerable risk of offsetting side effects. As the government covers its added deficit by borrowing in the private capital market, it encroaches on the financing available to private parties. Those who are thereby "crowded out" of the credit market will suffer a loss of spending, investment and income opportunities. In this sense, the "idle" resources mobilized by the government are not free, after all; there is thus no free lunch of the kind suggested. Deficit spending redistributes, as much as, or more than, it creates; this is now rather well understood.

Many had hoped that countercyclical deficits would be self-correcting, as they would produce higher incomes and thereby larger government tax revenues. In this way, most of the unfavorable consequences for the credit markets would be avoided. Experience has not generally borne out that hope.

Expansionary fiscal policies that concentrate on government spending increases have been even more detrimental: They have shifted additional resources and activity over to the public sector and to subsidized private sectors. That shift has tended to reduce overall economic efficiency, while unfairly rearranging economic opportunities again and again. One source of such distortions it the growing government debt that will have to be repaid some day through tax collection—a delayed encroachment on the private sector's own spending opportunities.

Growing budget deficits in the 1970s and 1980s led to a huge buildup in the federal debt, above and beyond the rate of growth in the whole economy or in the general price level. It gradually became apparent, even to fiscal activists, that this buildup might "overtax" the financial market's ability to absorb such debt; the more government bonds the public is asked to hold, the fewer private debt instruments it is likely to want to take on—to the detriment of businesses in need of borrowed funds. In that way, government also has to subject itself to the discipline of the market. This is, anyhow, something it always ought to do.

While public finance is mostly thought of as a macroeconomic matter, it clearly has a "micro" dimension as well. The big macro picture is actually nothing more than a statistical summation of a large number of micro pictures—and these are the ones that really matter from an individualistic perspective. There is no such thing as macro human welfare, despite what many macroeconomists and policymakers have tried to tell us. The summed-up economic consequences for all the citizens tell us little or nothing about the fate of the affected individuals.

Consider, for instance, a fiscal policy shift in the expansionary direction. New public spending or a broad tax cut can indeed lead to a short-term increase in business activity and employment, as the policymakers wish.

Yet the newly hired workers' net gain will often be much smaller than indicated by their new incomes, because they lose some of their leisure and opportunities for work outside the organized labor market (e.g., in the home). Moreover, if many new jobs are created in a particular industry (one especially affected by the new spending), other private businesses will have greater difficulties in filling upcoming job vacancies—forcing a change in the relative supplies of particular goods and services. Labor scarcities might then lead to new upward wage pressure in certain sectors, with secondary effects on shareholder profits and property values.

Very often the expansionary policy move will then in due course overstimulate—and require a policy reversal. The business cycle will then be aggravated, rather than alleviated. It is actually quite possible that misguided "stabilization" policies have, perversely, been a main cause of business cycles. In any case, each fiscally induced distortion tends to redistribute and reallocate, at the ultimate expense of efficiency and equity at many micro levels.

The Preferable System. What we now call fiscal policy should essentially be abolished. We ought instead to have a benefit-and-cost based program of spending, taxation, and borrowing, with each spending proposal evaluated on its own public-good merits. The policymakers should concern themselves with what each spending program can achieve in terms of public-good production and how it could be financed by letting the beneficiaries foot the bill.

We should stop looking at the government's aggregate spending level and aggregate tax revenues as policy targets in themselves. We should abandon the sweeping macro view that diverts attention from the merits and costs of individual programs; a combination of unworthy programs can never be worthy as a totality, and a failure to carry out worthwhile programs can never be corrected simply by adjusting total government spending to a "desirable" level. To escape the term's unfortunate present-day connotations, we ought perhaps to stop talking about "fiscal policy" altogether. Instead, we might concentrate our attention on matters of "government programming," "public program execution," "federal program financing"—and the resulting "private-sector resource deprivation."

With respect to the financing of legitimate government programs, the fundamental choice is between taxation and borrowing. This should entirely be a question of timing—the timing of the public's benefits from the programs to be financed. The rule should be: Government spending for immediate national consumption purposes ought to be tax- (or fee-) financed immediately by those who benefit from it; but spending with delayed benefits ought to be paid for, through taxes, when these benefits actually materialize. In particular, government spending for national collective goods ought to be debt-financed whenever their benefits are delayed beyond the current year. The spending is then in the nature of investment, to be financed in the same way as it normally would have been done by a responsible business firm.

The "current" budget should thus always be balanced, with no over- or undercharging of the programs' beneficiaries. Today's beneficiaries will then no longer be able to simply transfer the costs to future taxpayers, through a theft-like mortgaging of the latter's prospective incomes. The "capital" budget, showing the government's investment accounts and the associated financial transactions, will, by contrast, normally not be balanced, at least not the way "balance" is now construed.

Public investments should be financed by borrowings—most easily through bond issues. The bond issues should be structured so that repayments will be due when the actual benefits—the investment returns to the public—are expected to materialize. The capital budget should thus be fully debt financed. But each year it will show tax receipts of a magnitude that matches that year's debt repayments—i.e., repayments of borrowings connected with projects that are still productive and thus not fully depreciated; the repayments will include both amortization of principal and interest. Such a capital budget will almost always be unbalanced in the traditional, cash-based sense; yet it could be regarded as "balanced" under a more sensible, normative interpretation.

If public investment is on a strong uptrend, most years will then tend to show a deficit in the capital budget as fresh borrowing will exceed repayments on old borrowings. This deficit will be stimulatory only in the same sense as the investment spending of a large, growing business firm: It will attract some resources from the rest of the economy—as it should. But this result will be based on the budget's project-specific merits, not on countercyclical investments in substandard projects.

Many governments in Europe and Asia have adopted fiscal systems that attempt to follow this dual-budget principle, or a "pay-as-you-get" system of public finance. Yet they have not tried very hard to match the maturities of newly issued government bonds with the maturities of the associated benefits. Recently a number of American economists have proposed that the U.S. government also move toward separate capital budgeting—a first step toward greater fiscal rationality and reduced public hysteria over the "deficit," as now construed.[64]

If the U.S. government adopted this budget approach, it could no longer adjust the deficit just to manipulate the overall level of demand or the resulting level of economic activity; and this would be a healthy constraint on the administration and Congress. Experience shows that such efforts are not very successful even in the short run. In the long run, they tend to create cumulative distortions on the capital markets, on the nation's international balance of payments and on the allocation of resources between the public and the private sectors.

An overactive use of fiscal policy for stabilization purposes has created serious inefficiencies and inequities in our national economy. Deficit spending in excess of true government investment needs has cut into private investment that would have contributed more to national productivity. And taxpayers have unfairly had to pay the overdue bills for projects that matured a long time ago, for the benefit of an earlier generation that they may not even have met. The results of fiscal activism have been costly and inequitable.

Monetary Policy. Some of the same reservations and criticisms also apply to monetary policy. Both policy branches have been used extensively for the dubious purpose of managing aggregate demand. Monetary policy has sometimes been allowed to concentrate on stabilizing the price level, while fiscal policy has been assigned to controlling employment and economic growth. But the two policy branches are much too intertwined to permit such a clear separation of purpose.

Monetary policy has traditionally been carried out through control (by the Federal Reserve authorities) over bank credit and demand deposits or over the entire "money supply" (which includes coins, notes and, by some definitions, other types of bank deposits as well). Through such control, the Federal Reserve is believed to be able to prevent an inflationary excess (or an economically depressing shortage) of money. Is price stability, then, a public good worthy of government attention? And could or should it be achieved through the kind of monetary policy controls we now have?

The answers seem to be a tentative yes and a no. A stable money value is indeed a kind of broad collective good: It can facilitate trade and financial planning; it can make financial contracts more reliable—and these are beneficial results for the whole national economy. But this does not necessarily mean that government authorities ought to control the amount of money in circulation, for doing so interferes with private economic activity in many unacceptable ways. Monetary freedom should not be sacrificed on the altar of price stability.

Consider the typical consequences. If, in a recession, people get access to an expanded amount of money and credit, they will usually spend more freely, for the moment. The new spending may mobilize some of the seemingly idle resources and produce higher recorded incomes and more jobs. But the newly added money will upset the balance between money (and other financial assets) and physical assets in the economy, sooner or later forcing their price relationships to change. The value and price of money will fall, while the money prices of real assets go up—and of course, this describes inflation.

The inflation will impoverish those who were already holding financial assets with fixed interest rates. But interest rates on new financial assets will begin to rise so that lenders will be compensated for the declining value of money. The same will happen to yields on debt instruments (bonds, in particular) that are repriced (downward) through sales in the secondary markets. The increased interest rates will discourage some of the new credit-financed spending that might be contemplated.

The monetarily induced expansion of spending can thus affect both the price level and, temporarily, economic activity. But the authorities cannot foresee how the effects will be distributed between prices and activity, nor how soon the effects will emerge.

Monetary policy today suffers from two awkward problems. One, it gets entangled with fiscal policy inasmuch as fiscal deficits create special pressures for monetary expansion, which facilitates the deficits' financing; monetary policy is then not allowed to concentrate on its most natural function, price stability. Two, monetary policy cannot easily be executed without creating sectoral distortions and inequities—almost like an arbitrary set of taxes or controls. Is there an ideologically respectable way out?

Toward a New Monetary Control System. The crux of the matter is that "money" really means two different things. One is the standard unit in which we measure prices and values (a yardstick that indicates economic importance). The other refers to the type of asset with which we can make payments and discharge debts—essentially, cash. In the first sense, a dollar resembles an inch or a liter. In the second, it is a kind of IOU issued by banks (in the form of deposits) or the government (in the form of bills or coins) and intended to be used as a common medium of exchange. The two aspects of money need to be distinguished, or monetary policy might be seriously misdirected.

A steady, well-known unit of value appears to be a true public good. It permits firmer, better understood valuation, and it helps make the monetary aspects of contracts clearer and more definite. Therefore its "production" might well be entrusted to government. Besides, production of a reliable monetary unit can be almost costless, so the risk of a maldistribution of the costs will be very small.

So one should not object to a scheme under which the federal government decided how much a dollar is really worth; this would meet our public good criterion. But how could it do so without resorting to control of money and credit? By confining its monetary control to the unit-of-account function.

The government could simply announce that a "dollar" from now on will be worth perhaps a certain quantity of gold or silver. Or—even better—it could construct a "basket" of regularly traded commodities of homogeneous quality, with a fixed allotment of each (for example, a certain amount of steel, plus a certain amount of wheat, plus a certain amount of crude oil, plus a certain amount of cotton, etc.), and declare that the basket is, by definition, worth $1,000. The commodity basket should be broad enough so that it will be representative of the products used, directly or indirectly, by nearly everybody in the economy; that would make it more relevant and more indicative to all of us.

Once the unit has been defined, financial instruments denominated in it would appear on the market (issued, most likely, by banks). Some of those instruments would be usable for payment purposes; they would serve the same purposes as checks today. But the amounts and characteristics of such contracts would be determined solely by the private market; monetary policy would have no role in these matters. Yet to make the unit fully credible, the authorities might have to be prepared to redeem certain instruments (e.g., all insured checks or bills of a certain minimum value) in equivalent amounts of actual commodities.

Conceivably a similar stable money unit could be created through private collective action. But this presumes that a sufficiently large number of parties agreed on the scheme, stuck with it—and convinced the markets that the agreement would not break down. Thus one might envision a broad-based agreement among banks, securities firms and other corporations that defined a "dollar" through a similar commodity basket. Once known and accepted throughout the economy, this dollar would presumably be invoked in most private contracts, so that payments stipulated to be made in it became enforceable in court.[65]

If either public or private initiative produced a "dollar" along these lines, inflation could become virtually impossible. Nobody would need to be cheated out of real value as long as he had relied on the common, value-stable money unit. Those who wanted to obtain securities, bank deposits or salary contracts with fixed real values could indeed do so; they would no longer be at the mercy of the value uncertainty and value erosion that now results from erratic inflation.

But even with governmentally defined money, banks could be free to set their own loan and deposit policies, unregulated by the Federal Reserve. The government would not need to, and should not, regulate those private transactions. Doing so is a violation of the banks' right to voluntary exchange. And such market interferences inflict inefficiencies and inequities on both the banks and the borrowing, and depositing, public.

Banks, or other financial institutions, should not be subject to government controls not applied elsewhere in the economy. That is blatantly discriminatory and violates the neutrality principle that would govern the **libegalitarian** system. They should be allowed to make the amounts and kinds of loans that are consistent with their own long-run profit interests—which depend on their credibility and their ability to honor their loan and deposit contracts with the public. Banks would become as safe as the public wanted them, given the costs of safety. And, of course, if depositors insisted on insurance, banks would respond by taking out such insurance, while passing on the insurance costs to their depositors. This is how the private market should and would work in a properly deregulated financial system.[66]

In short, monetary policy should no longer be a government task, apart from the provision of a stable monetary unit. Discretionary monetary and fiscal policies—under which the government judges the economy's needs from season to season, and year to year, and adjusts its programs accordingly—should both be removed from the list of government functions.

The market instabilities we observe in almost all economies are, to a large extent, the perverse result of misguided government stabilization efforts. A **libegalitarian** economy would probably also exhibit some instabilities. But they would merely be a healthy sign of freely made market choices and constructive reallocations of resources.

Chapter VII
THE "LIBEGALITARIAN" SOCIETY

THE STRUCTURE OF RIGHTS

Political ideologies can be characterized by the rights they assign to different socioeconomic groups. Ideologies are, pre-eminently, formulas for rights distribution.

In a perfectly totalitarian dictatorship, all rights have, by definition, been confiscated by the central leader. That he cannot, in practice, control all aspects of social life is a different matter. Also, the fact that he may need to provide most people with a certain minimum amount of sustenance services, just to keep them producing for him, is secondary—it is not indicative of any true social rights. Rather, each person is at the mercy of the ruler's personal preferences, tempered only by the practical difficulties and costs of satisfying those preferences.

In nontotalitarian societies, the rights picture tends to be more complex. If rights are to be reasonably stable, predictable and enforceable, they will need to be laid out in an accessible public document—a social contract, or a constitution. In time, the constitution may seem to be the very source of those rights. It becomes not just the medium, but also the message.

A national constitution can assign rights in two alternative ways—by listing those that are to be granted or by specifying those that are being denied. Theoretically either method could be used in setting up a complete system of rights, with clear rights assignments for every conceivable social conflict situation.

But our language is not quite perfect enough to allow this result. And legislators are usually not willing to go that far anyway. Obscure language can make it easier for special-interest groups to reinterpret the constitution in their own favor. Apart from this political reality, constitutional precision is made difficult by the conceptual ambiguities of the underlying values and principles. Moreover, it is difficult to get broad support for specific constitutional provisions as long as the public does not have a good understanding of their ideological and programmatic implications.

Three Basic Categories. Where specific individual constitutional rights exist, or are denied, they will tend to fall into three main categories: rights to *own*, right to *do* and rights to *receive*. This taxonomy is a good starting point for ideological comparisons.

The right to *ownership* is subject to a variety of restrictions in different societies. The essential reality behind ownership is resource control or disposition. Ownership rights concern the degree and circumstances in which various types of resources are placed in private, rather than governmental, hands.

In regard to a person's human capital, restrictions on resource control and on the exercise of ownership rights tend to be especially obnoxious. They strike at the heart of our immediate, private existence. Luckily they are difficult to enforce, as long as we have a modicum of privacy, a personally managed home and some labor market access.

The most extreme example in which ownership of human capital is denied (except through execution) is slavery. Of course, it entails a nearly complete absence of personal control over one's whereabouts and activities and hence over the employment of one's talents and skills. On a more moderate scale, a military draft entails a temporary loss of similar resource control—in effect, a confiscation of muscle and brain power, in exchange for mediocre, nonnegotiable compensation.

Apart from these special examples, the right to human-capital ownership is reasonably secure in the western world today. Still, income taxes can undermine that right, and so can business or consumer regulations (e.g., by reducing the human-capital returns embodied in particular consumption opportunities).

More complex issues arise with regard to ordinary (nonhuman) physical or financial assets and the right to draw benefits from them. All fully socialist systems categorically deny their citizens the individual right to own such resources. These are, of course, collective national property. Consider the Soviet peasant without land of his own. Even though he presumably draws some worker benefits that can be traced to publicly owned land, these benefits convey zero ownership control for him. So in no meaningful sense does he have any land ownership "rights."

In modern western democracies, the rights to own nonhuman capital are clearly much more extensive. But let us not forget the many limitations that exist. Some European countries long ago expropriated the lavish estates that used to belong to the aristocracy. Much land in the United States is under public control and unavailable for private ownership, including most sea shores and many mountain areas. Many types of businesses are outlawed, here and abroad. In much of Western Europe, private ownership of cigarette factories, brandy distilleries, railroads or electical utilities is impossible.

The United States is a bit more liberal in this regard; but many localities forbid personal ownership of casinos or firearms (as well as addictive drugs). Gold bullion ownership was outlawed until recently in the United States. Local zoning ordinances can disallow the right to own tall buildings or specific types of commercial establishments in particular neighborhoods. And some animals must not, by law, be in any individual's possession. Prohibitions such as these have made noticeable dents in the American structure of ownership rights.

Real estate taxes in the United States can be viewed in two different ways. When they simply serve as substitutes for taxes on rental income, they may not produce any special, added ownership limitations (other than those that might be embedded in the entire income tax system). But when real estate levies go beyong the general level of income taxation, they become *de facto* taxes on real estate wealth per se and hence a special encroachment on real estate ownership.

However, the value of ownership stems from the assets' potential use and from their productivity to their current and prospective owners. I wish to own, either because my assets will produce direct benefits for me, or because my assets, or products derived from them, can be sold to others who in turn will benefit. All economical use of a tangible asset is in the nature of production, and production paves the way for beneficial consumption—these are just basic definitional relationships. Since to produce is to "do," the right to *do* is essentially the right to engage in a productive activity, through the use of needed assets or resources.

Restrictions on what we may do can have roughly the same consequences as restrictions on what we can own. The prohibition on growing marijuana sharply lessens the value of land with little other economical use, especially if the landowner has strong expertise and interest in that pursuit. Bans on seal hunting reduce the potential returns on seal hunters' investments in hunting equipment or hunting skills, even though there may be no restrictions on owning such resources per se.

185

New York City's rent controls severly impinge on the right to own and profitably operate apartment buildings in that overregulated city. Throughout the nation, numerous business regulations prohibit us from owning firms that operate contrary to government standards—in effect, prohibiting ownership of physical assets with particular characteristics. Many such regulations obviously restrict the rights of stockholders and entrepreneurs to pursue their chosen endeavors, and their loss of rights is reflected in reduced income and wealth. This list also includes business taxes in excess of cost-based fees for government services received.

All these production restrictions are economically equivalent to a full or partial expropriation of private assets. While the restrictions might not be severe enough to stop us from owning particular assets, they clearly reduce the benefits of so doning. Their effect is to diminish the capital embodied in those assets, pushing us to look for other, less desirable assets instead.

Rights limitations of these kinds, as well as prohibitions of behavior that is considered immoral or unhealthy, have long enjoyed wide popular and political support in the United States. Many of the restrictions are simply taken for granted, as if no sane, responsible person ought to expect to enjoy the proscribed rights. Support for such rights limitations comes from both conservatives and liberals, in varying degrees; only the diehard libertarians escape this charge. This applies to a wide range of controls on what is going on in factories, retail stores, banks and homes—affecting each of us as workers, investors, borrowers, entrepreneurs and consumers. The list of denied rights to do is a very long one.

Rights to *receive* are unrequited acquisition rights—rights to obtain, not through exchange or production, but through gifts. These purported rights are perhaps best described by the notion of "entitlements," or unilateral claims to government-provided benefits. For example, many feel that each of us, or at least the poorer among us, have a right to decent food, shelter, schooling, medical care and a minimum pension, at public expense.

Rights to receive are mostly based on a primitive type of egalitarianism—the kind that tries to reduce some of the apparent gaps in income or consumption levels. But they also have pretensions of social cost-effectiveness: We all "deserve" to receive certain basic goods—in part so that we will not feel excessive envy (which may trigger social instability), in part so that we will be healthy enough to work and pay taxes (and not to have to steal.) Much of that "desert" is established through "means tests" and criteria for "need" that are only loosely related to true differences in lifetime opportunity.

When Ronald Reagan spoke approvingly of the social safety net, even he seemed to invoke rights of this kind. Of course, such rights have a flip side: The taxpayers will be stuck with nonrights to retain that portion of their incomes that goes into sustaining the entitlement programs; and the general public may suffer even more because of the negative effects on the recipients' incentives to work, save and maintain their health.

The "Libegalitarian" Approach. So how should we characterize our proposed **libegalitarian** system in these respects?

Needless to say, a fundamentally individualistic system must offer a very broad range of rights to each member of society, and these rights must be completely nondiscriminatory. The only constraint on an individual's right will stem from the requirement of full mutuality, without which the system would lose its interpersonal neutrality. Hence each person will have unlimited rights to define and carry out his lifetime amibitions, in all facets of his socioeconomic behavior—as long as he does not thereby infringe on the like rights of others.

Arguments to the effect that some persons' existence may be offensive to others should, of course, carry no official weight; they would contradict the underlying mutuality requirement. There should be no law disfavoring or favoring anybody on account of his race, gender, appearance or age, nor, per se, because of his profession, residence, marital status or habits. Special taxes or controls on dentists, Texans, widows or pipe smokers would be antithetical to our individualistic doctrine.

All the same, each person must have the right to express his own preferences in these, as well as all other, matters, provided he does so in a noncoercive way. He may express those preferences freely in the marketplace for ideas; yet he may not force anybody to listen to him by unilaterally appropriating communications media (e.g., airwaves) or by otherwise violating the property rights of others. By the same token, each person should be able to trade any private goods or services with whomever he wishes, on voluntarily agreed terms. He must have the right to judge for himself the merits of each possible deal, and to personally decide whom to trade with.

If a person's market transactions reveal any sort of bias in his selection of trading partners, that bias is to be officially tolerated—though it might be widely condemned in the private marketplace for ethical standards. Such biases should not be construed as attacks on anybody's basic human or civil rights. Instead they should be regarded as legitimate expressions of market demand or supply—a reflection of personal buyer or seller choice in the social game of market competition.

The **libegalitarian** ideology is also completely supportive of ownership rights, as long as they are mutually reconciled. No resource category must be disallowed from private possession. Each of us should be allowed to own any type or amount of any physical, financial or intangible asset as long as it has been legitimately acquired, through personal effort (read: production), voluntary exchange or private donation. No type of resource ownership can be outlawed, for some individuals would then be singled out for discriminatory treatment. Such extensive ownership rights would go well beyond those that satisfy other ideological camps, including the social-liberal wealth redistributors and the environmental conservationists, not to mention the antiproperty Marxists.

A **libegalitarian** (or a libertarian, for that matter) cannot flatly prohibit anybody from owning koala bears, unlicensed breweries, beautiful lakes, Colombian artifacts or firms that "monopolistically" (but without government protection or privilege) dominate their industries. Nor can there reasonably be any upper limit on permissible personal wealth or any special penalties on successful wealth accumulators (as through disproportionately large tax obligations).

Asset ownership, and asset control, is a key ingredient of a free society, and selective limitations on it are clearly inequitable. No existing or conceivable asset will ever be so important, or so dangerous, that it could not rightfully be made available for sale and for individual ownership. If somebody could afford to buy Manhattan, by all means let him do so. Both he and all the sellers among us would probably be better off as a result—that is the overwhelmingly typical result of voluntary exchange.

The **libegalitarian** right to do—to act and produce, socially and economically—is equally broad and general. Basically, everybody should be free to act, as long as he respects the like rights of others, along with their rights to property and voluntary exchange. No activity should officially be illegitimate, however objectionable a majority might find it. This rule might initially strike many as overly liberal or dangerous; but let them shut their eyes and minds if they cannot stand the sight or thought of it.

The right to do—to use or dispose of a resource—presumes a clear delineation of personal property; this is a *sine qua non* of an individualistic social system. One important consequence is that, with property arrangements fully in place, no environmental curbs on private activities will ever make sense. There will always be a legitimate owner, whether an individual or a group organization, with a full right to dispose of the property, by selling or not selling. And clear property lines will give society a better handle on what really should constitute a crime: All crimes can then be subsumed under the concept of property infringement, or theft, and they can be stripped of their irrelevant moral connotations.

Respect for ownership and voluntary exchange is incompatible with all wasteful government activities—those that do not meet public-good criteria. Excessive public-sector production unnecessarily reduces the value of the nation's total resources, through pressures on resource availability to the private sector and on taxpayers. Nor should there be any tax levies that go beond the costs of financing legitimate public goods—which, by definition, provide cost-effective benefits to each taxpayer.

These principles, moreover, preclude any redistributionist taxation programs and deny any associated rights claims. The **libegalitarian** ideology thus has no room for rights to receive without a *quid pro quo*, either through underpayment of legitimate taxes or through pure unilateral transfers. Of course, gratis receipts are ethically acceptable as long as they are truly voluntary gifts by the other, private party. But receipts from the government, i.e., from the taxpayers, are not: Taxpayers are practically incapable of unanimous giving, and governmental redistribution is intrinsically coercive.

When the government makes handouts, it is engaging in collective embezzlement of taxpayer money, a type of theft. This "right" must be rejected, given our ideological premises. Neither proverty, nor poor health, nor other circumstances should suffice for overthrowing that rule.

But what about children and their rights to an adequate, ultimately productive upbringing? Isn't this a big unilateral gift from the rest of society? Not if we adopt the **libegalitarian** child-development approach: coupling the right to a standard-quality upbringing with a financing scheme that lets the beneficiaries themselves repay the costs. This provision removes any true gift element from the services a child obtains through his schooling and care.

Herein lies the biggest difference between the **libegalitarian** brand of egalitarianism and that of the social liberals. When the latter want to give children substantial rights to educational resources, they construe these transfers as gifts, without repayment obligations. They will then have to finance these resource transfers through theft-like taxes on the productive members of the adult generation, thus violating the property rights of latter. The difference is not merely semantic—it bespeaks two sharply different standards of lifetime equity.

Another ideological difference involves the social-liberal urge to give grown-ups the right to qualify for continuous income support, year after year (and the resulting systemic moral hazard, both to the government's budget and to the structure of economic opportunities). The public's "obligation" to accommodate those purported rights is another illegitimate encroachment on taxpayer rights and is inconsistent with **libegalitarian** values.

In short, the social-liberal society is geared toward cultivating the rights to receive, at the expense of the rights to own and to do. By contrast, the **libegalitarian** system is geared toward restoring and sustaining the mutual rights to resource acquisition, ownership and use, thereby facilitating the maximization of individual opportunities. The system endows each person with rights for life, rather than modifying his initial rights in response to his economic behavior over time. And those rights are broad and general, rather than discriminatorily linked to specific market situations, income levels or circumstances.

GAINERS AND LOSERS

Ideological reform is inevitably redistributive; all comprehensive socioeconomic changes are. Some people will be better off under the new regime, while others will be worse off, compared with the status quo.

The only conceivable exceptions to this rule involve reforms that are guaranteed to improve economic efficiency and, at the same time, make sure nobody will be worse off. This would imply an enlargement of the socioeconomic pie, with all or some slices increased but no slice reduced. Such reforms are theoretically possible.[67] Otherwise, large-scale reforms will produce intergroup and interpersonal trade-offs; some pie slices will shrink. This is typical of almost all reform programs, regardless of their scope or rationale. Besides, if we insist that nobody must be worse off, we will severely limit the range of permissible reforms.

A requirement that we not disadvantage any individual, or any major group, would really be ethically absurd. It would imply that all groups were fully entitled to their current incomes and opportunities, regardless of how these opportunities had been achieved. This kind of requirement would treat existing privileges as sacrosanct, even if they are, in themselves, objectionable. It would effectively limit the applicability of our ideological principles, wrapping everybody in a huge constitutional grandfather clause.

Instead we ought to admit that drastic constitutional reform cannot be undertaken without some parties losing some of their previous advantages. If those advantages have no ethical legitimacy, there is clearly no reason to sustain them any longer.

So the transition to a **libegalitarian** system will require transitional redistributions. On the other hand, once the transition has been completed, no further redistribution can be considered legitimate. Once everybody has been accorded an equal lifetime opportunity, his socioeconomic slice has automatically been defined, and no further reslicing will be appropriate. There will then be no question of weighing the gains and losses for different groups and trying to balance them against one another; so doing would upset the system's ethical equilibrium. This is in contrast to systems that concern themselves with the welfare of shifting majorities (e.g., by seeking to maximize total income or wealth, regardless of its initial or ultimate distribution). It is also in contrast to systems that intrinsically favor particular social groups (e.g., by attaching greater public-policy weight to the conditions of artists, the elderly or independent farmers).

What redistribution changes in potential income and wealth, and hence in opportunities, would occur if the United States of the 1990s were suddenly **libegalitarianized**? Who would be the gainers and the losers, relative to the status quo?

Pluses and Minuses. One can give only partial and tentative answers to that question. This is because we do not quite know how different groups would respond to the changes that would occur in their respective rights and opportunities, and we cannot foretell how their responses would impact on others.

In particular, we cannot estimate, even approximately, how businesses, workers, consumers and investors would react to the elimination of unwarranted regulations or excessive taxes or to the loss of subsidies that they currently receive. Market prices would change, but by how much cannot be foreseen. And the price changes would induce people to change their behavior in unpredictable ways, with unpredictable consequences for all the parties that they deal with in the market.

For example, it is impossible to predict how the elimination of big-city rent control would affect renters, on the one hand, and the real estate owners, on the other. Many affected renters would move to cheaper dwellings, while some would absorb the added rent by scrimping on other items. Many real estate owners would make immediate gains, but they would see part of these gains disappear as developers and builders gradually added to the supply of housing and competed for tenants. And they might be compelled by competitive pressure to upgrade their facilities, with a negative effect on profits. And how much would the price of marijuana actually drop upon the product's legalization, and with what consequences for demand, sales and producer profits?

Reforming the tax system would create another set of distributional effects. It is unclear what tax rates would be needed as taxes were directly linked to the costs of producing specific public goods, and became payable by the individual beneficiaries. It is reasonable to believe that they would go down overall, but one cannot project by how much or for whom. Going a step further, one also cannot foresee how different groups would spend their additional disposable (after-tax) incomes. These ambiguities are the consequences of giving each individual the right to choose—and not a sign that the **libegalitarian** system might be incomplete.

And most of us have multiple stakes in various product categories and markets. Directly or indirectly, we might experience both some gain and some loss from, say, decontrol of a product or activity or from the elimination of an income support program. Thus the individual automobile driver has a stake both in the freedom from strict speed limits and in the safety he enjoys because the pace of the traffic is moderate. But different drivers will add up the two consequences differently.

Our desires for education, medical care and many other services change drastically during the course of our lifetimes. A regulatory or tax change in these areas might therefore be gainful during one phase of our lives, costly during another. This is one more reason why one cannot easily add up and net out all the various effects of all the necessary **libegalitarian** reforms.

Major Gainers. Despite all these caveats, one can cautiously point in the direction of some of the major gainers. They would tend to include those who now grow up in poor, overcrowded homes, run by uneducated, negligent parents. These groups are currently underendowed by society, almost as if marked for life for relative failure. They would be much better provided for under the **libegalitarian** system, as they would have better guardians or receive compensatory child care outside the home; they would obtain larger initial human-capital endowments. And just as they would enjoy higher levels of capital accumulation and consumption as children, they would normally reap larger income returns and consumption opportunities as adults.

A second group of gainers consists of those who are now governmentally overregulated in their work, consumption or investment. They may now be effectively forced to cut back these activities below their preferred, cost-effective levels; or, worse, they may be pushed into other, less useful activities or spending patterns.

Consider a physician-to-be who is prevented from practicing by current license requirements, but who might in fact meet the test of a potential free physician market. Or consider an urban business entrepreneur who is now zoned out of the district in which his potential customers would do their shopping. If the respective regulations were removed, these parties would be potentially enriched, financially and in terms of lifetime opportunities.

Another gainer group are those who are now subject to unfair, discriminatory taxes. By **libegalitarian** standards, most Americans are currently taxed too heavily, for they do not receive their taxes' worth in government services; so this is a large, diffuse population group with legitimate claims to larger slices of the American pie.

Today's biggest tax victims include successful, well-educated professionals who, because of progressive income taxation, do not get the full, competitive returns on their extensive human-capital investments. The victims also include financial savers who have to pay income taxes on dividends that have already been subject to the corporate income tax. And they include buyers of French cognac, Hong Kong shirts, Japanese automobiles, European steel products and other items that are overpriced because of American import tariffs or other trade-restrictive policies. Conversely, these tax or control victims are among the big potential gainers from a **libegalitarian** reform program.

At the same time, the reform program may permit certain socioeconomic groups to gain from the expansion of particular government services. This could occur whenever the group strongly depends on government services that, by public-goods standards, are now in short supply.

Plausible evidence of such gains, for instance related to national security, is hard to produce. Yet the prosecution of crimes has surely left many victims grossly undercompensated, because of overly restrictive requirements for proof or inadequate payment of damages. Correcting these deficiencies in public policy would benefit many actual crime victims. In addition, more effective police forces and public security programs could reduce commercial and personal risks and bring down private insurance costs. And these gains would in many cases exceed the prorated tax costs of the new programs.

On the environmental balance sheet, property privatization, with clear, enforceable property lines, would make it easier to resolve environmental conflicts. Affected communities would then be able to get compensation for damage to their air, water supply, health or personal comfort. And the potential liability for damage would make some polluters stop their harmful activities altogether. In either case, the now-disadvantaged communities would gain, at the expense of the now-favored polluters, as **libegalitarian** principles began to prevail.

Major Losers. Many other socioeconomic groups would, admittedly, suffer some losses if a **libegalitarian** system was introduced in the United States. But their losses would merely consist of the disappearance of advantages that they now have but which are inconsistent with the new, non-discriminatory rights structure. So no apologies are needed for these consequences.

For the nation as a whole, one might wish to claim that the losses would be much smaller than the gains. This is mainly because the elimination of government price and cost distortions (through controls and excessive taxes) would make the economy much more efficient and thereby enlarge the total socioeconomic pie.

This would not, however, be a completely fair conclusion. We have no right to pretend that we can measure and compare the incremental satisfactions or dissatisfactions of different population groups. A larger pie need not necessarily produce larger overall human well-being—at least not if some of the just-described "losers" somehow had derived disproportionately large satisfactions from their initial privileges. No statistical method could ever tell us if this were the actual case. And note that maximum aggregate well-being (in any case, a very muddy notion) is not the goal of the **libegalitarian** system. Its goal is to maximize opportunities at the individual level, not their social totality or the actual outcomes over time.

The most we can claim is this: If the subjective reactions of gainers and losers were approximately symmetrical, the gainers' gains would exceed the losers' losses. The aggregate quantity gain to the national economy would then translate into a similar subjective quality gain for the national population.

One broad, prominent loser group would be made up of "entitlement" collectors. The group would comprise those who are currently at the receiving end of major income-support or social-service programs, despite an absence of initial socioeconomic handicaps. It includes the habitually unemployed, who nonetheless had received a standard amount of publicly supported education; the carelessly unhealthy, who had enjoyed adequate medical care during their childhood, and the food stamp recipients who would actually be able to earn a comfortable living wage in the labor market—many of these might fit the term "welfare chiselers." The group also includes the long-lived Social Security pensioner who had contributed much less to the system than he is now collecting from it. For all of these citizen categories, the loss of privileges would put them on an equitable footing with the rest of the population; so the loss should not be mourned.

Tax reform would produce many deserving losers, and not only because of the elimination of tax-financed transfer programs. Those who now benefit from government-provided police protection or environmental preservation but, because of the current tax structure, escape paying for these services, would lose these public favors. Other examples include individuals who now can claim large tax deductions for charitable contributions or medical expenses and thereby receive implicit subsidies. And they include, as well, some artists or health-care professionals who, as a result of those tax provisions, receive subsidized contributions for their activities.

The removal of various on-or-off budget subsidies would similarly disfavor a great many farmers who currently are paid for not growing wheat and corn, who can obtain government loans at below-market interest rates or who can sell their surplus butter to the government. Similar benefit losses would rightly be inflicted on low- and middle-income couples who now get home mortgage subsidies through government loan or guarantee programs.

By the same token, long-term tenants of rent-controlled apartments in New York City and other large metropolitan areas would lose this privileged status. And as the government started to apply businesslike cost controls on its own operations, many cost overruns by defense suppliers would no longer be feasible. Consequently, some of their undeserved profits would be wiped out, and the inflated salaries of their executives might be restored to appropriate, competitive levels. In a psychological sense, the loser list should also account for those whose personal moral or esthetic preferences would no longer be reflected in public law—for instance, those who oppose obscenity, defamatory writings, private drug traffic or behavior that "disturbs the peace."

Lastly a standardized system of child rearing would produce some indirect, antidiscriminatory losses for those who now get a better start in life. These groups—overeducated children, in particular—would have to accept a broader sharing of available educational and medical-care resources with other young persons. The upgrading of education in low-income areas would thus absorb some resources that currently go to children in superior private schools. Also, the requirement of equal social capital endowments in all children would preclude large inheritances. Curbing the right to parent-to-child wealth transfers would put those now born into wealthy families, or wishing to make such transfers, in the comparative loser category.

But, again, these losses would merely be the flip side of the restoration of rights to those who are currently, by **libegalitarian** standards, disadvantaged. The losses would be necessary to restore balance and equity in the distribution of lifetime socioeconomic opportunities.

THE NEW CONSTITUTION

The **libegalitarian** society will need a constitution, or its governing principles will not be clear and enforceable. Without a constitution—preferably a written one—there will be no legal protection against arbitrary, revolutionary changes. There will be no dependable authority that can determine the nature and boundaries of citizen rights, and every presumed right will be open to dispute and challenge.

Without a constitution, there could, practically speaking, be no legitimate government. Yet powerful private interest-group organizations might try to impose their rules and values on the rest of the population; and it is quite possible that one such organization would dominate and act like a *de facto* government. But it would soon need to establish a constitution that outlined its purposes and operating principles, with rules about its relations and obligations to the citizens.

Besides, constitutions are informative and educational. They communicate ideological values and political goals. They tell us how their authors—the nation's founders, the leaders of the most recent revolution or their hired theoreticians—want society to be structured. Especially if it is clearly conceived, internally consistent and sufficiently specific, a constitution can give us a convenient overview of a socioeconomic system.

Main Features. The **libegalitarian** society can be viewed as a territorial club that caters to the interests of those who inhabit a particular territory (nation). The inhabitants of that territory are, of course, the club members (the citizens). Its government will be no more, and no less, than the club's managing board.

The club needs a charter, or constitution, that spells out its functions in representing and mediating the interests of its members. Its constitution is, in effect, a comprehensive long-term contract between itself and its citizen-members. It should be designed so that it can protect the citizens' individual and collective interests, both internally (within the club) and externally (between it and the rest of the world).

The basic mission of the **libegalitarian** society is, to repeat, to provide maximum equal lifetime opportunities for all its citizens. By focusing on opportunities rather than outcomes, it leaves the responsibility for outcomes—for translating opportunities into actual results—in the hands of each individual. By addressing lifetime, and not current, opportunities, it recognizes the interconnectedness of different stages of a person's life and avoids encouraging exploitative behavior that could create fresh rights to "entitlements." This feature permits the **libegalitarian** society to promise long-term interpersonal equity; it is nondiscriminatory, fully and permanently. And by stressing the opportunities' maximization, it avoids imposing any predetermined limit on how much economic welfare each of us deserves.

The key steps toward such a society involve the distribution and use of economic resources—human, physical and financial. Equality of opportunity requires an equal start in life, societally speaking; and attaining such equality presupposes standardized upbringing of children (or equal social endowments of human capital).

But equality also requires equal access to the private market and to the services supplied by government itself; any alternatives would, by definition, be discriminatory. Equal market access implies a mutual recognition of property rights and a mutual respect for voluntary contracts—or some could preempt the opportunities of others. And it implies a free use of resources, within the constraints of such mutuality. In turn, that freedom allows resources to be used so that the benefits they produce can be maximized.

By the same token, the benefits of government (in the form of public goods) can be maximized only if the public sector lets itself be guided by the same cost-conscious, optimizing rules as private enterprise. And the costs of government must, analogously, be shared proportionately among the benefiting taxpayers—or inequities would arise on this plane. Government should be prevented from overproducing public goods or interfering in the production of private goods; but underproduction of truly needed, cost-effective public goods can be equally detrimental.

A Constitutional Blueprint. A **libegalitarian** constitution might read as follows:

> **1.** The fundamental aim of this constitution is to provide for the maximization of individual lifetime opportunities, equally shared among all citizens. Each citizen shall have an equal opportunity to pursue his or her personal objectives, through individual action, participation in private group organizations and access to the benefits of government. This shall constitute each individual's basic human right.
>
> **2.** All individuals shall be endowed with an equal amount of socioeconomic capital before entering adult life. This capital shall consist of such physical, intellectual and psychological capabilities that can be transferred to children and adolescents through care and education. The task of so endowing each child shall be jointly carried out by each child's natural or adopted parents and community organizations. These organizations shall monitor the treatment of each child in his or her home and shall demand corrective steps when these functions are inadequately performed by the parents. These organizations shall also offer remedial child development services to all children who would otherwise be disadvantaged.
>
> **3.** Each mature person shall have an unlimited right to develop or use his or her personal resources, whether obtained through birth, upbringing, gifts or personal effort, as long as the like rights of others are fully respected. In particular, each person shall have an unlimited right to enter into voluntary exchanges of goods or services with other individuals or organizations and to employ his or her resources in his or her chosen activities. Persons acting jointly, through a private organization or group, shall have a similar right to exchange or employ the group's legitimately acquired resources. No exchange or activity

shall ever be prohibited as long as its resource costs are fully borne by the person or group undertaking it.

4. Governments, at all levels, shall produce and supply such goods and services that collectively benefit the citizens residing within their respective jurisdictions, as long as the collective benefits of each unit of service exceeds its costs. The costs of such production shall be borne by the individual beneficiaries thereof in proportion to the benefits they receive, as determined by the expenditure each of them would willingly have made on a comparable amount of services in the private market. The costs shall be recouped through fees or taxes.

5. Each person shall have the right to full compensation for any deprivation of resources, services or goods in violation of pars. 2–4. This right shall include compensation for losses he or she might have incurred through:

a. an inadequate initial social resource endowment;

b. coercive acquisitions by other individuals or organizations of goods that he or she had rightfully acquired, or failures by other parties to fulfill contractual obligations;

c. an inadequate government provision of a public good or service relative to the taxes or fees that he or she had paid, or would have been willing to pay, for such services, and

d. government restrictions that improperly have been imposed on voluntary private exchanges or activities.

Some Ideological Comparisons. This skeleton constitution outlines a society that could not be fairly described by any of the conventional ideological labels. That is, of course, why it needs a new name—**libegalitarianism**, which suggests a fusion of libertarian and egalitarian principles.

The libertarian aspect is reflected in a shared belief in nearly unlimited private-market freedom. However, in the **libegalitarian** world, that freedom is complemented by an analogous freedom to avail oneself of a market-simulative government (which produces carefully defined public goods).

As an additional difference, freedom in the **libegalitarian** scheme derives its intrinsic value from the human benefits, or utility, it can produce. By contrast, most full-fledged libertarians take pains to avoid any appearance of being "utilitarian" (especially since the term often invokes the maximization of the aggregate utility of the whole society, as in the Jeremy Bentham definition). Yet the **libegalitarian** case for freedom is founded in freedom's utility to the individual (as well as, secondarily, to the market economy overall); it might thus be said to reflect an individualistic utilitarianism.

The new society would be highly "liberal" in the classical nineteenth-century sense (that of laissez-faire). But it would be even closer to the modern neoclassical model that seeks to maximize individual welfare through a cost-efficient combination of private- and government-sector activity. Yet its liberalism would be circumscribed in one particular area: Individual freedom would not encompass any special right for parents to define and supply the resource needs of their children. For granting parents that right is, of course, incompatible with equal opportunity.

As sketched here, the **libegalitarian** society might also be called "democratic," though only in a restricted sense. All socioeconomic power would reside in the individual citizens ("the people")—not in any subdivision of society or in any single institution (nor, of course, in a dictator). But the "democracy" would be of an individualistic, market-based variety. Economic power would stem from the individual's ability to supply resources and purchasing power to the market (and to a market-minded government)—and not from his use of the ballot. That power would be heavily circumscribed by a strict property delineation and by the prohibition against the use of government for redistributive or coercive purposes. This is in contrast with the more familiar political democracy that encourages majority control and transfers vast collective powers to legislators or the nation's chief executive.

Would the evolving society be "republican"? Yes, in the literal sense that government would involve itself only with truly public matters (fitting the label of *res publica*). But the notion of "public matters" would not bear much resemblance to the one that has evolved in the American republic over the last two centuries—a vague and open-ended notion. The term would have to be reinterpreted so as to mean "public goods" in the more limited, economic-theoretic sense; political majority decision would not suffice to alter the types of activities or goods that could fit the label. Needless to say, the **libegalitarian** public-goods program would in many respects be at odds with the contemporary program of the Republican party.

This society would be profoundly "egalitarian" in terms of lifetime opportunities, but it would not exhibit the superficial, transitory equalities so eagerly sought by contemporary social liberals. It would offer equal unrestricted access to the private market (just as the libertarian society), along with equal access to cost-based government services (just as the neoclassical-liberal model). And the equality of the resulting opportunities would be ensured through equal endowments of "start-up human capital" for everybody. No other known ideology seems to go this far toward true interpersonal societal equity.

Finally, a society built on a **libegalitarian** constitution would, to most people, not seem particular "conservative," at least not in the quasi-authoritarian, traditionalist sense. Yet it would, of course, permit private parties to preserve, among themselves, whatever private values, institutions and resources they wish. While it might have to impose income taxes on private churches, it would definitely not tear them down. And it would broaden the conservative free-enterprise principle so that it would apply also to nonmarket activities, including expressions of lifestyle, personal morality and artistic ambition—even to the point of permitting the burning of privately owned flags on private property.

Organization. The **libegalitarian** government would in all conceivable circumstances play a much more limited role than that of the current U.S. government, or almost any other government, today. If we envisioned retaining our existing political institutions, at least *pro forma*, some of their functions would have to be redefined drastically. This applies especially to Congress and the Executive Branch, but also to a wide range of public sector agencies.

The U.S. Congress should be, if anything, an instrument for articulating public demands for national collective goods and weighing their costs. It should no longer be a tool for satisfying special group interests at general public expense. It should be a spokesman for the collective wishes of the citizenry and not for the interests of individual Congressmen or of contributors to their election campaign. Developing techniques for ensuring this performance is a separate, politico-technological issue; it points toward "preference revealing" studies of voluntary private sector behavior and scientific sampling of citizen views—with legal recourse against Congressional failure to perform its job.

The national government would then resemble a huge private conglomerate, producing a fluid variety of national public goods that the citizens demonstrably found worth their tax costs. Its mandate would be much broader than that of almost any conceivable private enterprise. But the cost-benefit and taxation rules for public goods would not allow it the entrepreneurial license and experimentation that often characterize the individual firm.

The future **libegalitarian** President would be the implicit chief executive of this conglomerate producer-distributor. He or she would establish overall plans for the production of national collective goods and its financing. Undoubtedly, he would need to delegate most of the details to particular departments or agencies, so that the departments could develop the appropriate production, taxation and debt-financing techniques for their respective lines of production.

One can certainly envision a Department of State, handling military and economic-policy negotiations with other nations (and some circumscribed CIA functions). It would exist side by side with a Defense Department protecting the national territory. There might also have to be a new Domestic Security Department that coordinated national police activities (including those of the FBI).

National environmental issues, including those with international ramifications, could be the province of a Natural Resource Department (superseding the Department of the Interior and the Environmental Protection Agency). The Treasury Department might keep its tax collection function, while undertaking profitable financial transactions with other governments or intergovernmental bodies.

The national court system could continue to be supervised by the Department of Justice, which ought to establish consistent administrative procedures for the settling of legal disputes nationwide. There should be no reason to retain an independent judiciary struggling to undo or modify the actions of the executive or the legislature. But the Supreme Court might remain a permanent watchdog over how well other branches of the government obeyed the Constitution.

Most other federal departments should turn out to be unnecessary in the **libegalitarian** society. Among existing departments, the reformed society should have little or no need for the Departments of Commerce, Agriculture, Transportation, Labor, Energy or Housing and Urban Development, as their regulatory and subsidization functions would be abolished. Nor would there be any need for Departments of Education or Health and Human Services, at least not in the far-flung versions that exist today. However, the expanded government functions with respect to child development might require a new department devoted to setting nationwide standards for the education and care of minors—in schools, in day-care centers and in families. Let us call it the Department of Personal Capital Endowments.

The future **libegalitarian** Presidents should certainly be allowed to speak to us now and then so as to promote citizen-government communication, despite the inherent risks of misrepresentation and deceptions. But the most important Presidential address would be the initial one, which would mark the introduction of the new societal system. It might read as follows.

A PRESIDENTIAL ADDRESS

"My fellow citizens:
"We have reached a turning point in our nation's history. I am today proposing a far-reaching reform program that will dramatically change the principles, institutions and policies that govern the United States of America.

"We will create a new society—a society that will provide greater opportunities overall and equal opportunities for each and every citizen. It will give us a more efficient economy and allow our living standards to rise. And it will eliminate the inequalities that have resulted from unfair social policies and programs in the past.

"To achieve this, our government will from now on base all its policies and actions on two mutually supportive principles: basic social equality and maximum individual freedom. Everybody shall have received an equal amount of societal resources when he or she reaches maturity; that is what we mean by 'equal opportunity.' And everybody shall have full individual freedom to use these resources as he wants to; that is, of course, the meaning of freedom in the socioeconomic context.

"Similar principles of equality and freedom have figured prominently in our history and in our previous constitution. But they have been poorly articulated and inadequately carried out; and there have seemed to be irreconcilable conflicts between them. But after consulting with some top political theoreticians, I am now fully convinced that equal opportunity and individual freedom can indeed be simultaneously achieved. The two principles are complementary, and not in competition with each other.

"Our reform program is based on a view of the individual and society that almost everybody seems to share. The individual depends on society, up to a point; but each person also depends on himself. There are limits to what society *can* do; it is not all-powerful. There are additional limits to what it *should* do, for societal actions tend to be costly, and we must leave sufficient room for individual action. We need to respect these limits better than we have in the past.

"Equal opportunity must mean that society gives everybody—every child and youngster—an equal start in life. Therefore society should, in the jargon of experts, endow each child with an identical amount of social developmental capital. That capital is the foundation for each young person's prospects for achieving a happy, satisfying life. Beyond that, we will make sure that everybody will have unrestricted opportunities to employ, cultivate and use that personal capital in accordance with his personal needs and interests.

"Let me elaborate on how we propose to achieve these

202

ambitious ends. My administration will take all the necessary steps to give each child an adequate amount of physical, psychological and intellectual care and attention, inside or outside his family environment. We will no longer allow any child to be brought up in conditions of malnutrition, poor medical care or psychological neglect. And we will insist that each child get a basic education tailored to his innate potential.

"From now on, the child's interests will take precedence over those of his parents. The family shall be subject to stricter social quality control. Parents who perform their child-rearing duties adequately will receive financial support that matches the costs of those duties. They will be given the same financial support whether they are working outside the home or not and regardless of their personal incomes. But parents who do not may lose their roles as guardians, temporarily or permanently. These rules are fair and nondiscriminatory to parents, as well as to children.

"All children will attend schools that draw students from diverse ethnic and family backgrounds. Schools will be publicly financed, but may be privately run as long as they offer standard high-quality programs and facilities. Each child will at birth be given a medical insurance policy that covers the cost of all needed medical care until it reaches maturity. The quality of child rearing, schooling and medical care will be monitored by my new Department of Personal Capital Endowments. But private citizens will be free to investigate the prevailing standards and procedures and to challenge these in court.

"However, the resources that go into a child's development and care are not a gift from society; they are essentially on loan until the mature person can repay them. The costs of child support shall therefore be financed through government-backed bonds that mature over a person's typical life span, or about seventy years. And each grown-up person shall be obligated to repay these obligations in annual installments, with interest rates equivalent to those in the open market. Persons who can demonstrate that they have received substandard amounts of developmental capital will be allowed special, compensatory reductions in these obligations.

"Once we have offered equal opportunity to every young person, we can in good conscience give him, as an adult, full responsibility for his own needs and interests. We will no longer have any reason to give special government help to the grown-up poor, sick or unemployed.

"Those who want to protect themselves against the risks of such misfortunes can do so on their own initiative and at their own expense. They can, of course, educate themselves so as to earn more and afford better health care; they can avoid unhealthy habits; they can save up some of their incomes for future emergency purposes; and they can take out private insurance policies as extra safeguards. However a person does it, he should be fully accountable for the costs, and not be allowed to dump them on the taxpayers.

"We can, as a result, eliminate all 'entitlements' to grown-ups, for they are unearned and unfair burdens on the taxpayers. We will no longer have what some people now, very misleadingly, like to call a 'welfare state.' But we will be able to raise the general level of individual welfare, especially by letting the hard-working majority use their own incomes for their own purposes and not forcing them to subsidize the less-productive minority. To be blunt about it: The new system will not permit any citizen groups to become parasites on the general public. Instead of a 'welfare state' for favored minorities, we will build a 'welfare society' for everybody.

"From now on, unemployment benefits will be available only to those who have taken out private insurance against the loss of their jobs. And social security will be a matter of personal financial planning, and not an 'entitlement.' These policy changes will produce large budgetary savings and allow the federal tax burden to be sharply reduced.

"The government will now be consistently nondiscriminatory, not favoring or disfavoring anybody. There will be no more privileges, or penalties, for people who happen to find themselves in particular economic circumstances; who have particular job or consumption preferences; or who belong to particular ethnic, sexual or age groups. We will abolish the unseemly patchwork of interest-group privileges that have been established in the past in the name of civil rights. Instead, civil rights will now be for everybody.

"Let me give you some of the details of our specific reform plans. Public nondiscrimination will mean that we will no longer harass tobacco smokers with compulsory, patronizing health warnings on cigarette packages. Nor will we restrict the private choice of medications by insisting that they be declared safe by government bureaucrats.

"We will discontinue the outrageously wasteful farm support programs that have penalized our taxpayers, and many of our farmers, too, for so long. Our auto, steel, television and textile manufacturers will have to do without tariff or quota protection against incoming foreign goods; if they can't hack it in the global competition, they ought to look for other things to do.

"What, then, will our government be doing in the future, except looking after the education and well-being of minors? Do we really need any government at all for responsible, individualistic grown-ups? Yes, we do. Our national government should do the things that we agree need to be done but which cannot efficiently be handled by the private sector. The government will devote itself to producing services that cannot be made available just to individual buyers but which, by their nature, automatically benefit large portions of the population.

"But in doing this, the government should be businesslike—i.e., cost-conscious and attuned to its customers, our citizens. It should act like a conglomerate business corporation whose services we have all subscribed to by choosing to live in this country. Like a well-run corporation, it should weigh the costs of potential activities, undertake those activities that are worthwhile to its customers and charge each of these accordingly. But it should no longer dabble in things that are not worth their costs or which could be better taken care of by the private sector.

"The national government will in the future concentrate mostly on protecting our national wealth against potential external and internal damage. Externally, the main threats are, of course, military, and we shall continue to maintain an adequate defense while trying, through diplomatic means, to persuade potential foreign aggressors to leave us alone. We shall be ready to negotiate further arms reductions with our adversaries abroad, while opening the doors to more trade and easier cultural contacts.

"Internally, we shall set up a stronger national system of property preservation, both on the private and the public plane. The constitution will protect private wealth by forbidding unreasonable taxes on income and harmful controls on economic activity. We will also strengthen the police and court system so that it will be easier and cheaper to collect adequate damages for property infringements, contract breaches and outright thefts.

"But the courts will be obliged to be fair and even-handed when they assess damages for such involuntary property losses. Crimes will no longer be treated differently from torts and contract violations. They all call for full restitution, no more and no less, and with no extra punishment for acts that, in the popular mind, carry a moral stigma. That is the extent and limit of personal accountability. We shall thus put a stop to the current practice of giving outlandishly large damages to plaintiffs in a lot of dubious liability cases.

"Nor will we throw people in jail for driving home safely and harmlessly after an evening of liquid entertainment. We will declare a truce in the misguided, costly 'war on drugs' and let each person take responsibility for his drug habits, however risky they might be to him. And we will reform the entire criminal justice system so that nobody will have to endure jail terms, or pay fines, completely out of proportion to the damage he actually has caused.

"To improve the efficiency and consumer responsiveness of the economy, we will quickly privatize many of the enterprises that are now in public hands. For instance, postal service, transportation and university education will be fully transferred to the private sector, where the various services can be more cost-effectively supplied.

"Any remaining public lands, air or waters that cannot practically be privatized will be at the disposal of the general public, for appropriate fees. But such public property will be protected against any excessive damage by polluters, despoilers or abusers. For instance, those who want to exploit a public ocean shore to such an extent that it loses part of its value to nature watchers and swimmers will have three options: buy the beach at a fair market price from the public, quickly restore the beach to its original condition or pay the government for the cleanup costs. I will instruct regional, state and local governments to implement these policies through the needed environmental protection programs within their respective jurisdictions.

"Whenever we continue or institute a government program, we will always try to ensure that it can be adequately and fairly paid for by the beneficiaries. Like in a private market situation, nobody shall have to pay for something not worth his while. The taxes we must levy on ourselves must therefore be no higher than what we would have been willing to pay voluntarily for similar services in the market. These calculations will not be easy to make. But we will do our best to estimate the monetary value that each of you receives through government programs, and we will tax you accordingly.

"And as an extra guarantee, the new constitution will allow anyone of us to take the government to court if it has failed to obey these rules. You can thus seek damages from the government whenever it has underproduced public goods that you really needed or whenever it has overcharged you for public goods that you received.

"In most cases, taxes shall be proportional to our respective incomes, since higher incomes imply larger benefits from income-supportive government activities. However, everybody needs a basic income just to subsist and to be able to work, and we will therefore offer tax-exempt allowances corresponding to the cost of a minimum tolerable standard of living. The allowances will be considerably larger than those we have had in the past; those have been unrealistically low. In this way, the government will calculate each person's *net* income, and this income will be subject to a general proportional income tax.

"Furthermore, the new tax laws will redefine taxable income so that it will more accurately reflect each person's true benefit from participating in the national economy. For example, the rental value of owner-occupied homes will from now on be taxable, for income in kind can no longer be accorded a special tax privilege; yet there should be no special real estate taxes, because we should no longer confiscate wealth. Charitable contributions will no longer be tax deductible, since such tax treatment constitutes discriminatory government support for particular private activities.

"Corporate profits will no longer be subject to a separate tax, since this practice unfairly results in double taxation for stockholders. And we will, from now on, be able to go to the liquor store without being clobbered with a tax bill there, too.

"Overall, the role of our new government will be supportive and not coercive. It will fill the gaps that are unavoidably left by the private sector, provided we are willing to foot the bill. It will secure the individual's right to get a fair chance in life—and to enjoy the benefits of participating in the private economy, unobstructed by the government.

"Government from now on will be a source of national wealth and individual welfare, rather than a destroyer of resources or a manipulator of their use. This will be a better society for all of us, except for those who in the past have managed to obtain special, unfair privileges for themselves.

"We invite citizens of other countries to come over and join us in perfecting our new society. Their presence within our country will enrich our lives, as well as—I believe—their own. And I hope that those who remain abroad will work for similar economic reforms in their societies.

"On this hopeful note, I wish all of you good luck."

APPENDIX: A BRIEF IDEOLOGICAL GLOSSARY

Affirmative action has become one of the most contentious principles in modern American politics. It is an outgrowth of the movement for *civil rights* (see below) of the last several decades. It aims to reduce racism, sexism and other sources of social inequality, especially in employment and education.

Almost all large private organizations, as well as public agencies, are required by law to maintain affirmative action programs. The beneficiaries mainly comprise blacks, Hispanics, women, the handicapped and, in some locations, homosexuals. These requirements have been quantified through explicit or implicit hiring and employment quotas or "goals" (now the favored, less drastic term). The beneficiary groups are believed to have suffered from systematic *discrimination* (see below) in the past. But the obligation to undertake remedial affirmative action is not tied to specific proof that the employer (or college, etc.) has engaged in actual discrimination.

Most observers agree that affirmative action can help minority-group members overcome some of their labor market handicaps—and that this will usually be at the expense of their employers or white job applicants who lose out in the job competition. Those handicaps seem to be un-evenly distributed among the various minority groups, and the ben-eficiaries from these programs may or may not individually deserve that benefit.

Because affirmative action relies largely on the private sector for en-forcement, it is not a very costly item in the government budget. Yet it imposes indirect costs on private corporations, with uncertain payoffs in terms of additional job experience for minority workers or a more harmonious and equitable society.

Since affirmative action is ostensible egalitarian in spirit, it appeals to American liberals. Since it is a type of business regulation, it appeals much less to conservatives. As a government regulation, it is of course incompatible with true laissez-faire or with libertarian ideals.

The **libegalitarian** will be fairly sympathetic to the underlying goal but negative in regard to the methods. The sanctity of voluntary exchange should not be sacrificed in labor or other negotiable matters. The long-run remedy for educational handicaps is better, more standardized education—not on-the-job training at others' expense.

In this view, a permanent system of legal ethnic or gender classifications, to be forced upon contracting private parties, is strongly objectionable. It is at odds with any credible notion of equal opportunity. If, because of a failure to solve related problems in education and upbringing, affirmative action is today the best available course—which is unclear—provisions ought to be made for its gradual self-destruction.

Capitalism is, literally, not a very descriptive term, since all economic systems have a foundation of capital. Most often, the term refers to private ownership and control of the physical means of production (i.e., plant, machinery and land); that human capital—manpower and skills—is privately owned is usually taken for granted. In this sense, capitalism is approximately synonymous with free enterprise.

The merits of capitalism lies in the associated production efficiencies, as well as in the ethical appeal of free choice in the generation and use of capital. Such choice, if well-informed and motivated by profit seeking, will tend to produce such capital allocation and capital use that creates maximum profits. This will benefit both the capital's owners and, indirectly, the economy at large; Adam Smith's "invisible hand" will usually see to that.

Capitalism is often attacked on two grounds. One, it seems based on greed. Yet the capitalist message does not include any prescription for how capital, or income derived from it, ought to be used; charity is definitely permitted.

George Gilder, in *Wealth and Property* (New York: Basic Books, 1981), even goes so far as to claim that the essence of capitalism is giving, not taking; to him the capital-accumulating investor "gives" his investment to the rest of the market economy (though typically with an expectation of adequate returns). A more reasonable interpretation is that, greedy or not, the capitalist enhances economic opportunities for others—those working in his factory, producing and selling him raw materials, or supplying him the goods he wants to purchase with his investment income.

Capitalism can be criticized more intelligently on an egalitarian ground. True, everybody has in principle an equal right to accumulate and employ capital; subsequent inequalities in capital ownership will then be self-inflicted and presumable fair. But capitalist systems have, in practice, allowed capital to be passed on from generation to generation, thereby creating very unequal initial capital endowments throughout the population. Capitalists have tended to be family-minded conservatives who seek to pass on capital and wealth along hereditary lines, and capitalist systems have permitted them to do so. In this sense, capitalism seems inegalitarian.

In theory, capitalism could be combined with provisions for equal initial capital endowments for the young, at least as far as transferable resources are concerned; brains and beauty we cannot so transfer. Much of the **libegalitarian** program is devoted exactly to this proposition. Its goal is to eliminate the unequal opportunities connected with a family- or government-imposed maldistribution of capital, while ensuring that all capital can be put to optimum individual use.

Civil rights until the 1960s involved mainly "political" rights—especially voting rights and rights to assembly and association—that had historically often been denied blacks and other minority groups. After most of these rights gaps had been eliminated, the civil rights focus shifted to housing, public accommodations, employment and college admission (and, in the 1980s, club membership). Meanwhile, there have been frequent suggestions that the term should be broadened so as to also denote basic, humane living conditions. The implicit distinction between "civil" and other potential rights then becomes very obscure. (See, similarly, *human rights* below.)

The blurriness of the civil rights concept is reflected in the large, expanding catalog of questions taken up by the American Civil Liberties Union. Those questions include the sale of heavy drugs, school discipline, tax treatment of churches, prostitution, "comparable worth" for female workers, "workfare" requirements for welfare recipients and many other controversial matters.

The term's open-endedness also poses awkward ideological problems, even for those who support equal opportunity. On the one hand, there may be a strong ethical case for restoring and protecting particular rights that some groups have been deprived of in the past—for instance, through discriminatory laws or policies. On the other, claims to particular civil rights raise questions about why those rights deserve special treatment. Moreover, there are, normally, conflicting interests. Rights to private employment (or housing) can violate the rights of employers and other employees (or landlords and other renters)—yet all market rights ought to carry equal weight in a truly nondiscriminatory society.

A standard justification for that differentiation is that employers and landlords are in a stronger market position and are prone to exploit their weaker bargaining partners; and their market behavior can often seem discriminatory. To a libertarian or a **libegalitarian**, this justification has little or no validity, for government has no right to disturb and bias what ought be to a free bargaining process.

Admittedly, some civil rights "privileges" probably have helped restore some of the lifetime opportunities that have been lost through unfair public-policy treatment in the less liberated past, e.g., in regard to voting rights, and they may have performed a useful public-educational function in highlighting private-sector irrationalities. But these are transitory considerations. Selective civil rights ought not have a permanent role in a functioning equal-opportunity society. Such provisions impose special costs that will be unfairly borne by small segments of society.

The long-term goal ought to be a society with firm constitutional rights of a broad, nondiscriminatory nature. In the marketplace, everybody should have a "civil right" to unobstructed voluntary exchanges and to property protection. In the public-policy area, he should have a "civil right" to cost-effective public goods, financed through fairly allocated taxes. Children should have "civil rights," too—and these rights refer to an adequate societal investment in their care and education, matched by a future obligation to repay the costs of that investment.

Collectivism is nowadays not a frequently used term (except in historical descriptions of Soviet or Chinese agriculture). Macroeconomically, it normally suggests collectively owned resources used to produce collectively sought goods. It contrasts, of course, with a system of individually owned resources used to generate individually desired goods.

"Collectivism" smacks of socialism or even communism, i.e., a governmentally centralized system. But private parties can also behave collectively, and the theoretical concepts of collective goods and collective action are not limited to the activities of the public sector. Consider corporations, trade associations, labor unions, cooperative housing organizations, bridge clubs and so on; even the family is a small collective of sorts.

"Collective goods" are goods that cannot be individually produced and distributed, but whose existence automatically produces shared benefits to a group with a common interest. Some collective goods deserve the label *public goods* (see below), because their benefits are widely and diffusely distributed throughout a politically defined region. Others do not, because they serve only limited citizen groups. The public/private distinction is not always terribly clear, and those with a progovernment bent will tend to apply the public-good label more liberally.

A public concert producing music for an appreciative audience is such a shared good (while, for music haters, it might be a collective "bad"). Increased profits by a publicly held corporation also create collective goods within the circle of shareholders. In the former situation, there is no formal group organizaiton arranging the collective-good production; in the latter, there is. In neither situation is there an uncontroversial case for government involvement.

The standard ideologies show varying degress of appreciation for collective-goods problems. Socialism is, of course, forbiddingly collectivistic. In practice, it gives government the right to define the collective goods that are to be produced, from military programs to public transport and communication services to hospital care. Even the provision of ordinary private consumer goods—food, clothing and so on—takes on a public-collectivistic character as the socialist government tries to ensure their availability or rig their prices.

In the United States, the modern liberals tend to argue that public goods are underprovided, while individual and private goods are overproduced—this is evidenced by the alleged "private affluence" in the face of "public squalor" (in the words of J. K. Galbraith a few decades ago). Today, the big-city Democrats similarly talk about our "declining infrastructure" (crumbling bridges, highways in disrepair, etc.), as well as unmet "needs" for quasipublic health-care facilities for the poor and educational institutions for the young.

The ideological conservative draws a sharper line between public and private goods and between the public and private spheres of production. He (or she) might deny any necessary public-good aspect of health care, education and much of the economy's infrastructure. To him, public highways and national parks are examples of how government has invaded the private sector and taken it upon itself to produce fundamentally individual goods (i.e., road and park access). Yet he will regard private enterprise and a functioning law as vast systemic goods, worthy of government support. Together with defense and internal security, these institutions will almost always be on the public-good list.

The main libertarian spokesmen have been noticeably uncomfortable over the collective-good question. It could easily undermine their case for perfect laissez-faire. The anarcholibertarians (Rothbard, especially) tend to deny the existence of public goods or to advocate that they could better be produced and distributed by private organizations. This is the theoretical basis for "voluntary defense associations," proposed to take the place of the Pentagon. More moderate libertarians (like Hospers) acknowledge a limited number of public goods that they do not believe the private sector could sufficiently supply. They thus share much of the **libegalitarian** position in this matter; see *public goods* below.

Conservatism, literally interpreted, suggests the maintenance of the status quo; but the term begs the question of what, precisely, is to be conserved. When Mikhail Gorbachev has attacked Soviet conservatism, his target has been rigid, oppressive authoritarianism or the lack of economic freedom in that system. But in the United States, conservatism refers to the preservation of the centuries-old American values of free enterprise, patriotism, family and a foundation of nonspecific religion. It connotes a distaste for government control, income redistribution, social engineering and moral laxity.

The principles that define American conservatism (as interpreted, for instance, by *National Review*) make it impossible to locate it along either of the primary ideological dimensions, collectivism and centralization. The conservatives' 19th-century economic liberalism, stressing individual entrepreneurship and laissez-faire, is clearly anticollectivist. Reliance on the family, and family-selected private schools, is also in tune with their antigovernment theme. But conservatism has unmistakable collectivistic elements in its stress on broad social-religious values, traditions and "law and order."

Libertarians find fault with conservatism because of its restrictions on individual freedom outside the commercial marketplace, for instance, in matters of sexual behavior and personal morality. They also object to the conservatives' desire to provide a strong, tax-financed national defense and their readiness to intervene in the affairs of other nations. Liberals and social democrats dislike the conservative tolerance of income and wealth disparities, and they want to subject business to more severe regulations in the name of public welfare.

The **libegalitarian** system proposed in this book weds the economic individualism of conservatives with the moral-cultural individualism of many modern liberals (but rejected by the religious-conservative New Right). Yet it tempers that individualism with a recognition of the need for "public goods," whose production inevitably has to be collective and governmentally managed; this feature distinguishes **libegalitarianism** from libertarianism.

Discrimination has become one of the most used, and most severely misused, terms in the American economic-political vocabulary. It ought, literally, to refer to a healthy ability or willingness to distinguish between socioeconomic phenomena that are, indeed, different and therefore deserve to be dealt with differently. Rational economic choice presumes this ability, among consumers, job seekers, investors and entrepreneurs.

But the term discrimination is now mostly reserved for situations in which the speaker thinks that the distinction being made is nonexistent or unworthy of recognition. The economic implications of a true difference may seem unfair, and the difference therefore ought not to be acted upon.

Most publicly aired discrimination questions today concern the employment or housing of ethnic minorities, women, handicapped or gays. Liberals argue that these groups deserve an extra chance because they seem historically to have been disadvantaged; and crude job, salary and housing statistics seem to bear out that observation. "Quotas" and numerical "goals" are, of course, among the favored remedies for it; but they lead to compensatory, or "reverse," discrimination. Conservatives see less evidence of significant discrimination and less merit in such corrective measures.

So what is the **libegalitarian** solution to this awkward problem? It must be admitted that antidiscrimination laws interfere with free choice and voluntary exchange, and that they invite unfair abuse. It should also be acknowledged that many minority groups have suffered both from childhood handicaps and from difficulties in overcoming them in the marketplace.

The long-run remedy, then, is to abolish all antidiscrimination legislation and restore free choice in hiring, housing and other private-sector pursuits. (Should stockholders discover serious mismanagement in matters of hiring, they can sell their stock; or they ought to be able to sue for breach of their implicit performance contracts with managements.) Public agencies should automatically be expected to pursue cost-effective hiring policies or be subject to legal remedies. And the problem of childhood disadvantages for minorities should be resolved through equalized access to schooling and child care, if necessary, by cutting back on parental control and prerogatives. In this way, all remaining societal "discrimination" can be attributed to the unbiased choices of autonomous individuals and should be accepted as such.

Entitlements usually denote rights to receive government transfer payments (without any goods or services rendered in exchange), especially in the form of income support, unemployment benefits and Social Security. Entitlements are essentially gifts from the general taxpayer. They are a key feature of the social-liberal welfare programs adopted in the United States over the past three decades, with grudging support from many conservatives.

Entitlements of this kind are clearly inconsistent with personal responsibility and individual freedom, as well as with a limited, public-goods system of government. They imply that society, and the productive taxpayers, are responsible for those receiving entitlements; and of course, the tax liabilities cut into the taxpayers' personal economic freedom.

Entitlements are anathema to a true libertarian, for they imply a theft-like government intrusion in the private enterprise system. A **libegalitarian** will, in principle, feel the same way. He might, however, offer a few qualifications: Each child might be said to be entitled to an adequate upbringing and education, financed by society at large. And one could give the entire concept a much broader meaning. In a sense, we are all entitled to whatever the national constitution offers us, including each valuable freedom or opportunity; entitlements will then equal rights.

This is essentially the approach taken by Nozick, in *Anarchy, State, and Utopia* (New York: Basic Books, 1974), ch. 7, as he elaborates an "entitlement theory of social justice" while rejecting the quasiegalitarian entitlement principles of John Rawls in *A Theory of Justice* (Cambridge: Harvard University Press, 1971). In Nozick's scheme, entitlement to an asset or service depends not on "need," but on the legitimacy of the process through which the asset or service was acquired (as through a voluntary exchange transaction or gift). For the most part, this is a sophisticated restatement of the traditional libertarian view.

Democratic systems generally make us entitled to most (though by no means all) of the fruits of our own labor. They also entitle us to certain services from the government and the chance, under special circumstances, to receive various gratuitous transfer payments. But the extent of these entitlements varies considerably along the ideological spectrum, with a maximum on the social-democratic left.

The **libegalitarian** system would offer three fundamental entitlements: one, the right to an adequate upbringing and basic education, offered on a credit basis; two, the right to unlimited voluntary exchange, unimpeded by government, and three, access to cost-effective public goods, paid for by the beneficiary. Altogether, these rights add up to an overall entitlement to participate in a maximum-benefit, equal-opportunity society.

Equality is a much-admired social principle with supporters across a wide variety of ideologies. It benefits from a number of psychologically satisfying associations: balance, evenness and, by extension, justice; it might also seem like a cure for envy. But the principle easily collides with the inevitable reality of change and variety, a reality that is a source of both individual pleasure and societal benefit.

To be meaningful, the concept of equality needs to be put into a specific quantitative framework. There must be an understanding both of what factor is being compared and of how that factor is to be measured. Very often, public discussion about equality suffers from ambiguity on either of these scores.

Some equalities pertain to what we own or earn; others to what we are allowed to do. Some seem to be connected with government policies, others with private market transactions. Consider equal incomes, equal wealth, equal freedom of speech, equal marriage opportunities, etc. Some of these equalities seem verifiable by accepted statistical measurements. This is the case with income, wealth and other conventional economic variables. Not so with freedoms or opportunities. For instance, how do we count work in the home, favors received from friends or spouse, and the pleasure of living in an agreeable climate?

Much of the public debate concerns income and wealth, as judged by conventional statistics. But there is little understanding of the interconnections between the two factors—or of the perverse wealth effects of many income-equalizing programs. In particular, the egalitarian liberals of today normally adopt a time-limited perspective, stressing the immediate income situation while ignoring the longer-term wealth position. They rarely concede that policy actions to equalize income (as through tax-financed transfers) often create unfair penalties on legitimate wealth accumulation in the past, while creating disincentives for wealth buildups in the future.

It would be more natural for a true egalitarian to concern himself with the equalizing of wealth rather than of income. And he might go beyond what we usually regard as wealth and look at the freedoms, rights and opportunities that make wealth accumulation possible.

By extreme contrast, a libertarian will be content to prescribe equally complete freedom for everybody to engage in voluntary exchanges. He will thus tolerate all inequalities stemming either from personal effort or from inborn or early environmental differences in individual capabilities. Yet he cannot claim to offer equality of opportunity.

To others, equality of socioeconomic opportunity is the highest principle of social justice. Such equality will have to encompass all potential relations with government and access to all private markets. But the markets might produce price relations that put some of us at a relative advantage or disadvantage. This might suggest inequality, of sorts. Yet to a **libegalitarian** (or a libertarian), the latter type of inequality is just a normal expression of private market freedom—and no cause for social redistribution efforts.

But opportunity is subject to change under the influence of personal ambition and exertion. So equality of opportunity ought to be offered on a lifetime basis. Society will then have to equalize all persons' initial endowments of potentially wealth-creating resources. Identifying those resources—and equalizing their distribution across the population—then becomes a central economic-political task. This is a main goal of a **libegalitarian** system.

Fiscal policy—i.e., the combination of government expenditure programs and taxation rules—is one of the main expressions of a nation's ideological goals. On the expenditure side of the government budget, fiscal policy demonstrates what productive functions, and what redistributional tasks, the government has taken on. On the revenue side, the budget indicates the government's policies toward the distribution of disposable income and wealth.

The one major facet of government that fiscal policy, as conventionally formulated, does not embody is regulation. The traditional items in a government budget do not reflect the reallocation and redistribution of resources that the government achieves through regulatory controls or privileges (apart from administrative costs and receipts of fines). But if they were honest, governments would present a full picture of their activities, inclusive of the implicit taxes and subsidies it imposes through regulations. Such broad public accounting would turn government budgets into a kind of "economic impact statements" of much greater value to policy analysts and intelligent voters.

Very often, fiscal policy is analyzed on the basis of the budget's bottom line, the surplus or deficit (as variously measured). This practice owes a lot to the Keynesian economic revolution, which encouraged the idea of the budget is a key countercyclical instrument (surpluses being contractionary and deflationary, deficits expansionary and inflationary).

More sophisticated, up-to-date economic thinking acknowledges that the budget bottom line is not everything, by far: The composition of expenditure and the tax structure can, in themselves, affect the country's macroeconomic performance. Neoclassical economists (who tend to be skeptical of simple-minded Keynesianism) are especially aware that the private sector's responses to fiscal policies can lessen or even nullify the first-round effects of fiscal programs. As stressed by the "supply-siders" of the Reagan years, there will be private-sector feedbacks, with complex interactions between governmental and private economic activity.

Can we then fairly speak of a liberal, or a conservative, fiscal policy? Well, yes, if we carefully analyze all the budget specifies, examine their effects (along with the potential private sector offsets) and place them alongside acknowledged liberal and conservative principles. This is a tall order, barely worth the trouble considering the muddiness of those principles.

Yet it is roughly correct that liberal American budgets are bigger than conservative ones, especially in peacetime. And historically, liberals and Democrats took the lead in deliberately adopting budgets with planned expansionary deficits.

But nowadays either ideological camp is willing to tolerate large budget deficits. While liberals are still more prone to invoke a need to stimulate the economy, conservatives remind us of their reluctance to raise taxes. At the same time, both camps ritualistically demand a return to "responsible" fiscal policies in the form of budgetary balance (or a resemblance of balance over the business cycle). And they distort the budget debate by lumping Social Security benefits and taxes together with ordinary expenditure and income tax receipts, even though Social Security ought to be viewed as a separate public saving-and-pension program.

Further ambiguities result from the fact that the official budget includes both consumption and investment items (along with pure transfers). It is the American practice to combine these items together in a "consolidated" budget, whereas many other countries prefer to present separate "current" and "capital" budgets.

That distinction is especially relevant for those who are concerned about the budget's long-term distributional consequences. Capital items, unless completely senseless and wasteful, will generate benefits in the future. It therefore seems reasonable to let future taxpayers pay for them— by borrowing now and collecting the taxes needed to repay these borrowings later on. Otherwise, there will result a kind of intergenerational inequity.

In all, the American budget debate is painfully dishonest and ideologically muddled. In this respect, matters would be much improved in an anarcholibertarian society: There would be no government budget (zero expenditure, zero tax revenues and perfect balance) and hence no chance for fiscal trickery. But this society would suffer from all the weaknesses connected with inadequate national defense, poor environmental management and a highly unequal treatment of children.

The **libegalitarian** alternative would offer a functioning government— scaled-down, cost-conscious and constrained by firm constitutional principles. Government would be businesslike and concerned with both efficiency and equity among the taxpayers. The budget would acknowledge the distinction between current and capital expenditure items—as do private firms. More generally, the **libegalitarian** budget would only contain spending that is for well-recognized public goods and can be equitably tax-financed by the beneficiaries.

In practice, the **libegalitarian** budget would be much smaller than the current U.S. budget, especially for two reasons: Many government programs (e.g., involving farm support, public higher education and excessive military spending) would no longer exist; and expenditure for children's upbringing would be financed through separate borrowings, on each child's behalf. In addition, the Social Security system would be entirely privatized and thus removed from the budget. Each person could then regard the government budget as a logical complement to his own private budget.

Free speech stands out as an especially cherished right in Western societies, and also a highly romanticized one. It can be a consumption-type leisure activity, with immediately gratifying effects on personal welfare. Or it can be a kind of investment activity, spreading information or points of view for the future benefit of the speaker. The immediate, observable costs are often low; and so the net returns can be high, if the message has the sought-after impact.

But the benefits of successful speech can be at the expense of other parties, who would have preferred a different message. Unobstructed political speech can topple a tyrant—just as it can promote another one.

Nearly all political parties and movements in modern democratic societies subscribe to the free-speech principle, although with qualifications. The litmus test is their willingness to tolerate speech that many find offensive, vulgar or subversive. Controversies have arisen primarily on two planes: One concerns the outer limit of the free-speech rule, or exceptions in which greater social interests might prevail, after all. The other concerns the very definition of "speech"—and the awkward possibility that simply redefining a type of activity as "speech" could suddenly remove a legal prohibition against it.

Both liberals and conservatives are willing to make some exceptions in cases of national security threats, obscenity or damage to a person's reputation (libel, slander). Conservatives tend to be a bit more restrictive, especially in matters of security and morality, and less inclined to classify nonverbal behavior (e.g., clothing, sexual or drug habits) as "speech."

A more consistent approach is possible if we can clarify property relationship and make free speech a matter of legitimate property use. Speech always depends on some natural or manmade communication medium—airwaves, newspapers, megaphones or telephone lines—that should be treated as property. All private parties could be allowed to control all speech-related uses of their property, never mind whether the speech's content oversteps majority limits of propriety. No private media should be forced to broadcast anything against their will—no equal-time provisions, no obligation to carry Presidential messages. But of course, there must then be a free market for these resources, so that anybody could buy his wanted media access.

However, if some property technologically has to be in public hands, and this property offers communication avenues, the government ought to accommodate all public interests in the property's use. It would have to do this by auctioning off access (say, to advertising space in the undivided sky) to the highest bidders. By contrast, a public TV channel existing side by side with private channels might confine itself to information related to the government's public-good functions or to basic educational material. And a local government need not tolerate unlimited shouting from the steps of the town hall as long as comparable private forums are available.

Libertarian and **libegalitarian** ideas will here tend to converge. Communication resources can and should almost always be in private hands—the hands of those who built or purchased those resources. Speech ought to be free in the same sense, and to the same extent, as other private products or activities—not free of cost, but free of government regulation—even if it offends listeners or third-party targets. Unregulated speech must include liquor advertisements, pornography and racist slurs—all subject to the terms of agreement with the media owner.

The government in an equal-opportunity society should let the speech-market processes run their course and not step in and bias the process in either party's favor. Both maximum freedom and equality of opportunity require a free market in ideas, or idea "production" will be discouraged and idea "consumption" choice will be unduly curtailed.

Free trade usually refers to the ability to conduct commerce with foreign nations without governmental obstructions, e.g., without import tariffs, quotas or special taxes. But it is actually a much broader concept. All interpersonal transactions can be regarded as trade—in the grocery store or in the mutual accommodations of family members and office coworkers. So free trade can be viewed as a very general principle of noninterference by government in interpersonal or interorganizational affairs.

To anybody with appreciation for individualism, the principle should seem entirely legitimate. We all like that kind of freedom; and when intelligently used, it seems to make us better off, individually and as a nation. Occasionally, third parties might be adversely affected (e.g., through negative "externalities"). But almost all such cases can be dealt with through means (like better property delineation) that leave the general free-trade regime intact.

Commitment to free trade varies fairly systematically along the ideological spectrum. The nineteen-century classical liberals (beginning with Adam Smith) were staunch free-traders. Socialistically inclined planners in all parts of the world have been disposed toward protectionist foreign-trade controls, supplementing similar regulations at home. Yet so have many governments (e.g., in Latin America) best described as authoritarian-conservative. And so have both liberals and conservatives that have been beholden to politically powerful interest groups (farmers, manufacturers, labor unions) that fear competition from more-productive foreigners.

Two major rationales are given for these antitrade positions: The market mechanism is not perfect enough to tolerate completely free trade, and government interferences in the trading economies distort the competitive positions of exporting and import-competing firms. So true international economic efficiency might, in some cases, require compensatory trade restrictions.

Both a traditional libertarian and a **libegalitarian** will, in principle, oppose all anti-free-trade measures. To both, voluntary exchange is a supreme value; yet there has to be a supportive, extensive system of private property. For the diehard laissez-faire libertarian, the ideal is a combination of complete property privatization and no government—and thus no regulations of trade.

The **libegalitarian** system is a bit more complex. There will be a government, but its actions (in spending, taxation and public-sector administration) will be carried out through an emulation of private free-trade practice. When the government produces and distributes public goods, it will be able to reap any available free-trade gains of its own. The benefits of free trade will thereby be extended beyond what is feasible in a purely libertarian system (in which public goods will be absent or in short supply).

Members of a hypothetical global **libegalitarian** society would have an unobstructed right to buy Toyotas, South African gold and seal skin coats at the prevailing world market prices. These prices would be established through free competition among all private and public-sector parties. Each person would similarly have full rights to travel, to invest and to work wherever he wanted, while paying his way and meeting his contractual obligations. And he would have full, fee-based access to the services supplied by all governmental units anywhere in the world, including a global law enforcement agency.

Human rights ought, literally, to stand in contrast to animal or plant rights. But the term has instead come to denote a more limited set of freedoms or opportunities—primarily the right to not be unfairly prosecuted or punished, to not be maltreated by the police and to participate in the democratic political process. These rights are usually considered political.

Typically, human rights are described through their relative absence in countries with gross police brutality, heavily politicized trials and no legal recourse against gross abuse by the authorities. Their limited existence is regarded as a manifestation of fascism or severe authoritarianism. The concept partially overlaps that of *civil rights* (see above). Both rights concepts suffer from some of the same definitional and operational ambiguities.

The leading international human-rights spokesmen (e.g., the United Nations and Amnesty International) seem to be of two minds. On the one hand, they have focused most of their ire on political rights abuses in South Africa, the Soviet Union and right-wing dictatorships in Latin America. On the other, they sometimes broaden their concern for "basic" human rights to include education, medical care and a minimum standard of living. They do not sort out these varying demands and resource claims, and they do not acknowledge the redistributive implications of the rights they wish to confer.

To get a fuller concept of human rights, one has to spell out the entire range of individual rights that a particular ideology or society will offer. If they are really broad, no classification is particularly helpful. Ideally, all rights stem from a fundamental individual right to equal opportunity, attained through a fair start in life and the chance for voluntary exchange.

In short, "human rights" would better be defined as a synonym for individual rights. It should not be used as a special label for a selected list of freedoms that leaves out so much else. The strongest, unbiased supporters of such comprehensive rights will be found among the classical liberals, contemporary libertarians and, particularly, **libegalitarians**.

Laissez-faire is the battle cry of all individualists and enemies of government. Let people do what they want to do, individually and privately, rather than coercing them to support the presence of government. But let us also make sure that, somehow, everybody will respect the boundaries of private property, the sanctity of contractual obligations, and the ethical necessity of voluntarism—through persuasion or social pressure. This is the message.

Stated that simply, laissez-faire is an immensely appealing principle of social organization. It responds to our need for personal choice and for translating that choice into personal decisions in all areas of life. But these aspirations have to be weighed against the view that the laissez-faire world is too disorderly and fragmented, that it is prone to "market failures" or other costly instabilities, or that it breeds an unacceptable degree of inequality.

American conservatives fight bitterly for nearly unlimited laissez-faire in traditional "economic" areas, while opposing business regulations and punitive taxes; but they do not accord us similar freedoms in moral matters. The moderate center is a bit weaker on economic laissez-faire (e.g., in its tolerance of antitrust laws and strict environmental controls) but a bit laxer on moral questions (e.g., homosexuality and abortions). To today's liberals, freedom of speech and personal morality often counts for more than the freedom to exploit commercial market opportunities and to reap the fruits of one's labor.

Both libertarians and **libegalitarians** dismiss these distinctions and accord individuals the same freedom in all aspects of behavior. They will also agree that free markets in themselves are not unduly unstable or prone to failure. Much of the market "failures" that we have seen have been due to destabilizing government actions. Any true, autonomous market instabilities are just health symptoms of the market's inherent dynamism and adaptability.

However, anarcholibertarians and **libegalitarians** will part company when it comes to public goods and equality of opportunity. The former claim that the private market itself will fill the needs for defense and law enforcement, while both conservative-libertarians (e.g., Hospers, Nozick) and **libegalitarians** will argue for a limited government role in these areas. To the latter, cost-effective *public goods* (see below), financed by the beneficiaries, will enhance, rather than limit, the extent and benefits of laissez-faire in purely private pursuits.

The other source of disagreement is the potential for great social inequalities in a laissez-faire world. Anarcholibertarian will say okay—if freedom creates inequality, so be it. Here, the **libegalitarian** shares the concern of socialists and modern liberals about unequal opportunity, while making equal opportunity a higher priority than free markets per se.

Liberalism has become another value-laden misnomer that confuses the ideological debate. To Adam Smith, "liberalism" meant individual freedom, private enterprise and free international, as well as domestic, trade. To contemporary Democrats, it mostly means a "caring" and "protective" government that confers redistributive benefits to lower-income groups and restricts opportunities for selected market activities.

But modern American liberalism does not have a firm ideology or a clear agenda. It favors change but avoids radicalism. It has a lot of faith in the efficacy and potential goodness of government, both in regulatory and in macroeconomic policy matters; yet it appreciates a taxable, profitable private sector. It encourages new ideas and new policies; but it prefers to deal with upcoming issues ad hoc, instead of fitting them into an overarching ideological framework.

American liberals have sounded like Western European social democrats when arguing, in the 1960s and 1970s, for more activist fiscal policies or for wide-ranging industrial policies. More recently, many of them have shown a new skepticism toward government that puts them closer to many moderate conservatives. In fact, it is hard to differentiate "neoliberals" from "neoconservatives."

At the same time, the liberal support for free speech, privacy and personal choice in moral matters correlates quite well with libertarianism and **libegalitarianism**. All three "lib" movements share certain doubts about the sanctity and effectiveness of the family (e.g., in deciding matters of children's schooling). But on this score, liberals and **libegalitarians** are willing to give the public sector a substantial equalizing role, whereas the libertarians would rather retain the inequities of the private family (perhaps supplemented with a utopian free baby market).

Libertarianism is the systemic expression of the ideology of *laissez-faire* (see above) or, more loosely, individualism. It encompasses all that, in technical economics, falls under the label of *capitalism* (see above), yet it argues for similar personal freedoms in nonmarket activities as well.

Libertarianism glorifies the freedom of the competitive market, undisturbed by government controls or taxes. And it seeks comparable free bargaining and free choice in all interpersonal and individual affairs. It paints government as the basic social evil, disrupting the bargaining process and distorting the preferred allocation of private resources. In the libertarian view, the active, meddlesome government deprives us of our hard-earned wealth and weakens the overall efficiency of the economy.

The purest, most extreme form of theoretical libertarianism is anarchism—a system of absolutely no central authority. It is entirely dependent on private exchanges, private contracts, privately sustained property rules and private arrangements for internal and external security. The law is that of the jungle—which might be idyllically harmonious or destructively chaotic. The economically strongest will survive and prosper.

The vast majority of political and economic analysts dismiss the anarchist social model as a foolish pipe dream. They point to a basic deficiency: There will be a shortage of *public goods* (see below), because there will be no central authority that can arrange and finance their production. Thus, in the absence of a government with taxation power, most citizens would refrain from (financially or otherwise) providing for national defense, police, courts and other broadly needed services, and they would try to get a free ride from those who do provide such services on a private basis.

Some libertarians (e.g., Hospers and Nozick) have tempered their free-enterprise faith with calls for a limited government ("minigovernment") with carefully defined functions. These functions essentially belong to the public-goods category (e.g., defense, security and law enforcement), even though they may not be formally linked to the public-goods concept. This group of libertarians can be described as conservative libertarians, and their thinking often converges with that of neoclassical conservatives (like Milton Friedman and other members of the "Chicago school of economics").

Libertarians have consistently supported the nuclear family (established through free bargaining and unregulated contracts) as an adequate institution for bringing up children. They have willingly tolerated the large inequalities that this institution seems to produce. They have regarded freedom and equality of opportunity as incompatible social goals, with clear priority given to the former. This is another area in which libertarianism parts company with the **libegalitarian** system introduced in this book.

Monetary policy—i.e., policies affecting the creation of money and the availability or price of credit—is one of the major government tools for influencing the national economy. It can affect the economy's efficiency in important ways, and it can influence the way the total pie is being sliced.

Experience indicates that monetary policy can sometimes affect the overall level of output, at least in the short run. A policy of expanding the supply of money tends to stimulate production and/or raise the rate of inflation. Contractionary monetary policies have usually the opposite effect. But after the initial adjustments, output and real income will revert to their previous trends; if the money supply increase is continued, the entire effect will soon be concentrated on the price level.

Since money conditions influence interest rates, changes in monetary policy will affect borrowers and lenders in opposite ways, at least during an initial adjustment period. Monetary policy hence has both macroeconomic-efficiency and income-distribution implications.

The powers of present-day monetary policies largely stem from the fact that government has nearly monopolized the definition and creation of money; it has made money, in its central aspects, a government institution.

Within the current rules of the game, the Federal Reserve System can closely control the total amount of bank credit and the amount of money (demand and checking deposits, dollar bills and coins) in circulation in the United States. It does so by buying and selling government securities on the capital market and by regulating the ability of commercial banks to borrow temporarily from the Fed itself.

The typical progovernment liberal has generally viewed monetary policy as a helpful accompaniment to *fiscal policy* (see above), which to him is still the primary tool for managing the economy and distributing national income. Certainly the growth of social-liberal spending programs in the 1930–70 period was greatly aided by the expansion of money and credit. But as certainly, this monetary expansion was inflationary, and most of the benefits were short-lived or illusionary. Even the liberals have gradually accepted this analysis. Traditionally, conservatives have been less aggressive in the use of monetary policy, but liberal-conservative differences on these issues are now small.

Libertarian writers are split on the question of whether the definition and creation of money really ought to be a government function. Anarchists will tell us that adequate private monetary instruments would be created in a true laissez-faire system. Each private bank could offer its customers its own deposit money, or groups of banks would set up equivalent deposit types.

Still, more conservative-minded libertarians regard the definition of money as one of the few legitimate government tasks. They feel that government ought to establish a monetary unit of account—preferably one that is stable relative to most goods and services—just as it effectively defines our physical units of measurement (pound, inch, centigrade, etc.). This is a costless public-good function that helps communication, accounting and valuation.

This is also the **libegalitarian** position. If the private financial markets do not themselves come up with a standardized monetary unit, the government ought to be allowed to do the job. But otherwise, banking and financial services ought to be handled by the private sector, for the resulting goods are essentially private.

Public goods are, in modern economic and political-science theory, contrasted with private or individual goods. Public goods are goods that cannot be produced and distributed to individual consumers or users (i.e., to private-market buyers). Because of their technical nature, they will have to be made available, if at all, within the entire community. They are a sub-category of "collective goods" (see *collectivism* above), but with ben-eficiaries that are identified primarily by the area where they live.

Sometimes the groups that would benefit from the production of public goods can conveniently organize themselves into a special "producing" organization (e.g., a neighborhood association cleaning up a shared street, or a funds-collecting charity group supporting its favorite cause). The public goods they thereby produce for themselves are essentially privatized; private collective action might thereby obviate the need for government involvement.

At other times, such private efforts are impractical or too costly relative to the perceived collective benefits. It might then be appropriate for some level of government to take on that function. This will usually be the rec-ommendation of most economists and political scientists, anarchists excluded.

Conservatives implicitly accept public-good reasoning when they call for a strong national defense or law enforcement. But they rarely invoke the term, perhaps out of fear that it will be casually applied in support of many other, unneeded public programs. American liberals occasionally use the term as a vague justification for new types of government spend-ing or regulation (e.g., involving the environment, public health or mass transit); but they, too, neglect to establish rules about efficient, fair produc-tion levels or financing methods. Many libertarians regard public-good talk as a betrayal of free-enterprise principles, even though well-designed public-goods activities by the government could enhance the economic benefits of free enterprise.

By contrast, the formal public-goods principles play a big role in the **libegalitarian** system proposed in this book. In this system, public goods are recognized as individually beneficial, potentially worth their costs and amenable to fair financing arrangements. (Also see *taxation* below.) With-out access to public goods, we could not maximize our incomes, wealth and economic opportunities.

Regulations are do's and don't's issued by the government to influence the behavior of private organizations and individuals (or government agencies). Their variety is so large that it is difficult to typify them. But some take aim at production or exchange activities in the otherwise pri-vate market; examples include fire-hazard restrictions on factories, affir-mative-action rules on employment practices, and prohibitions on prostitu-tion or liquor advertisements. Other regulations pertain to interactions between private parties and government agencies (e.g., rules on how to file income tax returns, or acquire a physician's license).

Modern economics has rather convincingly demonstrated that effective regulations almost always are counterefficient. They hinder private production or exchanges, as if by driving a wedge between private transactors or obstructing resource use. The regulating authority might defend these inefficiencies as the necessary social "price" for the sought-after behavior modification, along with a healthier environment, safer products, more benevolent business practices, etc. But almost universally, regulations are unnecessarily crude for their own purposes. They lack the flexibility of the price mechanism or a price-simulative tax system.

Liberals and socialists usually have little patience with these antiregulatory arguments; why not just stop the bastards? By contrast, American conservatives tend to acknowledge the drawbacks of harsh regulations, at least when they pertain to traditional business matters. But they typically do not approach matters of personal morality or propriety in the same way; they fail to see the inequities of controlling private behavior (prostitution, drug use at home, etc.) without negative effects on the general public.

The **libegalitarian** society would have complete property lines and allow full, cost-determined compensations for any actual crossings of those lines. Its two "regulatory" devices would be (a) free, competitive pricing of individual goods, and (b) benefit-related taxation that financed legitimate public goods. Otherwise, it would be regulation free. For to regulate is to take, and "takings" without acceptable *quid pro quos* are illegitimate in a free, fair society.

Social democracy is a mixed, but left-leaning, economic-political system located somewhere between modern American liberalism and the Eastern bloc regimes we knew before *perestroika*. Social democrats are usually attracted to theoretical socialism but see pragmatic reasons for delaying its implementation (or they fear that it would degenerate into old Soviet-style communism).

On the current American scene, social democrats can be found within the far left of the Democratic party—among the followers of Hubert Humphrey, Edward Kennedy and Walter Mondale. Their political programs resemble those of the (capitalized) Social Democrats in Scandinavia, as well as various union-supported, anticapitalist parties in Continental Western Europe and the British Labour Party.

In social democratic systems, a popularly elected government honors most of the traditional democratic political rights. But many economic tasks are handled by the state, and the government strongly influences the distribution of income and wealth. Business is subject to a broad range of controls, justified by concerns about consumer or worker protection, macroeconomic stability or industrial structure.

Yet social democratic spokesmen have been forced to admit that those controls (as well as severe taxes) will reduce private incentives and impair the private price mechanism. So they sometimes enlist the reluctant cooperation of big business in navigating between their collectivist-egalitarian ambitions and public demands for increasing real incomes and economic freedom. Artists receive a great deal of government financial support, in the name of the masses' cultural enrichment. Equality—as construed by social democrats—and efficiency seems to be in a constant battle.

From the **libegalitarian** vantage point, one merit of this system is its attempt to equalize initial opportunities, through standardized schooling and extensive public child-care facilities. Otherwise, most social democratic interventions in the private economy must be considered harmful and unfair. They reduce private economic opportunities and impair the allocative mechanism of the market. And despite its ostensible egalitarianism, the social democratic system leads to gross inequities between the productive taxpayers and many undeserving beneficiaries of the *welfare state* (see below).

Special-interest groups are voter or citizen groups that share particular socioeconomic goals and have enough political clout to publicly pursue those goals. Such groups can be formally organized, like trade associations, consumer advocacy organizations or the National Rifle Association. Or they might simply consist of unidentified members of the public who cast their votes, or contribute money, to those who speak for their shared cause.

In this broad sence, special-interest groups crisscross the entire political landscape. Each of us belongs to a number of such groups, based on our individual wants and preferences in both private-market and public-policy matters. Bicycle riders, lung cancer patients and Christian Scientists are just a few examples.

American conservatives traditionally support the interests of the entrepreneurial or wealth-accumulating classes, whereas liberals and social democrats have heeded those of unionized workers, environmentalists, artists, blacks and unwed mothers. More important, there are ideological differences regarding the proper social mechanism for accommodating these interests—through organized private markets, through negotiations between large private organizations (labor unions versus employer groups, professional associations, etc.) or through government (public-sector enterprise, regulation, taxation or subsidy).

The libertarian and right-of-center view is that most special interests can be accommodated adequately by the private market. Such interests translate into consumer (or investor, or worker) demands that can find outlets through buyer pressure for changes in products or services. Yet this technically presumes that the government does not substantially distort the relevant markets.

Especially critical policy questions arise when well-functioning private markets do not, or cannot, exist—especially because what the interest group wants is a *public good* (see above). On this score, the **libegalitarian** position will differ from the libertarian one and overlap with much centrist or liberal thinking. Thus, special interests directed toward public goods may require public-sector production. But **libegalitarians** will insist that any government action meet both cost-effectiveness and equity criteria, as laid down in the neoclassical public-good theory.

Subsidies are, basically, government favors to individuals, firms or other private parties. They can take two major forms: one, cash payments or tax rebates offered, without any *quid pro quo*, to particular groups of citizens; and (perhaps less obviously) two, the benefit of regulatory protection, effected through restrictions on the activities of competing firms or individuals.

Current examples in the United States include federal cash support (or loan guarantees) to farmers, publicly financed tuition deferral for college students, income and property tax exemptions for churches and other "nonprofit" organizations, import restrictions, and food stamps, given to low-income persons.

But the term is slippery. It presumes a neutral starting point or a baseline. Ultimately, that requires a "control" society, with or without government; but we have no standard model of what this society would look like.

To a libertarian, all government payments would constitute (illegitimate) subsidies. The **libegalitarian** model similarly rejects all subsidies—except when they have been mislabeled and actually represent payments for services rendered (e.g., a tax rebate for extra antipollution efforts). By this standard, a nonexistent national defense would be an inappropriate *de facto* subsidy to those who get a free ride from private defense arrangements; the same holds for those who could foul the ocean beach with impunity. Conversely, since much government assistance to college students today will be repaid later through extra income-tax payments, there may in the end be no subsidy element in the full lifetime context.

Taxation is, of course, the main method for financing government activities and transfer payments (and interest payments on debt incurred through past government borrowing).

Ideological tax questions will always be linked to questions about the merits of the government programs they finance. Taxes can then be looked upon in many different ways, each relecting a particular ideological perspective.

To an anarcholibertarian, taxes are a mechanism through which governments, by virtue of their omnipotence, can rob us of our rightful income. All taxes are coercive, and used for illegitimate collectivist purposes; without any government at all, no taxes, of course, are necessary. All non-anarchists will concede that some taxes are necessary contributions to the financing of government activities, from which many or all of us collectively benefit. Conservatives tend to be a bit more selective and critical (unless the taxes are for the defense budget), while liberals are more ready to give up some of their incomes in this way (especially to finance redistribution programs).

Modern economists believe that taxes are an important macroeconomic tool through which the national government can adjust aggregate demand and help ensure low-inflation economic growth. Yet the conservatives in their ranks will add that this interventionist view fails to account for private sector feedbacks and for the damage done to the price mechanism. Students of public finance might add, in turn, that, for reasons of macroeconomic efficiency, taxes ought to be just high enough to finance truly worthwhile public-good production within the government sector.

The latter taxation principle is a key part of the **libegalitarian** society outlined in this book. (Also see *public goods* above.) This model points to a new tax structure tailored to the financing of cost-effective public goods. In short, the ideal tax is effectively a user fee, set just like the price in a private market and payable by the users of the services that the fee finances. (Also see *fiscal policy.*)

Welfare state usually suggests a system of ample, tax-financed public assistance programs, including cash transfers and outright public-sector services (health care, education, etc.). Its principal aim is to reduce observable income and wealth disparities at public (taxpayer) expense. It reflects a view that individuals often cannot take care of themselves but that government can, indeed, provide more "welfare."

The vagueness of the term "welfare state" makes many uncomfortable. We cannot easily observe other people's relative well-being, and we cannot add different individuals' well-being into a meaningful total. So the idea of raising aggregate "welfare" through income redistribution is suspect. If we nevertheless use the term, we will need to translate it into something that is socioeconomically measurable—perhaps personal real income, or personal consumption, per capita. But neither "welfare" measure accounts for the benefits of leisure or informal work in the home.

Moreover, spokesmen for more equalized "welfare" are usually oblivious to the longer-term aspects of their favored redistribution programs. Especially, they ignore the detrimental effects on work, saving and skill-investment incentives. Our individual freedom to rearrange our lifetime economic affairs is correspondingly reduced.

The cradle-to-grave "welfare" typified by the Scandinavian system appeals primarily to those with a strong left-liberal or social democratic persuasion. Many of its aspects are unappealing to moderates and conservatives and of course to the antigovernment libertarians.

But if "welfare" is redefined so as to denote opportunity instead of outcome, the concept could probably gain greater credibility. In fact, the socioeconomic model of **libegalitarianism** could conceivably, despite the risk of misinterpretation, be said to be an "equal lifetime welfare system." But by emphasizing lifetime aspects, this system would differ very fundamentally from contemporary liberal or social-democratic "welfare states."

NOTES

1. These commentators seem to disagree with Abraham Lincoln's statement that "important principles may and must be inflexible."

2. A broad-based survey of popular American values and beliefs, reported in the *New York Times*, December 25, 1988, indicated that 90 percent of the citizens want government to ensure that everyone has an "equal opportunity to succeed." Unfortunately the interviewees were not asked about their appreciation of individual freedom or about the reconciliation of these two values.

3. Generally, the notion of opportunity has been too abstract and fluid to get a clear, consistent treatment by economic and political analysts. In particular the time frame within which a person's opportunities (since birth?; as of today, looking X years into the future?; or when?) are evaluated, is obscure.

A search through the contemporary economic-political literature reveals not a single serious attempt to define the individual's socioeconomic opportunity on a full lifetime basis, rather than as of a particular moment in time. A major reason for this neglect may lie in most writers' unfamiliarity with the economic analysis of timing and, in the technical capital-theoretic jargon, intertemporal transformations. It will be argued in this book that better intertemporal analysis would go a long way toward clarifying ideological choices and developing a more satisfactory ideological scheme. (Some of the misunderstandings of these timing matters in recent political-theoretic literature are explored in the author's "The Intertemporal Dimension of Distributive Justice," *Reason Papers*, Fall 1976.)

4. Efforts to apply economic concepts and theory to broader aspects of social

behavior are examined, in an entertaining fashion, in Richard B. McKenzie and Gordon Tullock, *The New World of Economics* (New York: Richard Irwin, 1975).

5. These philosophers include, for instance, Robert Nozick; see his deservedly much-praised *Anarchy, State, and Utopia* (New York: Basic Books, 1974), pp. 35–42. Nozick seems sympathetic to giving constitutional protection to some types of animals, but does not resolve the man-animal rights conflicts in any clear-cut way.

Nobody so far seems to have suggested any formula for weighing animal concerns against those of humans whenever conflicts arise. Nor has any of our proanimal social thinkers come up with any system for classifying animals into categories of different moral worth. We will also not attempt to do this. So the question of human-animal relations will remain a loose end in our ideological scheme. Of course, the simple (and perhaps cynical) solution is to treat animals as private property and let each person define his own animal relations. In this way, we will remove animals entirely from any further socioethical consideration.

For a brief discussion of the environmentalist aspect of animal rights, see ch. VI.

6. Herbert Spencer, *Social Statics* (New York: Schalkenbach Foundation, 1970), p. 69: "[E]very man may claim the fullest liberty to exercise his faculties compatible with the possession of like liberty by every other man."

7. Adam Smith, *An Inquiry into the Nature and Causes of the Wealth of Nations* (New York: Modern Library, 1937); Milton Friedman, *Capitalism and Freedom* (Chicago: University of Chicago Press, 1962).

8. The basic theory is presented in Mancur Olson, *The Logic of Collective Action* (New York: Schocken Books, 1968).

9. See Paul Samuelson, "The Pure Theory of Public Expenditure," *Review of Economics and Statistics*, Nov. 1954, pp. 387–89.

10. Most libertarian writers and commentators say very little, if anything, about equality (although Robert Nozick, *op. cit.*, pp. 235–39, is a partial exception). Their commitment to freedom is nearly unlimited, and to them, equality conjures up a socialistic leveling of incomes, restrictions on personal choice and stifling cultural homogeneity. Some writers sympathetic to libertarian ideals (e.g., Milton Friedman, *op. cit.*, p. 195) wiggle out of this perceived dilemma by invoking an "equal right to freedom"—a much more limited form of equality.

The farther leftward we go on the ideological scale, the more we hear about equality. In the gray middle, there are attempted compromises: The social democrats in Scandinavia and in the left wing of the U.S. Democratic party deliberately seek a trade-off between the two principles, as if too much of either would be harmful or unfair; this is apparent from their party platforms and voting records.

11. In special cases, the usual distinction between freedom and resources becomes blurred. A freedom can then take on the characteristics of a resource and achieve a degree of fungibility. Consider air rights (the freedom to build in, or to

pollute, a certain air space), which can sometimes, under current laws, be sold and bought by real estate developers or factory owners.

12. The modern theoretical analysis of human capital is attributable to Theodore Schultz and Gary Becker. See especially Becker's *Human Capital: A Theoretical and Empirical Analysis*, 2nd ed. (New York: Columbia University Press, 1975).

13. One modern political theorist who has raised similar questions, and provided some of the same answers, is James M. Buchanan. See his *Liberty, Market and State* (New York: New York University Press, 1985), especially chs. 12 and 13.

14. Among income support programs, Social Security has been the main exception to this rule. Its main benefit program—old-age pensions—has not been based on any means test. Recent changes in the federal income tax code, however, have made Social Security income taxable for higher income groups, thus introducing a regressive feature into this program too. For a more detailed discussion of how Social Security should be structured, see ch. V below.

15. These perverse results of current welfare programs are extensively analyzed and discussed in Charles Murray, *Losing Ground* (New York: Basic Books, 1984). See also Richard Vedder and Lowell Gallaway, "AFDC and the Laffer Principle," *Wall Street Journal*, March 26, 1986, for a demonstration of how public poverty relief actually can increase, rather than decrease, the "supply" of poverty. And note the parallel with changes in taxation: As argued especially by the "supply-siders" connected with the Reagan administration, higher tax rates can, by changing the incentives to work and to save, have the perverse result of reducing, rather than increasing, tax revenues.

16. Possibly one could alternatively speak of "outcomes" in a purely expectational sense. This would allow us to sum up conditions in future time periods and calculate a prospective "outcome" encompassing the remainder of a person's life experience. For example, a realistic prospect of a particularly high future living standard would, under this definition, qualify as a particularly favorable outcome. Outcome would then include, or become synonymous with, opportunity. This perspective would be very much in line with the **libegalitarian** philosophy.

17. A column in the *New York Times*, August 17, 1988 ("About Education") describes the child-care experience of the Scandinavian countries, which rely heavily on child-care centers. The column finds this experience positive and perhaps worth emulating in the United States—both because it is "democratic" (presumably meaning "egalitarian") and because children in the Scandinavian day-care centers, according to the report, seem so "happy."

18. A number of articles in the daily press have discussed these problems from various perspectives, but without putting them in a coherent general ideological context. The undeniable existence of a "dual family system" in the United States today is one of the main themes of Senator Daniel Moynihan (D., N.Y.) in an article in the *New York Times*, September 25, 1988 ("Half the Nation's Children With-

out a Fair Chance"). The major new legislative proposals in this area are described and evaluated in Douglas Besharov, "The ABCs of Child-Care Politics," *Wall Street Journal*, March 9, 1988, and in Lawrence Lindsey, "Better Child Care, Cheaper," *Wall Street Journal*, July 5, 1988, both of whom are skeptical of the merits of child care outside the family. The views of Congressional Republicans are explained in "The Day-Care Reform Juggernaut," *National Review*, March 10, 1989.

19. Mary Jo Bane, in *Here to Stay* (New York: Basic Books, 1976), similarly proposes that parental and caretaker expenses for child care be regarded as "loans" to the new generation, to be financed through the general Social Security system. Her scheme, however, does not make explicit provisions for the repayment of these funds (see pp. 129–31). She sees these "loans" as generational rather than as individual obligations, which leaves the intragenerational distribution of the repayment burden undefined. However, this ambiguity could be removed by establishing a special "children's trust" within the Social Security system, with its own borrowing authority and tax provisions.

20. Among those who advocate a complete reliance on voluntary defense agencies is Murray Rothbard, as in *For A New Liberty* (New York: MacMillan, 1973), especially pp. 247–52. By contrast, more realistic, centrist libertarian scholars accept the need for tax-financed national defense. See John Hospers, *Libertarianism* (Los Angeles: Nash Publishing, 1971), pp. 433–64, who stresses the freeloader aspect of voluntary defense agencies and the resulting insufficiency of the likely defense effort. Or see Robert Nozick, *op. cit.*, pp. 12–25, who demonstrates that a defense association that is sufficiently dominant and strong will *de facto* constitute a kind of state.

21. In nearly all criminal cases, the prosecutor must prove both that the accused caused a criminal act (*actus reus*) and that he was of a guilty mind (*mens rea*).

22. How much general property protection really is offered by the U.S. Constitution is still a matter of serious dispute. Under some interpretations, many of the federal or local governments' policies and programs might actually be constitutionally illegal. The Supreme Court has not fully resolved these matters, and future challenges of government policies might conceivably force modifications of many government policies on this ground.

For example, one prominent legal scholar has recently argued that the Constitution's prohibition of uncompensated "takings" (in accordance with its eminent domain, or "takings," clause) casts doubt on the legality of many contemporary government programs: progressive income taxes, business regulations, zoning laws and many other aspects of public policy. See Richard A. Epstein, *Takings* (Cambridge, Mass.: Harvard University Press, 1985), especially part IV. Indeed, if Epstein's views were put into practice, the **libegalitarian** society would be much closer to realization.

23. See, e.g., Rothbard, *op. cit.*, p. 246.

24. Taxes, as usually defined, are a mixed-economy phenomenon. But in a deeper sense, the citizen's obligation in a totalitarian society to accept a government-selected job is a huge *de facto* tax, equivalent to the value of the work performed, less any paid-out compensation. In a conventional sense, the most heavily taxed people on earth are, allegedly, the Swedes. In a broader sense, inmates of Siberian and Cuban labor camps have surely been even worse off this respect.

25. For a description of the benefit approach to taxation, see, e.g., Charles Allan, *The Theory of Taxation* (Harmondsworth, England: Penguin Books, 1971), ch. 8. Or for a brief summary, see the latest edition of a standard introductory economics textbook such as Campbell McConnell, *Economics* (chapter on the public sector of the American economy).

26. The debate over the U.S. federal budget deficit in 1988 and 1989 produced a lot of cynical commentary about the meaning of "tax" versus "fee," with suggestions that all payments to the government should honestly be considered taxes. Unfortunately, no major public figure stood up and informed the public of the useful distinction between payments for public services actually received and payments for services or cash given to others—i.e., between exchange-like and redistributive taxes; this would have been more instructive. And, unfortunately, no libertarian-spirited observer pointed out to the Congress and the public that any tax that does not at least resemble a fee is ethically suspect.

27. Taxable income should include wages and salaries, in cash or in kind. It might also include earnings from stock ownership and nonincorporated business activities. But if such "income from capital" is taxed in this way, there will be no reason to impose a general profit tax on corporations and businesses at the same time. This entails "double taxation," which unduly penalizes organized business activity and which violates both efficiency and equity criteria.

28. The proposed tax system would somewhat resemble the tax reform plans offered by some of the "flat-tax" advocates in the early 1980s (and which had some influence on the actual simplifications undertaken in the U.S. tax code during the first Reagan administration). However, the system proposed here would be much "flatter" and much simpler. And it would be much fairer, too, since it would be fundamentally nonredistributive, whereas the U.S. income tax system still incorporates many progressive, redistributive features.

29. The virtue of the private market as a mechanism for information sharing, and the complex coordination it thereby provides, is emphasized by the "Austrian" school of economics. For a lucid elaboration, see Israel Kirzner, *Competition and Entrepreneurship* (Chicago: University of Chicago Press, 1973), pp. 213–31, and Kirzner's citations of F.A. von Hayek.

30. A mostly favorable summary evaluation, by Gary Becker, of the current all-volunteer system appeared in *Business Week*, February 8, 1988.

31. The merits of ending draft registration and, instead, creating a reserve volun-

teer force are discussed in Doug Bandow, "It's Time to Drop Draft Registration," *New York Times*, July 23, 1987.

32. The most prominent proposal has been one sponsored by Senator Sam Nunn (D., Ga.). It calls for the creation of a Citizen Corps of men and women, 18–26 years old, in return for future educational vouchers and small cash allowances. For a well-reasoned critical appraisal, see George Roche, "Stop National Service Before It Starts," *Wall Street Journal*, June 7, 1989. Another proposal has, rather surprisingly, been offered by William F. Buckley, in *Gratitude: Reflections on What We Owe to Our Country* (New York: Random House, 1990).

33. Among the most extreme illustrations is a jury award of $11.2 million to the surviving dependents of a woman who died of toxic shock syndrome, allegedly because she had used Playtex tampons. Another infamous case involves a woman who said she had lost her psychic powers after a CAT scan—and was awarded nearly $1 million. For a critical analysis of these damage awards and the underlying legal principles, see Peter Huber, *Liability: The Legal Revolution and Its Consequences* (New York: Basic Books, 1988).

Another vehicle for grossly excessive sanctions is the U.S. Racketeer Influenced and Corrupt Organizations law. Despite its sinister-sounding name, RICO has been used for imposing uncalled-for penalties on peaceful demonstrators, political lobbyists, securities traders and many other nonracketeers; and the law is now widely believed to be unconstitutional. See "Two Cheers for This Bill to Reform RICO," *Wall Street Journal*, June 27, 1990.

34. See Huber, *op. cit.*

35. However, the Supreme Court in June 1989 ruled (in a commercial dispute between industrial-waste disposal firms) that the Eighth Amendment's prohibition of "excessive fines" applies only to criminal cases. Yet the question does not seem to have been permanently settled.

36. On the constitutionality of these awards, see editorial, *Wall Street Journal*, December 9, 1987.

37. Huber, *op. cit.*, offers evidence that the threat of damage suits, or the cost of liability insurance, now adds very substantially to the prices of various consumer goods, from step ladders to children's vaccines to sporting goods.

Aaron Wildavsky, *Searching for Safety* (New Brunswick: Transaction Books, 1988), ch. 8, criticizes these awards for their economic shortsightedness: They might seem to offer protection against risks, but in the end they discourage development of many lower-risk, more effective products. To him the failure to balance short- and long-term consequences of these kinds is symptomatic of society's overemphasis on "anticipatory" protection (avoidance of specific, foreseeable risks), at the expense of experimental creativity that fosters more "resilience" to new, upcoming hazards (and, ultimately, lowers risks).

38. The main exponents of this approach are connected with the economics-and-

law faculty of the University of Chicago. In this regard, they combine the liberality of neoclassical economics with the illiberality of law-and-order convervatism, with ambiguous ethical implications. One of the seminal articles is Gary Becker, "Crime and Punishment: An Economic Approach," *Journal of Political Economy,* March–April 1968, pp. 169–217.

Much of the Chicago School thinking was incorporated in a 1988 proposal by the U.S. Sentencing Commission for new Federal rules regarding punishments for corporate crimes, including fraud, tax evasion and violation of food or drug legislation. Commendably, the proposed rules take an "economic" approach, basing punishments on actual private and social losses. But less commendably, they seek to enlarge punishments by numerical factors that measure the difficulty of discovering the crimes and apprehending the criminals—a formula for arbitrary inequities.

39. The case for decriminalizing and legalizing drugs has been repeatedly made by *Reason,* the leading popular libertarian periodical.

40. A recent summary analysis of available evidence is provided in Federal Reserve Bank of San Francisco, *Weekly Letter,* June 24, 1988. Among the findings are that the minimum-wage hike proposed by Congress in 1988 would slightly raise the measured unemployment rate. But, more important, it would drive many unskilled workers out of the labor force altogether (thus leaving them unaccounted for in the official unemployment statistics). In addition, it would boost the price level and the inflation rate—another sign of its distortive macroeconomic influence.

41. Perhaps the most eloquent articulation of this view is that of Thomas Sowell, a leading conservative-libertarian scholar in the field of minority-group economics and sociology. See his several books on this broad subject, including *Race and Economics* (New York: David McKay, 1975), *Ethnic America: A History* (New York: Basic Books, 1981) and *Civil Rights: Rhetoric or Reality?* (New York: William Morrow, 1984).

42. Many Constitution watchers have focused their attention on whether the Supreme Court will uphold or overturn its ruling in the 1976 case of *Runyon v. McCrary.* The ruling, based in part on a 1866 civil rights law, seemed to entitle minority group members to the same right "to make and enforce contracts" that has always been enjoyed by the white majority; this right might compel private parties, for the sake of racial balance, to enter into employment and other commercial contracts they do not wish to make. A Court ruling in June 1989 upheld this minority right when it comes to the making of employment contracts. For a critical analysis, see Michael Greve, "Runyon Decision Doesn't Deserve to Stand," *Wall Street Journal,* June 29, 1988.

43. A middle ground position is taken in David Kirp *et al., Gender Justice* (Chicago: University of Chicago Press, 1986). This scholarly work supports government efforts to curb "discrimination" in employment, taxes and other social-pol-

icy areas, yet it wants to preserve a great deal of individual autonomy and privacy—even though private choices might produce sex-differentiated outcomes. For instance, the authors oppose job quotas—which are an encroachment on private market choice and do not respect the market's true gender preferences.

44. Laws forbidding sexual discrimination are, of course, not confined to employment matters. They have occasionally been applied even to small-scale retail transactions. For instance, the press has reported that a San Francisco laundry facility was ordered to reduce its charges for women's shirt laundering so as to make the charges equal to those for men's shirts. As part of the settlement, the laundry also agreed to launder 3,000 women's shirts free, in recognition of its longstanding shirt-segregationist behavior.

45. The current fashion of claiming victimhood for one's own professional, social or ethnic group (such as artists, students or veterans, as well as the legally recognized minority groups) is explored in Joseph Epstein, "The Joys of Victimhood," *New York Times Magazine*, July 2, 1989.

46. Unfortunately, public policy has taken a different tack: The 1990 "Americans with Disabilities Act" forces private business firms to bear much of the cost of accommodating the disabled (regardless of what or who is to blame for that condition). The law is a new blow to labor market efficiency and makes a further dent in the business-generated opportunity pie.

47. Another controversial aspect of the AIDS crisis is that of compulsory blood testing by doctors, hospitals, prisons and other agencies; some rules to that effect have already been legislated. A large majority of voters and public-policy spokesmen seem to favor such rules, in the name of public health. But forcing private parties to abide by them is a violation of individual rights—the rights to privacy and to freely negotiate the terms of our transactions with private (and public) institutions; it represents true victimization by the government. Understandably, the ACLU issued a policy statement in 1986 to the effect that it opposes involuntary AIDS testing, based on "basic constitutional guarantees" and "civil rights." Yet there might be situations in which, say, unregulated private hospitals would voluntarily adopt similar rules, and would see them accepted by many patients; this would be an unchallengeable private matter.

48. William Safire, in *Political Dictionary* (New York: Random House, 1968), p. 121, uses a similar basic definition of "civil rights": "those rights guaranteed to an individual as a member of society." To him, a "human right" (pp. 313–14) now basically refers to a "moral claim on some political freedom"—a surprisingly limited definition. But presumably Safire is merely reporting on common usage, without endorsing its unfortunate normative implications. The English language does not comfortably distinguish between rights that are actually honored by the authorities and those that the speaker finds morally valid but are not recognized.

49. Remarkably, the *New York Times*, in an editorial published on April 4, 1988,

offers another proposal: permit increased immigration, so that "hard-working, tax-paying Asians and Latin Americans" would be able to "support the retiring baby boomers." The historical parallels to such an exploitative labor-importation scheme are embarrassingly obvious.

50. John Makin, in "Social Security: Nothing But a Ponzi Scheme," *New York Times*, October 8, 1988, develops these themes further. He cites data on the relationship between tax payments and subsequent benefit receipts for different generations of Americans—they have indeed been grossly out of balance. He characterizes the trust fund as "bogus" and chides politicians for currying favor with the growing generation of older citizens by promising irresponsibly generous benefits.

51. Among those proposing such a reform are Makin, *op. cit.*, and James Bovard, "Trillion-Dollar Trouble," *Reason*, July 1988.

52. Harry Schwartz, in "The Right Medicine," *National Review*, March 10, 1989, argues convincingly that there is no true "health-care crisis" in the United States and that the proposed "universal health insurance" reforms would make the system much worse. In the same spirit, an article in the *Wall Street Journal*, January 27, 1988 ("Market Tests Britain's Health System") offers a persuasive critical evaluation of the nationalized health-care system in Britain.

53. Meanwhile Britain has begun to rethink its own nationalized health care system: The Thatcher administration in 1989 announced a series of tentative steps to make British national health care more competitive and more price sensitive (while not yet abandoning compulsory participation). It would be ironic indeed if the United States were to imitate the British system just as the latter's failures have become serious enough to produce a significant retreat.

54. A similar term ("health fascism") is used by a liberal columnist in the *Wall Street Journal*, June 16, 1988 (Alexander Cockburn, "The Great American Smoke Screen"). Referring to smoking restrictions in the workplace, the article approvingly cites labor spokesmen who view the antismoking drive as another means, along with urine testing and lie detectors, of "keeping workers in line." Moreover, since the smoking habit is more prevalent at the lower end of the income scale, there seems to be a certain class bias in the new restrictions; "almost half of the industrial proletariat will be turned into 'legal addicts.' "

55. According to an article in the *New York Times*, June 22, 1988 (Peter Passell, "Who Should Pay Smoking's Cost?"), smoking now costs the American society about $65 billion annually in health care and lost worker productivity—representing more than $2 a pack, on average. However, since smokers typically die earlier than nonsmokers, they actually save the government a lot in Social Security benefits; and, overall, nonsmokers thereby "reap a grisly financial windfall." Indeed, the case for high tobacco taxes is weak. Under fairer, market-based arrangements, private insurance premiums would be adjusted so that smokers would re-

capture the collective good they transfer to nonsmokers, through reduced old-age claims, from the pension insurance pool.

56. This is, again, the argument made so forcefully by Wildavsky, *op. cit.*: The government's excessive preoccupation with short-run risks prevents the experimentation and societal "resiliency" that could create better and, yes, safer products in the future.

57. These critics now include the editorial writers of the *New York Times*, despite its tradition of favoring egalitarian-liberal market interventions.

58. Unfortunately, many environmentalists do not appreciate the need to balance demands and supplies or the various conflicting interests on the two sides of the resource-use equation. They seem to find reliance on the price mechanism crass and cynical. This misguided attitude is reflected in an article that mockingly suggests similar markets for clean fruit (with tradable pesticide residue rights) and for safe streets (with tradable rights to street crimes); it also proposes a United Nations program for tradable torture rights, distributed among participating countries. See Todd Gitlin, "Buying the Right to Pollute? What's Next?," *New York Times*, July 28, 1989.

59. A similar proposal is discussed in a task force report prepared under the sponsorship of members of the U.S. Senate and titled "Project 88: Harnessing Market Forces to Protect Our Environment." The proposal is summarized and evaluated in the *New York Times*, October 19, 1988 (Peter Passell, "Private Incentives as Pollution Curb"). The proposal is, in part, based on an estimate (put at $3 billion a year) of the cost saving of such an air-use system, as compared with a uniform emission standard tailored to the same air quality requirement.

60. The total taxpayer cost of the U.S. farm support program in recent years has been estimated at $30 billion annually. Almost the same amount is being spent by taxpayers in the European Community. For further data, see *New York Times*, July 12, 1987 ("Plotting a Global Attack against Farm Subsidies").

61. For a more detailed critique of the American farm program along similar lines, see James Bovard, "Farm Bill Follies of 1990," Cato Institute, Policy Analysis No. 135, 1990.

62. President Reagan in 1987 appealed to all foreign governments to work with him toward the elimination of all trade-related subsidies and controls on agricultural production over the subsequent ten years. There have been no significant follow-ups on the proposal so far. Any multilateral action to be taken would presumably be coordinated through the offices of the General Agreement on Tariffs and Trade, which has been dedicated to improving the international market mechanism. GATT negotiators in 1989–90 tried to find politically acceptable compromise formulas, with little success.

63. Another industry—yes, an "industry"—that benefits from tax-supported fed-

eral programs is the performing arts. The acrimonious debate over the funding practices of the National Endowment for the Arts in 1990 was a useful public reminder of this fact, never mind the sanctimonious arguments presented both by its pornography-obsessed opponents and its grant-seeking or art-consuming supporters. Some art, and artistic experiments, may well produce some long-term cultural or educational public (or broadly collective) goods. But the arts community needs to do a much better job in demonstrating those potential benefits—or its claims on the public purse will remain ethically unsubstantiated.

64. These economists—who wish to introduce federal capital budgeting—come from opposing ideological camps. See, on the left, Robert Heilbroner, "How I Learned to Love the Deficit," *New York Times*, September 4, 1988, and, on the right, Alan Reynolds, "Public Investment, Not a Binge," *Wall Street Journal*, July 27, 1987.

65. For instance, each major business contract might include the following clause: "By 'dollar' in this contract, the parties mean the amount of value represented by the commodity basket defined, for this purpose, in the agreement reached by. . . on. . . ."

66. Thus bank deposit insurance ought not to be provided by the taxpaying public, as largely done, today, through the Federal Deposit Insurance Corporation. The moral hazard, and resulting inefficiency, of this type of system has become painfully clear during the nationwide savings and loan crisis. The insurance program backing the savings and loans' access to the money market severely weakened their incentives for prudently balancing the risks and returns on their loans and investments. They consequently were seduced into making hundreds of billions of irresponsible, if not fraudulent, credit decisions, for which the taxpayers now have to foot the bill.

67. They would satisfy the so-called Pareto condition, which exactly defines that combination of results. The Pareto criterion is often invoked by neoclassical economists in defence of particular tax or regulatory reforms. When it is satisfied, equity complications can more easily be pushed aside, and it might be easier to rally political support for the reform that is being advocated.

INDEX
(n = note; g = glossary item)

246